Gods in the Global Village

The World's Religions in Sociological Perspective

Lester R. Kurtz
University of Texas, Austin

PINE FORGE PRESS
Thousand Oaks, California ◆ *London* ◆ *New Delhi*

Dedicated to Jeannie Kurtz
and the memory of Merwin Kurtz,
my first teachers

For information, address:

 Pine Forge Press
A Sage Publications Company
2455 Teller Road
Thousand Oaks, California 91320
(805) 499-4224
E-mail: sales@pfp.sagepub.com

Production Manager: Rebecca Holland
Designer: Lisa S. Mirski
Cover: Lisa S. Mirski

Map on p. xix prepared by: Sarah Beth Asher

Printed in the United States of America

99 00 01 02 11 10 9 8 7 6 5 4 3

Library of Congress Cataloging-in-Publication Data
Kurtz, Lester R.
    Gods in the global village : the world's religions in
sociological perspective / Lester R. Kurtz.
        p.   cm.—(Sociology for a new century)
    Includes bibliographical references and index.
    ISBN 0-8039-9037-5 (pbk.)
    1. Religion and sociology.   2. Religious pluralism.   3.
Religions.   I. Title.   II. Title: World's religions in
sociological perspective.
III. Series.
BL60.K87   1995
291.1'78—dc20   94-40483
                                              CIP

Contents

ABOUT THE AUTHOR

Lester R. Kurtz is Associate Professor of Sociology and Asian Studies at the University of Texas-Austin and has been a visiting professor at Tunghai University, Republic of China, and Delhi University, India. He received a Master of Arts in Religion from Yale University and a Ph.D. in sociology from the University of Chicago. His book *The Politics of Heresy* (University of California Press, 1986) won the Society for the Scientific Study of Religion's 1987 Distinguished Book Award. He was Director of Religious Studies at the University of Texas, 1986–1989, and is chair-elect of the Peace Studies Association and of the Peace and War Section of the American Sociological Association.

His research focuses on the relationship between religion and social conflict; he is author of *The Nuclear Cage: A Sociology of the Arms Race* (1988) and co-editor of two forthcoming books: *The Web of Violence* (with Jennifer Turpin) and *The Geography of Nonviolence* (with Sarah Beth Asher). He is currently writing a book on Mohandas Gandhi's nonviolent legacies in India. He is a husband and the father of two daughters and hopes to bring a third daughter, Shanti, from India to join the family in the near future.

ABOUT THE PUBLISHER

Pine Forge Press is a new educational publisher, dedicated to publishing innovative books and software throughout the social sciences. On this and any other of our publications, we welcome your comments, ideas, and suggestions. Please call or write to:

Pine Forge Press
A Sage Publications Company
2455 Teller Road
Thousand Oaks, California 91320
(805) 499-4224
E-mail: sales@pfp.sagepub.com

Foreword

Sociology for a New Century offers the best of current sociological thinking to today's students. The goal of the series is to prepare students, and—in the long run—the informed public, for a world that has changed dramatically in the last three decades and one that continues to astonish.

This goal reflects important changes that have taken place in sociology. The discipline has become broader in orientation, with an ever-growing interest in research that is comparative, historical, or transnational in orientation. Sociologists are less focused on "American" society as the pinnacle of human achievement and more sensitive to global processes and trends. They also have become less insulated from surrounding social forces. In the 1970s and 1980s sociologists were so obsessed with constructing a science of society that they saw impenetrability as a sign of success. Today, there is a greater effort to connect sociology to the ongoing concerns and experiences of the informed public.

Each book in this series offers a comparative, historical, transnational, or global perspective in some way, to help broaden students' vision. *Gods in the Global Village* responds to the multicultural interests of today's diverse student population by treating classic issues in the sociology of religion—rituals, beliefs, ethics, secularization, religious conflict—in a variety of religious contexts. Lester Kurtz gives students the tools they need to understand religious life in today's world, first by considering the manifold global interconnections among beliefs and believers (as well as among those who oppose them), and second by introducing students to the fundamentals of each of the world religions: Hinduism, Buddhism, Judaism, Christianity, and Islam. With this knowledge base established, *Gods in the Global Village* goes on to help students understand the interplay between social change and religion, addressing such questions as why modernization seems accompanied by renewed religious conflicts or why, in a society like ours, which is characterized by separation of church and state, religion continues to be one of the fault lines dividing Americans from each other. As provocative as it is informative, this book will spark heated classroom discussion and careful reexamination of some of our conventional understandings about the role of religion in the modern and postmodern world.

Preface

The Buddha is said to have argued that if a house is on fire, we should not sit around debating how to put it out but should set to work immediately. A scholar's inclination, however, is to think carefully about a problem before writing about it, let alone acting on it.

Humanity's common house is on fire in a very real sense: even after the end of the Cold War and its reign of nuclear terror, we live in a time of acute crisis. Despite our technological advances and abundant natural resources, millions of people die of starvation every day and millions more are malnourished; wars and various armed conflicts between religious and ethnic communities plague the planet, which is itself still booby trapped for self-destruction with thousands of nuclear weapons. Peoples around the world find their familiar societies being torn apart by a rapid globalization of the economy and culture of the human community that is producing a dizzying pace of change. The Earth itself has been seriously abused by civilization and it is not clear that we have the will to stop further damage, let alone repair what we have already done.

This book focuses on a central aspect of that common crisis—the relationship among the major religious traditions that inform the thinking and ethical standards of most people in the emerging global social order. It would be a better book if I spent another twenty-five years writing it, but the topic's urgency justifies this preliminary attempt to use sociological tools to assess the state of religious life in a globalizing world. Trying to synthesize the material in this book has been a humbling experience, and I hope that my readers will accept it in the spirit in which it is offered—as a tentative analysis, a first step in a process that will require more research and more action.

Since Max Weber's plea in 1918 for a value-neutral sociology and the professionalization of academia and the social sciences after World War II, sociologists have been divided about the manner in which they may properly address social issues—or whether these issues should be addressed at all. Mainstream sociology, especially in the United States, has tended to favor the objective, dispassionate approach avoiding both personal biases and political positions according to the canons of science. Alongside this trend, however, a more critical sociology has persisted since the founding of the discipline, gaining added momentum in the 1960s, when questions were raised not only about the morality but even the possibility of objectivity in the study of pressing social problems. *Gods in the Global Village* falls clearly in the latter camp; it employs the scientific model to investigate religious life but does not pretend to be entirely value free. It is necessary, therefore, to begin our argument by outlining some underlying assumptions.

A major assumption of this book is that all knowledge is shaped by the social context of the knower; therefore, both religious traditions and our studies of them are shaped by the context in which we construct them. That is not to say that the pursuit of objectivity is not valuable— we must always try to overcome our own biases in our pursuit of the truth—but that we will never fully attain it. We cannot know the world in and of itself, but only as it is filtered through the categories of the mind. Like other scholars, sociologists cannot pretend to be objective because their biases, explicit or implicit, will shape their work; nonetheless all scholars should attempt to transcend their own social and disciplinary contexts.

A second assumption is that religious pluralism will be a necessary precondition of the global village for the foreseeable future. The question that faces us as a human community is not "Which religious tradition is true?" or even "Is any religious tradition true?" but "How can we enable the various religious and secular traditions to coexist peacefully on the planet?"

A third assumption is the belief that the sociology of religion—itself a pluralistic discipline—can provide invaluable insight into the most pressing problems of the late twentieth century. That is not to say that sociologists should therefore lead the way in solving these problems (as Auguste Comte thought) nor that they should simply loosen the soil for contemplative thought (as Max Weber contended). Rather, sociologists should use their analytical tools to assess religion in the global community and become involved in the lively debates about the future of humanity that will ensue.

Finally, in the classroom I believe it is important to inform my students of my biases from the beginning so that they do not have to play guessing games. I will do the same here, because I think my background shapes what I see and how I interpret it. I am the son of a Methodist preacher, from a long line of clergymen, who became politically conscious in the

1960s and has participated in civil rights and peace movements. I continue to be a practicing Christian although I have reinterpreted some of the church's doctrines in my own way. My study of the world's religions, along with time spent living in India and China, has further shaped my personal beliefs, as did two years working on a master of arts in religion at Yale Divinity School. My wife and two daughters are Jewish, and we go to Quaker meetings on a regular basis as well as attending other religious ceremonies from various faiths. The astute reader will detect these shaping influences in the pages that follow.

Lester R. Kurtz

Acknowledgments

As the author of this book I am responsible for any errors. The list of contributors to the work's form and content would fill several hundred pages and would include everyone from my family to authors whose work informed me to teachers both past and present. I would like to give special thanks to Sarah Beth Asher, who encouraged, edited, inspired, and informed this volume from beginning to end, as she does all of my work, and to my muses Poeta and Patience, who endured the process. Others to single out are the editors of the *Sociology for a New Century* series, Larry Griffin, Charles Ragin, and especially Wendy Griswold, whose guidance was invaluable. Of the Pine Forge Press team, Steve Rutter became as much a valued friend and colleague as a publisher, as did Rebecca Holland. Editor Victoria Nelson reshaped every page with care, and anonymous reviewers provided valuable suggestions. Finally, my students energized this project and influenced it in many ways, as did numerous friends, colleagues, teachers, and strangers from around the global village, especially Rebecca Chopp, Yuan Horng Chu, Steven Dubin, Christopher Ellison, Tenzin Gyatso, Robert Herrick, S. Jeyapragasam, Juan Linz, Fred Kniss, Edgar Polome, Darren Sherkat, Edward Shils, Gideon Sjoberg, Teresa Sullivan, David Tracy, Stephen Warner, Andrew Weigert, and Robert Wuthnow.

I give special thanks to those who reviewed the book:

Darren Sherkat, Vanderbilt University

Mark Shibley, Loyola University

Kristen Wenzel, Sacred Heart University

Lester R. Kurtz

KEY DEVELOPMENTS IN TH

World Parliament of Religions
Chicago
1893, 1993

Crusades
begin 11th Centur

Th
1

King
1010-9

M
57

Christian Gospels Written
ca. 73-83 C.E.

ISLAM
in North Africa
7th century C.E.

BUDDHISM
to North America
20th Century C.E.

CHRISTIANITY
to the Americas
15th Century C.E.

WORLD'S MAJOR RELIGIONS

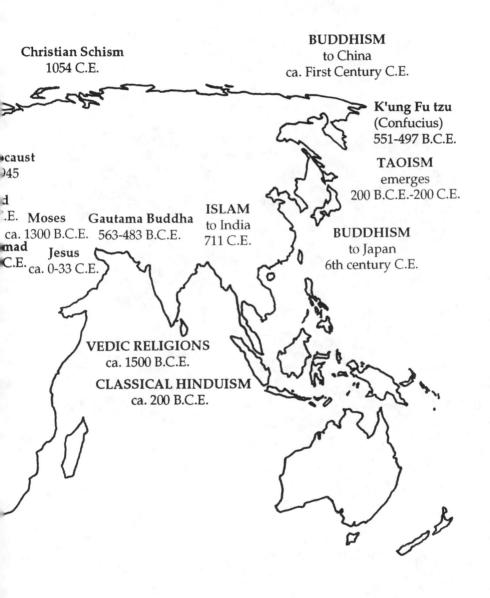

Christian Schism
1054 C.E.

BUDDHISM
to China
ca. First Century C.E.

K'ung Fu tzu
(Confucius)
551-497 B.C.E.

caust
945

TAOISM
emerges
200 B.C.E.-200 C.E.

d
.E. **Moses**
ca. 1300 B.C.E.

Gautama Buddha
563-483 B.C.E.

ISLAM
to India
711 C.E.

BUDDHISM
to Japan
6th century C.E.

mad
C.E.

Jesus
ca. 0-33 C.E.

VEDIC RELIGIONS
ca. 1500 B.C.E.

CLASSICAL HINDUISM
ca. 200 B.C.E.

Gods in the Global Village

1

Religious Life in the Global Village

Jews from around the world can now fax their prayers to the Wailing Wall in Jerusalem. Fortunetellers in China provide computer-generated astrological charts. Telecommunication satellites link isolated religious communities at separate ends of the earth; American television offers its viewers Christian preachers and Buddhist teachers. In the summer of 1993, representatives of religious communities met at a Parliament of the World's Religions in Chicago to establish a process for ongoing dialogue and to initiate a debate on a declaration of a global ethic. At lectures given by a Hindu teacher in Texas, a large color portrait of the Indian guru Sai Baba is framed by a vase of fresh flowers and a candle painted with an image of the Virgin of Guadalupe. In the middle of Colombo, Sri Lanka, sits St. Anthony's Cathedral, a pilgrimage center for hundreds of thousands each week, 90 percent of whom are not Christians but Buddhists and Hindus.

The pleasant coexistence of religious traditions is only one side of the story, however. In early 1994, an Israeli doctor entered a mosque in Hebron at the Cave of the Patriarchs, where Abraham is supposed to be buried, and murdered over thirty Muslims at prayer. He in turn was beaten to death, and violence broke out again between Jews and Muslims throughout the region. In India, Hindus and Muslims have been killing each other in a flare-up of a centuries-old conflict, now focused on the destruction of a Muslim mosque by Hindu nationalists at a disputed site in Ayodhya. Catholics and Protestants have been fighting one another viciously in Northern Ireland, and Muslim militants have targeted "officials, police officers, Christians and occasionally tourists" in an effort to replace the secular Egyptian government with a more traditional Islamic theocracy (Ibrahim 1994). The Ku Klux Klan still marches in the United States, using religious arguments to denounce African Americans, Jews, and others. In the former Yugoslavia, Serbian Orthodox Christians have been engaged in a campaign of "ethnic cleansing" of Muslims that involves wholesale slaughter.

The global village is becoming a reality economically and socially, if not politically, as every isolated corner of the planet is being knit together into a world system. This global order, emerging for several centuries, has become a reality in the twentieth century,[1] as all humans increasingly participate in a "shared fate" (Joseph 1993; cf. Durkheim 1915; Wallerstein 1984). Our economic and social institutions, our culture, art, music, and many of our aspirations, are now tied together around the world. But the human race is constructing a multicultural global village full of conflict and violence as well as promise.

Just as the Cold War between the United States and the Soviet Union ended in the 1990s and astounding progress was made in solving old conflicts, ethnic and religious nationalism exploded in violence around the world. Mark Juergensmeyer contends that rather than witnessing the "end of history" (see Fukuyama 1992) and emergence of a worldwide consensus in favor of secular liberal democracy, we may see the coming of a new Cold War, one between the secular West and numerous new religious nationalisms. "Like the old Cold War," says Juergensmeyer (1993: 2), "the confrontation between these new forms of culture-based politics and the secular state is global in its scope, binary in its opposition, occasionally violent, and essentially a difference of ideologies."

Social life may be fundamentally different in the next century, although many features of today's life will persist, just as there was much continuity between pre-agricultural and agricultural eras, premodern and modern times. A major task of the coming millennium will be to order our lives together and to create an ethos, or style of life, with a moral basis. The ethos must include sufficient agreement about common norms to facilitate cross-cultural interactions, international commerce, and conflict resolution while permitting considerable cultural diversity on the planet. The process of coming together, however, will not be an easy one. Religious traditions are central to that process because of their role in defining norms, values, and meaning; in providing the ethical underpinning for collective life; and in forging the cultural tools for cooperation and conflict.

Much of the best and worst of human history has been created in the name of its gods, and religious traditions continue to provide both an ethical critique of, as well as a justification for, much bloodletting. The central thesis of this book is that the sociological study of religion has important insights into the central issues of how we can live together in our multicultural global village as well as helpful tools for investigating the problems created by our newly created common life with its diverse norms and values. Our task here is to review those insights, assess the tools, raise questions, and develop some tentative conclusions about the role of religions in promoting chaos or community as humanity moves into the twenty-first century. Whether or not we can discover a means for sustaining a diversity of religious traditions and a wide range of ethical values and still live together remains an unanswered question.

The world's religion will be an integral part of the process, for better or for worse. Faith traditions "work" because they answer fundamental questions in a comprehensive way. That very strength, however, sometimes results in exclusivistic claims to a monopoly on the "Truth," which, in a multicultural global village, often precipitates fatal conflicts among competing religious claims and the people who make them. The very things that hold a community together can also tear it apart.[2]

Religion and the Globalization of Social Life

Our ancient ancestors sat around the fire and heard stories about their forebears—about the time when life first emerged in the universe, about lessons for living their lives. When people gather today, the flickering light comes from a television rather than a fire, but we still hear stories about the nature of reality as it is perceived in our own culture. Many of the Earth's previous inhabitants heard only one story about creation during their lifetime, but today most people hear more than one as the various religious traditions of the world—as well as newer scientific ones— diffuse widely through modern means of mass communication. We are surrounded not only by our own cultures but those of countless other peoples. Encountering these different perspectives on life is stimulating and enticing, but the overall process of cross-cultural contact is highly complicated because meaningful differences do exist among religions and sometimes provide the basis or excuse for confrontation.

Historically, religious ideas have provided the major organizing principles for explaining the world and defining ethical life for elites and masses alike, and they continue to do so, but modern critiques of religion have shaken them to the root. The globalization of our "lifeworlds" (Habermas 1987) will have as great an impact on religious life as industrialization did. Just when humanity most needs an ethical system that enables diverse peoples to coexist peacefully and justly, the traditional source of such guidelines are being daily undermined by the challenge of modern science and the increased cross-cultural contact.

Many conflicts occurred throughout the history of Christianity, of course, but none so radical as those precipitated by the crisis of modernism in the last two centuries. Scientific arguments called into question not just specific dogmas but the very notion of dogma. As the Roman Catholic pope put it in 1907, modernism lays "the axe not to the branches and shoots, but to the very root" of the faith (Pius X 1908b: 72). Cross-culturally, meanwhile, competing religious traditions were offering alternative religious explanations to fundamental questions about life and how it should be lived.

Even before the changes in society and culture associated with industrialization had time to become fully absorbed, however, the world changed again—just as profoundly—when the various human communities were thrust into intimate contact by late twentieth-century communications and transportation technologies and the globalization of an advanced capitalist economy that relies on far-flung networks of production and consumption. Most scholars in the nineteenth century predicted a new era of peace and prosperity, yet the twentieth century brought bloodshed on a scale never before experienced and prosperity for a privileged few, accompanied by mass starvation and misery for many more.

The communications and transportation revolutions of the twentieth century took off in the post–World War II era. By the time Marshall McLuhan (1960) introduced the term **global village** into our vocabulary, a new awareness of the interconnectedness of our lives was emerging. In the 1960s and 1970s, a massive increase in international trade transformed the nature of economic processes. Capital from the industrialized countries, in search of cheap labor, was shifted to so-called "less developed" nations so that much of the actual production process moved outside the United States and Western Europe and into Third World countries. By the early 1970s, the 500 U.S. major corporations were making 40 percent of their profits abroad.

These economic changes were intertwined with dramatic transformations in the civil society and political spheres as well. In 1900, there were about 200 nongovernmental organizations in the world, that is, noneconomic institutions organized to take care of some aspect of human life. By 1990, the number had risen to 6,000, creating a web of structures ranging from religious organizations to humanitarian, activist, and other civic organizations. Cultural diffusion, driven in part by economic developments, has resulted in a global greed for consumer goods among those people who can afford to participate in the system (and often a hope for participating among those who cannot afford to do so). In addition to nation-states, regional and international political alliances and institutions are playing an increasingly important role, right up to the United Nations, which functions as something of a quasistate at the global level.

At the close of the nineteenth century, the sociologist Emile Durkheim ([1893] 1933) observed that the emerging world system of his day showed two separate and contradictory trends: increasing unity and increasing diversity. This insight proved to be an enduring one. Even as our lives are becoming ever more intertwined, the people who exist in our every-day world are more and more diverse. Most people do not live in isolated homogenous villages but in heterogeneous cities. International trade, global social networks, and telecommunications locate us all in the same shared space. Even rural villagers are linked in an unprecedented way to the world economy as they send and receive goods around the globe.

Most people are ambivalent about the new world order. Many enjoy the material benefits, but they have come at a high price—including the destruction of many of the world's indigenous cultures and radical trans-formations of other societies as well as widespread ecological devasta-tion. The last two centuries have seen violence and misery on an unprece-dented scale, but a portion of the world is healthier, eats better, and lives longer than the royalty of past civilizations. In the nineteenth century, the people with the most advanced technology, Western Europeans, subju-gated most of the rest of the world; in the twentieth century they began slaughtering one another at an unprecedented rate as militarized conflict was industrialized and the technology of war created "total war," in which—for the first time in history—all humanity is involved and all are potential victims.

The sociology of religion provides one valuable approach to a serious study of the dilemmas plaguing modern culture. In the nineteenth cen-tury, science seemed to be replacing religion in the cultural centers of Europe; the Christian church cast its lot with the monarchy and appeared to be dying along with the old order. More than a century later, however, religion persists as a vital force in the world. Because of its persistent importance, the study of religion remains central to any adequate under-standing of the nature of human life. The discussion that follows provides a brief introduction to the history of the sociological analysis of religion, some of the analytical tools that can be used to explore current trends in religious life, and the series of themes that will inform this book.

Religion and the Sociological Tradition

Nineteenth-century sociologists, even as they mistakenly anticipated the imminent demise of religion, created a new approach to the study of religion that is rich with insights relevant to our lives. By identifying the very issues that define our present struggle, the intellectual quest initiated by Durkheim, Weber, Nietzsche, Marx, and Freud can help us as we move into a twenty-first century that teeters between destructive conflict and harmony.

Religion and sociology were always closely linked historically. The creation of the discipline of sociology in the nineteenth century was in fact largely an effort to come to grips with the crisis of faith and the revolutionary turmoil of the post-Enlightenment West. With the modern sensibility came a new level of self-consciousness about fundamental questions ordinarily taken for granted or explained by religious tradition. This intense reflexivity of the eighteenth and nineteenth centuries gave birth to the modern social sciences and explains why the earliest social scientists attempted not only to use scientific methods to explain social life, but to create a new basis for morality as well. From Immanuel Kant, Adam Smith, Auguste Comte, and G. F. W. Hegel to Karl Marx, Sigmund Freud, and Emile Durkheim, most of the major European intellectuals of this period sought to formulate a scientific moral basis for collective human life that would replace the religious foundations of European culture.

It is no accident that three of those intellectual giants—Marx, Freud, and Durkheim—were Jews living in a culture built on a Christian tradition that was being widely challenged by science and competing religious perspectives. Cross-cultural encounters and social and cultural revolution usually precipitate innovation, and the post-Enlightenment West was no exception. Moreover, the personal torments of these men—and of others who built the social sciences—were representative, in many ways, of the experience of millions buffeted by the storms of modernism.

The founder of sociology, the French philosopher Auguste Comte (1798–1857), was trapped between his traditional family—his father was a fervent Catholic and royalist who supported the monarchy and opposed democratic reform—and the rebellious democratic, anticlerical milieu he encountered when he left home. Comte became a champion of scientific inquiry, contending that antiquated theological thinking gave way first to metaphysics and then to science, or what he called "positive philosophy." He insisted that the methods of physics and the natural sciences could be applied to social life in order to construct a rational social order, solve the profound problems of human life, and elevate the intellectual over the rest of humanity with its coarser affective faculties.

Comte initiated a series of lectures outlining his master plan of human knowledge—the "Course of Positive Philosophy"—in which he proposed that a scientific sociology could solve the burning social problems of the day that the monarchy, the church, and the Revolution alike had failed to address. He insisted that religion was simply a residue from an earlier era and that science could replace it to everyone's benefit. Just as his lectures began, however, Comte suffered a mental breakdown and attempted suicide. The vociferous opponent of religion and champion of science eventually became a practitioner of "cerebral hygiene" and refused to read anything but the medieval devotional classic *The Imitation of Christ*. In his final years, isolated from his peers, Comte founded a "Religion of Humanity" in which he championed affect over intellect.

Karl Marx (1818–1883) came from a long line of Jewish rabbis, but his father converted to Christianity as a compromise to advance his position in the predominantly Lutheran community in Germany in which he lived. Marx's own disenchantment with religion was fueled by what he saw as the coopting of religion by elites to control the dependent classes; he attacked religious ideologies of repression with a moral passion, called upon the oppressed to turn from theology to politics, and was marginalized and exiled for his views. Similarly, Sigmund Freud (1856–1939)—himself a victim of anti-Semitism in Vienna—saw religion as a psychological defense mechanism to compensate people for the deprivations they suffered as a consequence of social organization, such as the repression of sexuality and the channeling of energies into building civilization rather than meeting personal needs. Freud advocated that the "illusions" of religion be replaced by rational mastery of one's environment.

Emile Durkheim (1858–1917), as the son of a French rabbi, was forced to make a sharp break with the Ashkenazi Jewish community that had nurtured him from infancy when he took up Auguste Comte's sociological banner. Durkheim's lifelong intellectual struggle to find a scientific substitute for the civic morality French culture lost when it rejected its Catholic past resonated deeply with his own personal trauma as he converted first to Catholicism and then to the anticlericalism of the Parisian intellectual scene of the late nineteenth century.

German sociologist Max Weber (1864–1920) spent his life struggling with the contradictions between the religious faith of his pious Protestant mother and the secular bureaucratic world of his politician father. He became increasingly estranged from his father, who died shortly after a visit to the younger Weber's home, where they fought violently and Weber asked his father to leave. After this event Weber fell into a deep depression for five years. When he recovered, he grappled with the issue that became the central agenda of his intellectual life: the tension between religious faith and modern Western rationality.

The groundwork for contemporary sociology of religion was thus laid by five men—Comte, Marx, Freud, Durkheim, and Weber—who were personally as well as intellectually caught up in the broad historical currents of change sweeping through Western civilization. Religion was one of the first phenomena to occupy sociologists because it lay at the center of the intellectual, religious, and political controversies of the time. When Comte coined the term **sociology** in the mid-nineteenth century and advocated replacing the "arbitrary" authority of the church with a new authority based on science, Christian clerics branded sociologists as the devil's workers. Sociologists and practitioners of religion have enjoyed a love-hate relationship ever since.

Tools of the Trade: Methods and Metaphors

The methodological tools sociologists use in studying religion are part of the intellectual heritage of Western European social thought from the seventeenth through the twentieth centuries. Like the other social sciences, sociology draws from the post-Enlightenment concept of the **scientific method,** which requires the investigator to disengage as much as possible from personal biases to gather and interpret information about the world.

The first task of sociologists, like other social scientists, is to gather data and attempt to define their subject matter with clarity. Sociologists of religion utilize standard data-gathering techniques such as social surveys and interviews, ethnographies (direct observations of settings), and textual analysis (of religious writings, speeches, etc.). All scientists simply look for indicators of the reality they are exploring, and instruments to measure them must be tailored to the phenomena in question. Social science methodologies have become more sophisticated in recent years, and many scholars make skillful use of traditional statistical methods. Because of the nature of their subject matter, sociologists who study religion tend to be eclectic in their approach and often draw upon techniques from the humanities as well, using such conceptual tools as **metaphors** and **sensitizing concepts** that illuminate the nature of a particular reality. Some of the best work in the sociology of religion relies on both metaphors and statistics.

Sociological definitions of religion. One of the first conceptual tools we must have to begin any intellectual inquiry is a good definition, but religion poses an obstacle. Weber admits that the term is impossible to define, at least at the beginning of a study (Weber 1968; cf. Plock 1987); William

James ([1902] 1960: 46) similarly advises us not to look for a single essence, but rather to explore the many characters of the phenomenon. Nevertheless, as Barbara Hargrove (1989: 21) correctly observes, we cannot beg the question of definition, because it will shape "the questions we ask, the behavior we observe, and the type of analyses we make."

The classic sociological definition comes from Durkheim (1915: 62), who says that religion is a *"unified system of beliefs and practices relative to sacred things, that is to say, things set apart and forbidden—beliefs and practices which unite into one single moral community called a Church, all those who adhere to them* [emphasis added]." Deleting the ethnocentric term "Church" gives us a still serviceable definition that points to the four major sociological components. **Religion,** then, consists of the beliefs, practices (rituals), the sacred, and the community or social organization of people who are drawn together by a religious tradition.

Every religion has a **system of beliefs** about the world and what should be considered **sacred** or held in awe (Durkheim 1915), or what is of "ultimate concern" (Tillich 1967), which are expressed in myths or stories that encompass a wide range of possibilities. Viable religious traditions usually incorporate some answers to the fundamental questions of the meaning of life and how the world was created; they offer some comfort, perhaps even joy, in the face of suffering and death. Such ideas are usually woven together into a series of narratives that include stories about unusual encounters with the sacred experienced by ancestors and other significant figures. The beliefs of a religious tradition never stand in isolation, either from one another or from the life of the **community** in which they are held. Any given religion is also part of a people's culture; in societies with little institutional differentiation, religion and culture are often essentially the same. Heterogeneous societies with multiple religious communities will develop a culture in which religion (even all religions represented in the society) constitute only a part of the culture, especially when there is a secular state. The fundamental "truths" they contain are persistently recalled and reinforced in **ritual practices** that also sustain the social order. Rituals include religious festivals, rites of passages (including births, marriages, and funerals) and the like, which hold the spiritual and material world together.

Sociological Metaphors About Religion

Sociologists have used a number of metaphors to describe elements of religious life, that is, analogies that sensitize observers of religion to aspects that might not be immediately apparent. Among the most common metaphors are three that we will employ throughout this book: the sacred canopy, the religious marketplace, and elective affinities.

Constructing a sacred canopy. Religious and cultural traditions are a result of the construction of what Peter Berger (1969) calls a **sacred canopy** over the life of a people. That is, they provide a sheltering fabric of security and answers for both the profound and the mundane questions of human life: What is the meaning of our existence? Why do people suffer and die? How can we get food for our family today? A particular social group's answers to these questions usually provide an overarching vision of the universe as well as a perception of how individual and collective life should be organized. That canopy may cover only a small subculture (such as a religious commune or an isolated tribe), or it may cover an entire national culture (such as Iran's). It may be used to legitimate a resistance movement or a national elite.

Meant to function in a small, homogeneous society, these unilateral belief systems are difficult to construct and maintain in a multicultural society. In pluralistic societies such as the United States or India, the belief systems of social groups differ so sharply that even the vaguest consensus is difficult to reach. Here the canopy metaphor is not adequate for describing the rich religious life of the entire society unless we think of it either as sewn from numerous differing threads or as a patchwork quilt. Perhaps a "force field" would be a more appropriate metaphor than a canopy, because it implies a dynamic system that has a reality of its own but one that is constantly changing. We will, however, cautiously use the sacred canopy metaphor in this analysis because it has been widely used in the past 25 years and it points to a key aspect of religious phenomena: believers do try to construct a sacred canopy that shields them from the vicissitudes of life, and they often think they have succeeded. The problem with the metaphor is that it presents an image that is too static for this dynamic phenomenon. We must keep in mind that the canopy is never a finished product; its construction is a process that is constantly underway.

Whether a society is small and homogenous or large and diverse, its religious symbols grow out of, and in turn act back upon, social life. Religion is a matter of what Berger calls **world construction,** that is, it is an attempt to make sense out of the universe. Although our natural and social worlds are given to us when we are born into them, humans are also cocreators of their own world. Certain fundamental parameters (e.g., the law of gravity and the inevitability of death) impinge on us. Yet we continue to form our own interpretations of the ecosystem, creating perceptional models that significantly affect the reality outside us. Because we are all involved in world constructions, this active creation of ours is a dynamic process that continuously acts back upon us, its producers.

Religion is at the core of the world-constructing process because it involves the highest level of the process: what a people holds sacred. Berger (1969) suggests that the construction of the sacred canopy involves three basic elements: externalization, objectivation, and internalization. The first element, **externalization,** is simply the ongoing outpouring of human beings into the world around them, both physical and mental. In our daily lives, our thoughts and actions affect and shape the world in which we exist. Through our activity, we create **material objects** (e.g., buildings, machinery, toys, paintings, books) and **cultural objects** (e.g., theology, money, institutions, social networks, etc.; see Griswold 1987) that change the world in some small or great way.

In the second stage of this process, our creations become objects external to us. This **objectivization** means that after we project our creations onto the world, they confront us, their original creators, as facts external to and separate from ourselves. Sometimes authors who create fictional characters find that they lose some of their control over those "people" as the figures develop personalities of their own. In the same way, once we create an institution—a university, a corporation, or a church—it seems to take on a life of its own, functioning independently and sometimes even in opposition to its designers.

Finally, in the third stage of world construction, we reappropriate the reality that has become objective and transform it from structures of the external world back into structures of our subjective consciousness through **internalization**. In other words, we **internalize** the outside world through the process of socialization. In relating to other people, individuals learn to accept their culture's sacred canopy as a given and natural reality. Each society, according to Berger, thus creates a *nomos*, a meaningful order that is then imposed upon the experiences and meanings of individuals and provides norms, or rules, for every situation and every social role. Traditionally, this process of constructing a worldview and nomos has been a religious quest, although it has become more self-conscious and dispersed since the arrival of the modern era. Broad theories of the universe and the ethical systems and rituals that grow out of them are now created by a variety of institutions, some traditionally religious, like churches, synagogues, and religious orders, and also by people who are deliberately independent of religious institutions, such as myth-makers and other shapers of culture, like writers, artists, scientists, journalists, entertainers, and intellectuals. Although the struggle to control the production of culture has been widespread throughout human history, clearly no one has a monopoly on it in the postmodern world (see Griswold 1994). Religious leaders find themselves competing in a cultural marketplace even when they try to make exclusive claims to the truth.

Religious marketplaces. Since cultural and social diversity are the distinguishing characteristics of modern life, individuals or groups in the global village can choose their religious orientations from a variety of options rather than simply accepting the specific sacred canopy transmitted to them by their family and friends in early childhood. Thus, a second central metaphor in the study of religion is that of the **religious marketplace.** Dissatisfied with the sacred canopy metaphor, recent scholars coined this image to emphasize the fact that in a multicultural society religious institutions and traditions compete for adherents, and worshippers shop for a religion in much the same way that consumers choose among options in the marketplace for goods and services (Warner 1993).

As Warner correctly notes, the reality addressed by the religious marketplace metaphor in the American case is not so much economic viability as the disestablishment of religion. It turns out, in fact, that the secularization so hotly contested in the post-Enlightenment European sociology of religion is actually the exception worldwide rather than the rule. Europe's established Christian churches of the Middle Ages were something of an anomaly, though one often taken as a universal norm by European and American sociologists of religion, and the extent of the Catholic monopoly may have been overdrawn (see Finke and Stark 1992). Although religious perspectives may be relatively uniform in small, homogeneous societies, they are never so in heterogeneous ones, and attempts to impose a single sacred canopy over such societies are never fully successful. The more pluralistic a society is, the more likely it is that people can choose their religious preferences. Students of American religion have thus found the marketplace metaphor helpful for examining various developments in the United States (Iannaccone 1991; Stark and Bainbridge 1985; Finke and Stark 1992; Lee 1992) in which people seeking religious experience make a rational choice among various "spiritual entrepreneurs" (Greeley 1989).

A number of forces shape the religious market: individual preferences of consumers (see Iannaccone 1990; Sherkat and Wilson forthcoming); the process of cultural production and the creators of the narratives embodied in a tradition (Stark and Bainbridge 1985); and the social world in which cultural constructions are found, including both the religious community with its norms that shape individual preferences (Sherkat and Wilson forthcoming; Ellison and Sherkat in press) and the broader world in which that group exists. The marketplace metaphor has its shortcomings too, of course. Ethical systems and beliefs of ultimate concern are not bought and discarded as easily as shoes or houses, and ancient religious practices persist in the most advanced technological societies.

As Iannaccone (1988, 1992) observes, subgroups gain from their distinctiveness in the religious marketplace, so that such issues as sacrifice and stigma—which are usually seen as costs when an individual is making choices—actually become benefits to a religious group that deliberately seeks tension with the dominant culture in order to provide participants with a distinctive identity (see Stark and Bainbridge 1985; Finke and Start 1992; Iannaccone 1994). Religious worldviews usually acknowledge that believers might incur costs or be labeled negatively for their beliefs but claim that future rewards will compensate them for any current sufferings. This insight suggests that religious particularism will thrive even as the globalization process intensifies; membership in a religious community labeled deviant by the mainstream becomes, for many believers, a way of protesting the trends of modernism and postmodernism, which they abhor. Whether they are located within the Islamic, Christian, Jewish, Hindu, Buddhist, or some other tradition, religious traditionalists, as we shall call them (see Chapter 6), cling to localized versions of a religious tradition in defiance of broader global developments.

Elective affinities. Since, as we have seen, a sacred canopy usually does not span the life of an entire society in the global village, it still may serve to protect a particular social stratum or group. Because religious beliefs and expressions are always closely linked to social life, individual social groups are drawn toward their own cultural styles and definitions of the sacred. Certain ideas seem particularly suited to some status groups and lack any sensible fit with others.

Weber (1947: 83) uses the metaphor of **elective affinities** to describe this relationship between ideas and interests (cf. Howe 1979). He takes the metaphor from Goethe's famous novel of the same name in which two people who are inexorably drawn toward one another despite the fact they are already married to other people. The concept of elective affinities is an extremely useful one for examining the relationship between culture and social structure, in part because it shows the connection between the two phenomena in a dynamic and nondeterministic way. Farmers and businesspeople are drawn to pragmatic theologies, for example, whereas university professors might prefer more abstract religious ideas. Affinities between the interests of some status groups and particular ideas or belief systems do emerge, but that does not mean that people have no free choice in selecting their own beliefs and practices.

The extent to which a religion is attached to particular social strata or ethnic groups varies over time and across traditions. Judaism has always been closely linked with a particular ethnic group and continues to be tied to the phenomenon of being Jewish by blood. Similarly, Hinduism is closely linked to the South Asian subcontinent; few people outside that geographical region are practicing Hindus unless their ancestral roots are there. The other major world religions are less clearly linked to ethnic groups, although Buddhists are most likely to be Asian (although they do not have to be) and Muslims are most likely to be Arab (although not necessarily). Some subgroups link their identity to religious traditions: Latinos are more likely to be Roman Catholic than Muslim or Quaker, for example.

These tendencies are partly a result of historic circumstances (such as who conquered whom), but may also be related to Weber's (1947: 83) notion of elective affinities between the ideas and the interests of particular social strata. Specific groups of people sometimes use religion as a way of promoting their own interests, but they also may find a given religious orientation more helpful in explaining the world as they experience it. Ethnic variations in religious expression become socially significant only when ethnic status is meaningful in a society—that is, when lifestyles and social status are based at least in part on ethnic criteria.

Religion has traditionally been linked to specific geographic locations in the social world. Because faith traditions can either sustain or subvert the social systems in those places, some traditions—or versions of them—attract a system's elites, whereas the rebels in a society have a natural affinity with other religious beliefs or interpretations of the same tradition. Elites in virtually every culture use religious legitimations to explain why they are in control and others are not. Similarly, the most effective dissident movements often employ religious arguments to legitimate their own position. Some of the most successful movements for social change are religiously motivated and religiously framed, which gives the struggle an intensity and legitimation otherwise unavailable, and makes it easier for reformers and revolutionaries to mobilize popular support. Religious traditions have provided both ideological support and institutional resources for a number of significant social change movements in the twentieth century, from the Indian Freedom Movement to the U.S. civil rights movement, from the People Power Revolution in the Philippines to anti-apartheid forces in South Africa and prodemocracy forces in Eastern Europe and the Soviet Union (see Chapter 6).

In the analysis that follows, we shall use the elective affinity metaphor to identify connections between religious traditions and various social groups in the global village. Of special interest is the common tendency for intense ethnic, class, and even gender conflicts to emerge along religious cleavages and to be framed in religious rhetoric.

Contemporary Approaches to the Sociology of Religion

Like the discipline of sociology in general, the sociology of religion has become more empirical and quantitative in its methodologies since Weber and Durkheim, largely because of the development of computer technology, statistics and social surveys and in part because of the theoretical orientation of modern researchers. Consequently, even though contemporary sociologists of religion usually examine the same issues as the discipline's founders and in much the same way, they are more precise and therefore often more narrow (see Wuthnow 1987).[3] Let us now examine four current theoretical frameworks that form yet another set of tools for the contemporary sociologist of religion.

The classical sociological tradition of Marx, Weber, and Durkheim has produced a "neoclassical" perspective—represented by Peter Berger, Clifford Geertz, Robert Bellah, and Thomas Luckmann—that tends to be **subjective**, emphasizing individual beliefs and attitudes, opinions and values. This perspective, which dominates much of current work in the sociology of religion, adapts well to survey methodologies and often uses the sacred canopy metaphor to frame its questions. The focus of these social psychological studies is usually on the problem of meaning and an individual's interpretations of reality.

In recent years, a second, **structural** approach explores patterns and relations among cultural elements. Its central task is the identification of structures (orderly relations and rules) that give culture coherence and identity. Structural studies by such scholars as Mary Douglas examine such phenomena as boundaries, categories, and elements of behavior (as opposed to attitudes, beliefs, and values), a category that includes discourse, gestures, objects, acts, and events that are amenable to observation. Thus, the structural approach examines not so much the content of the tradition's beliefs as the relationship between the religious system and the structures of social life.

A third, **dramaturgical** approach examines expressive or communicative properties of culture and its interaction with social structure. This approach, as Wuthnow (1987) suggests, explores the expressive dimensions of social relations over either individual feelings (the subjective approach) or structural categories (the structural approach). Much of this analysis focuses on ritual and its symbolic expressions of a moral order as a prototype of other symbol systems. It can be traced historically to Durkheim's (1915) and Malinowski's (1954) studies of ritual, embellished by Kai Erikson's (1966) exploration of witchcraft trials in colonial New England and more recent work inspired by Erving Goffman and others.

A final contemporary school—and one especially relevant for examining culture in the global village—is the **institutional** approach, represented in work by Guy Swanson and others. From this perspective, "actors who have special competencies" produce culture and sustain it through institutions that ritualize, codify, and transmit cultural products (Wuthnow 1987: 15). Proponents of this approach maintain that these social institutions of religion are often more securely understood than the more abstract notions of myth and ritual, and thus provide the firm empirical ground on which to address the larger issues.

In this volume, we will weave together elements of the four approaches—subjective, structural, dramaturgical, and institutional—as we analyze the world's religions, because each identifies a significant element of religious life. The subjective element is important in identifying how individuals are linked with the broader human community through the **worldview** and ethos options available to them in a diverse social setting. The various beliefs of religious systems are interconnected structurally and tied in patterned ways to each other and to the social system in which they are developed. Sociologists tend to be especially interested in religious institutions as key players in the social world, and the ways in which religious ideas are performed on the world stage. An individual Hindu, for example, interprets the world and acts in it according to the cultural patterns provided by his or her social networks and institutions as they collide with the institutions, beliefs, and practices of people from other religious traditions by means of the globalization process.

Anyone trying to understand religion in the global village will find in sociology a fruitful analytical framework. It is only fair, however, to warn the reader of some problems with the way sociologists look at religion. Religious traditions are, from a sociological perspective, comprehensible constructions of the human mind, yet they transcend comprehension. They comprise a collective effort to make sense out of life and death, but (like life itself) are riddled with contradictions and paradoxes. Religion tries to bridge the gap between temporal reality—what sociologists are rather good at describing—and the mysterious aspects of reality that cannot be easily examined, if they can be studied at all, by empirical methods. Consequently, sociologists often focus on those elements of religious life that are immediately observable: religious institutions, written texts and patterns of behavior, opinions about religious matters studied through surveys. Much of this subject does not fit neatly into our narrow conceptual boxes of survey instruments, however. We cannot discern by data gathering if the gods exist, let alone interview them face to face, so our conclusions seem always inadequate. Like astronomers looking for faint evidence from distant galaxies or archaeologists examining potsherds from the bottom of a 3,000-year-old well, we often have to choose between focusing on inconsequential details or constructing explanations that go far beyond what our data allow us to say.

The sociologist of religion tries to discern patterns, but since religious expression is so varied, the enterprise is fraught with danger. The sociologist of religion may also offend a person's religious sensibilities by subjecting his or her beliefs to rational scrutiny. The historical prejudices of the sociological tradition, developed primarily by white Western males, also stands in the way of objective observation. Even the language we use to discuss religion is riddled with prejudice. In talking about the deities of the world's religions, for example, it is difficult to generalize. If we talk about a "God," we imply a monotheism common in Western, but not Eastern, religions. If we refer instead, to "the gods," monotheists may object. Some, like Buddhists, are uncomfortable with the idea of a transcendental deity, since they believe that all creation is ultimately a unity.

Do the gods—or God—exist? The norms of science require us to be as objective as possible, yet science cannot answer this question because it involves a faith stance, not a strictly empirical one. Scientists examine phenomena indirectly by looking at indicators. If we could agree on what or who God is and what indicators might prove his/her/their existence, then we could test its reality. But we could not agree on the most basic indicators, and if we did, measuring them would be difficult as well.

Each of the sets of sociological tools we have examined here—definitions, metaphors, and theoretical frameworks—aids the task undertaken in this book. The sociology of religion, growing as it did out of the social turmoil of nineteenth-century Europe, identifies the struggles of late twentieth-century multiculturalism and points us in a direction that will assist us in understanding the current state of religion in the global village. The tumultuous history of the field betrays its assets and liabilities: the sociology of religion is relevant and valuable because it was born out of the early stages of battles we continue to fight. Yet those who forged it were partisans to the fight, and we must remain conscious of their limitations as well as of their insights.

Major Themes in the Sociology of Religion

Sociologists cannot answer questions of the ultimate meaning of life or the relative truth or fallacy of religious traditions, but they can examine systematically how these issues are dealt with in human societies. To undertake our analysis, Chapters 2, 3, and 4 will introduce the major religious traditions we have inherited from the premodern world and apply the conceptual and methodological tools of sociology to the task of understanding religious beliefs and practices. A short tour, in Chapter 2, of the central beliefs, rituals, and institutions of each major religion will focus on these traditions not as static belief systems but as dynamic processes that have changed dramatically over time as various civilizations have risen, fallen, and come into contact with one another. The historical and sociological nature of religious traditions is an essential starting point for our analysis.[4]

Chapters 3 and 4 elaborate on the "tools of the trade," as outlined briefly in Chapter 1. They discuss the conventional means by which some social theorists and researchers have tried to understand the relationship between religious and social life, primarily in the past century in the West. We will use the sociological studies of religious life to construct a comparative analysis of existing religions. Three themes emerge from the sociological literature on the nature of religious life as it has been practiced up to the modern period:

1. Religion is a *social phenomenon.* Each religious tradition grows out of, and in turn acts back upon, the social life of the people who participate in it.

2. Religious traditions contain a systematic set of *beliefs* that are acted upon and sustained by *rituals* and *institutions.*

3. Each tradition constructs a religious *ethos* that defines the taboo lines between acceptable and inappropriate behavior, defines identities, legitimates social orders, and provides guidelines for everyday life.

Once we have described the historical religious context of the emerging global village, we will examine the twin crises of modernism and multiculturalism, identifying another three themes that are usually implicit rather than explicit in sociological literature:

4. *The advent of the modern world created a crisis for religious communities,* challenging traditional beliefs with scientific critiques and competing views of the world.

5. *The multicultural context of the global village precipitated contradictory responses:* a revitalization of ancient traditions (e.g., fundamentalism), civil religion and nationalism, and religious syncretism.

6. *Religious tradition in the global village can promote chaos or community,* either facilitating the construction of a peaceful world or intensifying and justifying violence between conflicting social groups.

The focus of Chapter 5 is the crisis of modernism, as precipitated by the advent of science and intercultural contact that challenged the beliefs, rituals, institutions, and ethos of every religious tradition. As religious communities absorbed scientific teachings even as they found themselves confronting other faiths on a daily basis, people within each tradition struggled to find a way to solve the crisis posed by these assaults on the absoluteness of their belief system. Chapter 6 examines responses to modernism and multiculturalism in more detail; people within each community have tended either to develop protest theologies that revitalize their own tradition as a way of resisting elements of the modern world, or they create new religious approaches that synthesize elements of more than one tradition. Chapter 7 focuses on the relationship between religion and social conflict, first in the frequent link between religion and violence, and second, in the ways in which religious traditions develop nonviolent means of conflict. The book concludes by exploring the ways in which religious communities can either promote violent conflict and warfare or cultivate a global culture that facilitates the creation of a community in which diverse groups coexist peacefully.

Let us now embark on our inventory of the major religious narratives, practices, and communities inherited from the past so that we may assess the current state of religion in the global village and consider the possibilities of its future direction.

2

The World's Religions: A Sociological Tour

If a group of ten people were taken to represent the world's religious communities, three would identify themselves as Christians, two as Muslims, two would be unaffiliated or atheists, one Hindu, one Buddhist, and another would have to represent every other religious group, including various folk religions, tribal or shamanist traditions, and even Judaism (see Figure 2.1).

This example is complicated by the enormous numbers of people actually involved. On closer examination, for example, we will discover that each of these persons represents not only a religious tradition, but particular elements of the world's social organization as well. Some religious traditions are surprisingly underrepresented; for example, Jews do not get a full representative because their numbers are relatively small. Because of the broad dispersion of Jews around the world (in more than 100 countries), however, and their impact on religious and political affairs, their influence is much larger than the numbers would suggest. That groups such as shamanists would not get their own representative would not surprise most of the readers of this book. There are, however, more shamanists around the world (almost 10,000,000) than there are United Methodists in the United States.

In this chapter we will briefly examine some of the major beliefs and practices of the five major religious communities—Hinduism, Buddhism, Judaism, Christianity, and Islam. (Because of the diversity within each tradition, the discussion will be highly oversimplified.) Of special interest are the ways in which each of these traditions is organically related to a specific local social group and then changes over time as it diffuses and interacts with other religious perspectives. Although sometimes presented as immutable, each tradition proves in fact to be the product of centuries of transformation.

Types of Religious Traditions

Most efforts to classify religions are, out of convenience, theological: the texts themselves for most of the world's religions are readily available,

FIGURE 2.1

Approximate Membership in Religious Traditions

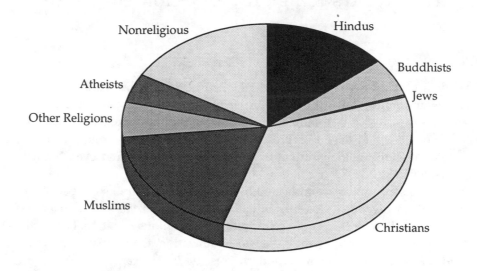

Source: Encyclopedia Britannica

although not always in good translation, so scholars can at least construct theological categories within which to place them. Do people believe in one god or many, male gods or female, or both? Are they more concerned with individual or collective religious issues, with the action of gods or humans? Is history presented as linear or cyclical? Was the world created by one god or many? Do people suffer because of their own actions or because of the actions of the gods?

The very questions we ask about religious traditions reflect our own culture-bound interests, however, and it is impossible to define "correct" or "orthodox" beliefs from within any given tradition, let alone to identify them from the outside. How are scholars to judge which sacred texts are significant, and how should they be interpreted? To what extent have time and translation altered the original sacred text; what was the socio-historical climate when it was produced; and how does it compare with the current context? How wide is the gap between what Redfield (1957) calls the **"big tradition"** (the "official" beliefs as defined by elites) and the **"little tradition"** (the version of a religion to which everyday people adhere)? How much of each of these traditions should be used to characterize a religion's theology? Which is more authoritative, the ancient or the recent versions of a tradition?

One theological distinction widely used by sociologists is that between **this-worldly** and **other-worldly** religious orientations—that is, does a religion emphasize ethical activity in this lifetime, or does it focus on what happens to people after they die or after a major transformation in the world, such as the coming of a messiah? Relying solely on religious texts to determine whether a tradition is this-worldly or other-worldly may be misleading, however; a text emphasizing rewards in the next life, for example, may serve to focus a believer's attention on how he or she lives in this one.

Other issues must be addressed outside the textual sources: Is the tradition more concerned with doctrine or with practice? What are the socioeconomic and demographic characteristics of the religion's practitioners? Have these characteristics changed over time? Are they similar around the world? To what extent do beliefs and practices vary between cultures and across social strata within cultures? Are certain kinds of people or social groups more likely to practice the tradition than others?

Those few broad, cross-cultural characterizations of religious traditions that brave scholars have attempted always fall short of the mark, but it is still helpful to get some sense of the varieties of religious life from a sociological perspective. Despite the impossibility of finding fully satisfactory answers, we will keep asking these questions throughout the book.

Evolutionary Schemes of Classification

A number of scholars of religion, especially during the nineteenth and early twentieth centuries, developed **evolutionary schemes** of classification as they attempted to make sense out of the broad range of religious behavior observed around the world during the colonial period. Using the metaphor of physical evolution, British folklorist Sir James Frazer (1854–1941) argues in his classic *The Golden Bough* that religion grew out of magic practices, an argument now widely discredited because of its ethnocentric implications about a model of progressive development leading from "primitive" to more "advanced." Frazer's theory was similar to earlier contentions by Auguste Comte that humans have progressed from a theological to a metaphysical, and finally to a scientific stage, in which arbitrary superstition gives way to rational scientific knowledge.

E. B. Tylor (1832–1917), sometimes called the father of modern anthropology, contended in *Primitive Culture* (1871) that the earliest and most basic religious forms were animistic, giving way first to fetishism, then a belief in demons, then polytheism, and finally monotheism. Marx and Engels ([1844] 1975) developed a theory of religious evolution as well, linked to their dialectical materialism. Because religion is an epiphenomenon of economic processes, they said, as the modes of production changed so did religion.

A more sophisticated evolutionary approach is Robert Bellah's (1964; 1970) typology of evolutionary stages. Not an entirely satisfactory model because it describes more the experience of Western culture than of all human culture, Bellah's typology is still helpful in examining some of the broad changes that take place over the course of human history. Bellah claims to describe not a unilinear development from lower to higher forms, but the ways in which religions and societies develop increasing differentiation and complexity of organization, thus becoming more autonomous relative to their environment. Such historical perspectives are important in order to understand continuities and discontinuities across historical epochs that shed light on the nature of contemporary religious beliefs, practices, and organization.

Sociological Classifications

Because the task is so difficult and the field lacks sufficient comparative research, sociologists have not developed a satisfactory scheme for classifying the world's religions. Ideally, a sociological approach would classify religions according to variations in the relationship between religious orientations and a variety of social criteria such as: (1) social strata, (2) different modes of production, (3) institutional and social diversity and complexity, and (4) various functions of religion.

1. *Social strata,* as examined by Weber ([1922–1923] 1946). To what extent do different strata have *elective affinities* with, and serve as carriers of, particular religious orientations, as suggested in Table 2.1.[5] One provocative treatment in the same spirit is the exploration of the differences between goddess worship in "partnership" societies and the warlike and hierarchical religious systems introduced by patriarchal invaders at the end of the Neolithic Age (Eisler 1988; Gimbutas 1982, 1989).

2. *Different modes of production,* suggested by Marx ("The German Ideology"), such as the relationship between the possible simultaneous emergence of monotheism and kingship during the agricultural revo-

TABLE 2.1

Weber: Elective Affinities Between Religious Ethics and Social Strata

Tradition	Strata	Characteristics
Confucianism	Literary prebendaries	Secular rationalism
Hinduism	Cultured literati (Brahmans)	Status stratification
Buddhism	Contemplative mendicant monks	World rejection
Islamism	World-conquering warriors	Disciplined crusading
Judaism	Pariah people Intellectuals trained in literature and ritual	Rationalist
Christianity	Itinerant artisan journeymen	Urban and civic

lution. Particular types of economic systems may have an affinity with specific kinds of belief structures.

3. *Degrees of institutional and social diversity and complexity,* as developed by Bellah (1964, 1970).

4. *Emphasis on different social functions* fulfilled by religious life, exemplified in Durkheim's ([1915] 1965) study of aboriginal religious life in Australia, and elaborated by a number of contemporary scholars. O'Dea and Aviad (1983) suggest that religion (a) provides support, consolation, and reconciliation; (b) offers a transcendental relationship that promotes security; (c) sacralizes norms and values of established society; (d) provides standards for critically examining established norms; (e) performs important identity functions; and (f) aids passage through the life cycle. Functional analysis also explores ways in which religion is dysfunctional in a social order.

Let us take a closer look at Max Weber's schema (see Table 2.1), which explores the religious determination of life-conduct in each tradition, beginning with the "directive elements in the life-conduct of those social strata which have most strongly influenced the practical ethic of their respective religions." Weber (1946: 268) argued that "these elements have stamped the most characteristic features upon practical ethics" in each tradition. The Confucians who received prebends, that is, a stipend from the state for their religious duties, were drawn to a secular rationalism that shaped the direction of the Confucian ethos. The high-status Brahmans of India promoted status stratification as a religious ideal, whereas the mendicant Buddhist monks who lived by begging and owned no personal property favored an ethic of world rejection. Islamic warriors promoted a theology of disciplined crusading; the intellectually oriented Jews coped with their pariah, or marginal, status through the cultivation of rationalist religious ethics; and the itinerant artisans of Christianity developed a civic ethic.

Weber does not contend that the tradition is a "function" of the social situation of the stratum which appears as its "characteristic bearer," or a mere reflection of the stratum's interest. On the contrary, he claims that "however incisive the social influence, economically and politically determined, may have been upon a religious ethic in a particular case, it receives its stamp primarily from religious sources, and, first of all, from the content of its annunciation and its promise" (1946: 270).

Weber's theory centers on his notion of the elective affinities between ideas and interests, as discussed in Chapter 1. Thus, the religion of intellectuals tends to be relatively theoretical and that of business classes more practical, because of the affinity between their respective material interests and the different orientations. Nonetheless, once worldviews are established, they have their own force: "Very frequently the 'world images' that have been created by 'ideas' have, like switchmen, determined the tracks along which action has been pushed by the dynamics of interest" (1946: 280).

Of particular interest to Weber was the development of an emphasis on ethical systems, especially religions that call for action in the world. He finds this call more frequently in religious traditions carried by civic strata, especially when "they have been torn from bonds of taboo and from divisions into sibs [kinship groups] and castes" (1946: 285). Out of these strata comes the tendency for ethical prophecy to emerge, which articulates the gap between the world as it is and as it should be, calling on believers and elites to close the gap by remaking the world.

Weber undertook a long-term historical-comparative study of the world's religions from a sociological point of view, thereby founding the discipline of modern comparative religion, but he relied upon secondary sources that, though in most cases the best scholarship of his time, are now considered inconsistent and, in some cases, highly unreliable. Because of the increasing specialization of academia, no one has attempted since Weber to undertake a similarly ambitious task. Because no one has undertaken Weber's comparative project, the sociology of religion tends to be unfortunately parochial and more focused on North American, and especially Christian, religious life than it should be.

Classification by Local vs. Cosmopolitan Religions

The world's religious traditions have thus been classified in a number of ways by social scientists, such as by the relationship between religious orientation and various social characteristics (e.g., social strata and modes of production) and by stages of evolution. For our purposes, it is helpful to look at the ways in which all the existing religious traditions have transformed from local to cosmopolitan orientations. This will become more apparent as we look at the five dominant religions currently practiced around the world.

Whatever the reasons, it is clear that changes in society do occur when religious and social life become more complex and differentiated. *When social circles expand and social institutions encompass increasingly heterogeneous populations, changes in both cultural and social organization proliferate.*

German sociologist Georg Simmel (1858–1918) proposed in 1908 that *"individuality in being and action generally increases to the degree that the social circle encompassing the individual expands"* (1971: 252; emphasis his). When homogeneous social circles originally isolated from one another come into contact, social differentiation increases at first, but gradually an increasing likeness emerges between the groups. Processes of "differentiation and individualization loosen the bond of the individual with those who are most near in order to weave in its place a new one—both real and ideal—with those who are more distant" (1971: 256).

The primal, **local religions** in relatively isolated locations focus on direct connections between life and existence as it is experienced locally, thus highlighting the continuities between human and natural life, the cycles of life and death, the significance of particular animals, plants, and elements of the local ecology. A particular mountain or animal species may be considered sacred and be featured in religious ceremonies because of its importance in the local environment and the lives of humans living there. As social circles and religious traditions expand across diverse cultures, a transformation occurs. At first, differentiation emerges within the circles and the traditions: encounters with other groups and religions with different characteristics accentuate the previously unnoticed differences *within* each group as well as commonalities between them.

When a religious tradition crosses cultural boundaries with a conquering force that imposes it upon indigenous worldviews and lifestyles, not only is the preexisting culture transformed, but the conquering tradition is as well. In the spread of Buddhism across Asia and the diffusion of Christianity along with the European colonialists, each tradition became more diverse as it adapted to a wide variety of local religious traditions and institutions. All of the dominant religions in the world today are, by definition, **cosmopolitan** rather than local, because they have diffused around the world over time and thus have been transformed. Even the traditions that remain more tribal—Judaism and Hinduism, and to a lesser extent Islam—have been so altered by encounters with countless local traditions that they have lost their geographic particularity as their beliefs and practices have become more varied. Primal elements run deep within each cosmopolitan tradition, however, and the continuity of symbols and stories across the centuries persists to some extent even among the most cosmopolitan sectors.

Hinduism

From one part of India to another, the rich mixture of cultures is reflected in a panoply of religious customs varying from region to region. Within each location, there are also extreme differences. A wide range of gods and rituals reflect and inform the diversity of roles and situations in which humans find themselves as they move through their life cycles. To some extent, gods and rituals are chosen by each temple, household, and individual on the basis of situational requirements, personal disposition, gender, caste, occupation, and stage in the life cycle. The underlying theme of this elaborate religious system is that each individual must discover his or her own path—with the aid of religious authorities—in order to cope with life's suffering, and eventually to escape it.

Hinduism is a religious tradition that encompasses layers of complex deposits from many different cultures over the centuries. Its remarkable diversity and doctrinal tolerance combine with a highly elaborated worldview and ethos that provide hundreds of millions of people with compelling answers to the basic questions of human life. Because of this religious anchor, they can live out their daily lives with a sense of dignity, despite widespread poverty and misery, and feel connected to a larger community.

As in many other societies, however, the stratification system is also sacralized, that is, made a part of the religious belief system. The exploitation of the masses by a small number of extremely wealthy and powerful families is legitimated by the traditional Hindu worldview. In recent decades, as these problems have been addressed by Hindu reformers, this ancient tradition is incorporating the egalitarian norms of modern culture under its sacred canopy alongside ideas and symbols that have endured for thousands of years.

The wide-ranging collection of beliefs and practices known as Hinduism dates back about 3,500 years,[6] linking contemporary and ancient India. Scholars dispute the origins of Hinduism; believers claim that it had no beginning. Contemporary Hinduism, however, probably emerged out of the encounter between the indigenous Dravidians and the Indo-Aryans who migrated into India from Central Asia or Iran about 1500 B.C.E. Some contemporary scholars believe that practitioners of the **Vedic religion**—that is, the faith based on the ancient Vedas now called Hinduism—encountered Jainism and Buddhism between the fifth and second centuries B.C.E., laying the foundations of modern Hinduism. Hindu ideas and practices evolved over the centuries across the subcontinent in a myriad of forms as various cultures of the region became intertwined, prefiguring the process of intercultural contact now occurring in the larger global village.

The strength of Hinduism has been its rich combination of highly rational with nonrational symbolism on one hand and its adaptability and theological tolerance on the other. Perhaps the most consistent theme in Hinduism is variety, and a central tenet of the perspective from the religion's earliest periods has been the belief that there are many paths to the "Truth," with the result that Hinduism has taken root and grown in a wide diversity of cultures on the Asian subcontinent. One of its most essential ideas is that people can reach their ultimate goal—to break the chain of rebirths in a process of liberation called *moksha*—by discovering one's own *dharma* (duties or responsibilities) and performing them well, thus enabling one to advance in a new lifetime or eventually to escape the cycle altogether. The idea that different paths lead to the same summit opens the door to remarkable flexibility in overall orientation and specific practices under a single broad sacred canopy.

At the center of the Hindu faith is a diverse collection of hymns, ritual chants, and collections of stories about encounters with the sacred in its myriad forms. The religion's beliefs are expressed in the hymns called the Vedas, which were originally transmitted orally, like most ancient religious literature, and compiled about 1500 B.C.E., at the time of the Dravidian-Aryan encounters. The Vedas themselves, according to tradition, were not authored—even by the gods—but have always existed, and were "discovered" by the sages who then transmitted them. Gods and humans interact regularly in these texts, creating stories that have been the lifeblood of social life in Indian villages over the centuries.

The Rig-Veda, which consists of ten books with liturgical chants and sacrificial formulas, is seen as the source of all truth and provides the basis for much of the material in other Vedas, each of which has a huge body of interpretive literature. Six or seven centuries before the Common Era, of philosophical speculations was a collection compiled as the **Upanishads**, first as part of a secret cult threatening the religious establishment, but later as a central component of Hindu literature. Finally, the massive epics of the *Mahabharata* and the *Ramayana* are the classics of Hindu literature, read and told by village storytellers, priests, and elders for centuries. The former consists of about 100,000 verses (twice the size of the *Iliad* and the *Odyssey*) and includes the famous **Bhagavad Gita**, the "Song of the Lord." The *Mahabharata* has been revived in the late twentieth century in a somewhat sensationalized form, in a television series that has riveted Indian audiences.

The gods serve as models both for everyday life and for the structure of authority in Indian life. Just as the gods' authority flows from their heroic deeds, so individuals with authority must prove their worthiness but are accorded considerable deference once they establish their legitimacy. The gods of Hinduism are highly specialized in character and function. They number, according to some estimates, about 33,000,000, and at least one god addresses each social and psychological need, whether it be safety (Vishnu), wealth (Lakshmi), or liberation from the pursuit of safety and wealth. The elephant God Ganesha is the overcomer of obstacles who aids people in need of courage or assistance in times of trouble. Most Hindus, however, believe that only one God stands behind the multitude of these manifestations.

This complex belief structure serves to unite the ethnic and economic diversity of a large majority of India's 800 million people. These social groups and subcultures interacting with one another across the vast Asian subcontinent are loosely bound in a shared worldview while maintaining their own autonomy. Each temple, and most households, has its own style of worship, choosing those gods and rituals that have an affinity with its interests. Nonetheless, the Vedic texts and Hindu epics, the stories of gods and humans interacting, stretch a loosely woven sacred canopy over the heterogenous social order of the Indian subcontinent.

A central task within the Hindu tradition has been making sense of these diverse cultures within a single geographical territory, and an effort to address that social problem lies at the root of major doctrinal developments within Hinduism. The famous teacher Shankara (c. 788–829 C.E.) attempted to systematize Hinduism by claiming that all reality is one (monism) and that we live in the illusion (*maya*) that individuals have a separate existence from the universe. The Supreme Reality, the Brahman, is unqualified and absolute in contrast to the world in which we live with its cycles of suffering, death, and rebirths. In the same way that actors perform a play, our lives have a provisional or dependent reality, dependent on the *Brahman*, or ultimate reality. Thus, the unity and diversity of the world are simultaneously affirmed in Shankara's school and the problem of social diversity is thereby solved theologically: there appear to be many gods, but there is really only one; there appear to be many social orders, but there is really only one. Shankara's ideas prevail in Indian philosophy today, reinforced by the elaborate institution of his monastic order, which controls many of India's most important Hindu temples.

A second major school of Hinduism was started by Ramanuja (c. eleventh century C.E.), who claimed that a single unified reality exists, but it is qualifiable. Matter, souls, and God all exist in the world, but the first two are simply qualities of God. The popular appeal of this perspective is that it does not involve the rejection of the world implied by the monism of the Shankara. According to Ramanuja, the material universe, including one's family and all the various gods are all aspects of the one ultimate God. A third major Hindu school emerged in Madhua's thirteenth-century dualism—called Duaita Vedanta—which views souls as distinct from God and matter. Madhua believed that at least some souls could become enlightened and that one can achieve *moksha* through devotion to Vishnu. The two major branches of Hinduism—the **Shivaites** (embracing the teachings of Shankara and Ramanuja) and the **Vishnaivites** (embracing the teachings of Madhua)—continue the dialogue between the monism of Shankara and the dualism of Madhua, respectively.

In the many manifestations of Hinduism on the Indian subcontinent, the boundaries among the natural, human, and divine worlds are often unclear, reflecting the reality of a life that is much more integrated across species than that most Westerners experience. Even in the modern cities of India, cows, pigs, water buffalo, goats, and sometimes monkeys and other animals live side by side with humans. People who exhibit great spiritual powers and are revered because of their accomplishments become deified in popular culture.

Hindu religion expresses this fluidity of boundaries among the diverse parts of a unified world in a number of ways: Hanuman is sometimes a monkey, sometimes a god; Ganesha is sometimes an elephant, other times divine. **Ram**, a name widely used to refer to God, is a legendary human hero and is also an incarnation of the god Vishnu. Major figures in human history become godlike and are treated as such. In addition to small shrines to Vishnu and Shiva, for example, one also finds shrines to Gandhi. People take some gods' names for their own, and even businesses may be named after a god.

The focus of Hinduism for most believers lies not so much in theological arguments but in the actual practice of worship, primarily in acts demonstrating respect for a god in one's home or temple. Humans and gods are mutually dependent: the gods require sacrifices, especially in the form of food, to stave off chaos and sustain nature; if they thrive, they offer benefits to humans. Moreover, Hindu theology reveals its social origins in the fact that each god represents an important aspect of human life.

Many Hindus believe in a single "godhead," made up of three elements: **Brahma,** (or Brahman) the Creator; **Vishnu,** the Preserver; and **Shiva,** the Destroyer. Each of these gods has a stylized form of presentation as well as a female aspect or consort: **Saraswati, Lakshmi,** and **Parvati,** respectively. Each of the mysteries of human life is thus personified in a particular god. Issues of creation and death are embodied in Brahma and Shiva, respectively. The tension between the two for preservation and survival is addressed in the person of Vishnu, who intervenes repeatedly at times of crisis to give people hope. The male aspects of God represent the rhythms of natural life, whereas the female aspects are more closely linked with human nature and therefore more accessible to ordinary people. A Mother Goddess movement emerged around **Durga-Parvati,** a body embodying the immanent active energy (*shakti*) of the distant and terrifying Shiva, who is transcendent and generally inaccessible to common mortals.

Part of the key to Hinduism's durability is its ability to incorporate other religious symbols. The god Vishnu plays a particularly important role in this process because he becomes identified in various **avatars,** or incarnations (including the ever-popular **Krishna**), with local deities as Hinduism becomes more cosmopolitan over time. Some Hindus reincorporated Buddhism by viewing the Buddha as an avatar of Vishnu; others have gone so far as to include Jesus in the list. During the late nineteenth century, several important Hindu authorities began to explore the relationship between Christianity and their native faith and found a number of parallels. Some became exponents of Christianity as well as Hinduism: Sri Ramakrishna had a vision in which he was embraced by Christ, and Swami Vivekananda called on his fellow monks to become Christs and

"to pledge themselves to aid in the redemption of the world" (Prabhavananda 1963: xiv).

Hinduism enables people to cope with life as it is. Some characteristics of one's life change over time; others, such as socioeconomic status,
nationality, ethnicity, and gender, will remain stable. Hinduism teaches
people that their happiness and fulfillment lies in discerning their own
dharma and carrying it out to the best of their ability. In our analytical
framework, given stages in the life cycle, occupational tasks, and other
roles show affinities with particular gods and rituals under a loosely woven sacred canopy that integrates the diversity of individuals, roles,
groups, and ethnic communities living on the subcontinent. At its best,
Hinduism enables people to identify, yet in some ways transcend, the
givens of their life situations; at its worst, it legitimates a system of social
stratification in which privileged and poor alike become convinced that
the inequalities of society are both fair and immutable.

The ancient tradition of Hinduism provides some interesting models
for the cultivation of religious tolerance within a broader social tradition.
Deities and their representatives alike are highly revered, yet they are not
exclusivistic. They must prove their worthiness by providing perceived
benefits, whether spiritual or material, psychological or social. The pluralism of Hinduism within this broad unity is accomplished by means of
an extraordinarily large perspective from which life is viewed, as shown
in Hindu cosmogenies. Just as the details of life on a planet seem unimportant when viewed from a distance in space, so the teeming particularity of subcultures, castes, families, and individuals becomes less urgent
from the universalistic perspective of the Hindu cosmogeny.

Buddhism

India is a land rich in religious pageantry and history, and it is in that
fertile soil that the seeds of Buddhism were planted. The enormous gap
between wealth and poverty at the time (which persists to the present)
helped to precipitate the founding of this religious tradition, which as-
serts that life is full of suffering that can be escaped by showing compassion to all creatures in the world. Paradoxically, a person gains merit by
serving others and rejoicing in their good fortune. From this starting
premise we can see that Buddhist thought is extraordinarily rational, yet
also deliberately nonrational; straightforward, yet often paradoxical. The
Buddha's Middle Path, in fact, attempts to unite a series of opposites that

people encounter (as the Buddha himself did) in their life experiences: materialism versus rationalism; asceticism versus indulgence; skepticism versus belief; reality versus illusion, and so on. In short, Buddhists accept the contradictions of the world but also strive to overcome them.

No religious tradition has flourished for so long in such disparate cultures as has Buddhism, which has adapted to a broad range of indigenous cultures and changes over time while retaining considerable continuity over the centuries (see Cousins 1984: 278ff). The complexities of these Buddhisms are compounded by their flexibility and diffusion over many cultures during a period of 2,500 years. More than half of the world's population lives in areas in which Buddhism has at some time been the dominant religion. Even in places where Buddhism has been politically suppressed (notably the People's Republic of China), it continues to exert a substantial influence both at the level of popular culture, where religious rituals often persist, and in the general culture, which bears the stamp of centuries of Buddhist influence.

As noted earlier, religious traditions emerge or change during times of social change, and Buddhism is a product of just such an era. The sixth century B.C.E.—the period when both the founder of Jainism and Gautama the Buddha emerged as vital religious forces in India—was a time of considerable social and cultural ferment throughout Asia. Cyrus the Great was extending the Persian empire into Central Asia, and the Indus Valley was rapidly becoming the richest province of the empire. At about the same time, **K'ung Fu tzu (Confucius)** was responding to a period of war and chaos in China with his teachings about respect and order in heaven and on earth. The Buddha's religious teachings flourished in an environment in which diverse cultures were encountering one another, and Buddhism itself (like the other major religious traditions) was constructed as a response to multicultural contact.

Gautama Buddha, also known as Sakyamuni and Prince Siddhartha, was born about 563 B.C.E. as the son of King Suddhodana. More interested in fathering a ruler than a monk, the king tried to keep his son bound to this world by surrounding him with luxury and shielding him from ugliness, sickness, decrepitude, and death. According to Buddhist tradition, however, Siddhartha slipped out of the palace and saw a decrepit, broken-toothed, gray-haired bent old man, thereby learning about old age. On a second ride, he saw a body racked with illness and learned about disease. On a third ride, he encountered a corpse and learned about death. Finally, he saw a monk with a shaven head, robe, and bowl, and learned about the option of withdrawing from the world of wealth and power into which he was born. The young Siddhartha escaped the palace at night and joined the wandering holy men of the forest, studying with various teachers and following a life of strict asceticism. He found that path no more satisfying than the life of indulgence in the palace, however, so he experimented with more moderate means of seeking fulfillment. In the midst of intense meditation under the famous *Bodhi* tree, he obtained Enlightenment, or **bodhi:**

> I thus knew and thus perceived, my mind was emancipated from the *asava* [canker] of sensual desire, from the *asava* of desire for existence, and from the *asava* of ignorance. . . . Ignorance was dispelled, knowledge arose. Darkness was dispelled, light arose. (Buddha 1954: 249)

Although he probably did not intend to found a new religion, a large number of followers gathered around Siddhartha, and their ideas became popular throughout Asia. The complex network of Buddhist traditions is difficult to characterize briefly, but we can identify two major branches emerging from the adaptation of Buddhism to local cultures during its diffusion in Asia. Different elements of the Buddha's teachings were emphasized in different regions of the continent, according to their affinities with indigenous cultures, interests of the local ruling classes, and so forth.

The basic teachings of the Buddha are summarized in famous images such as those of the lotus and the river. The lotus is a ubiquitous symbol in Buddhist art and literature. This waterlily is a beautiful pale blossom that emerges in its fragile splendor from the mud of shallow ponds, suggesting that purity can spring up from the anguish of the world; it thus becomes symbolic of the Buddha's teachings that humans can rise above the suffering of the world. Widely used in both Buddhism and Hinduism, the lotus image pervades Eastern thought. The river occupies a similarly archtypical spot in Buddhist imagery. Gautama Buddha himself was much inspired by the symbolism of rivers, which helped him to understand the unity in the diversity of life. A ferryman taught him to listen to the river, in which the water continually flowed and flowed, yet was always there; it was always the same yet at every moment was new. In just this way, the role of the Buddha figure would also vary widely with numerous reincarnations or manifestations that have made this religion, like Hinduism with its many avatars, so adaptable to indigenous cultures.

The Four Noble Truths are a series of four propositions about the nature of life that also encapsulate the Buddha's teachings:

1. Life is *dukkha* (usually translated as suffering, pain, or anguish, although these are merely subjective attributes of the larger phenomenon).

2. This suffering is rooted in *tanha* (craving, desire, attachment).

3. One can overcome *tanha* and be released into Ultimate Freedom in Perfect Existence (Nirvana).

4. Overcoming desire can be accomplished through the Way, or the Eightfold Path to Nirvana.

The suffering of which the First Truth speaks is the pain that seeps into all finite existence. Like an axle dislodged from the center of a wheel or a bone slipped out of its socket, life becomes dislocated, especially on six occasions: in the trauma of birth, the pathology of sickness, the morbidity of decrepitude, the phobia of death, and the entrapment in what one abhors and the separation from what one loves. The cause of this disloca-tion is complex and may come from a former, present, or future life (see Gard 1962: 113ff). Once the cause of suffering has been realized, however, it can also be overcome, by means of the fourth principle. As the Buddha put it, "I lay down simply anguish [*dukka*] and the stopping of anguish [*nirodha*]."[7] This last principle asks that we follow the Eightfold Path, which requires:

1. *Right knowledge:* This is to be sought not by itself but in conjunction with the other seven attributes.

2. *Right aspiration:* Seek liberation with single-mindedness.

3. *Right speech:* Master one's use of language, so that it moves toward charity. Because it is an indicator of motives, one should avoid false witness, idle chatter, abuse, slander, and the like.

4. *Right behavior:* This lies at the center of the moral code of the Five Precepts, which we will examine in a moment.

5. *Right livelihood:* Avoid occupations incompatible with spiritual ad-vance.

6. *Right effort:* Will and exertion are important.

7. *Right mindfulness:* Note the importance of the mind and its influence on life ("All we are is the result of what we have thought").

8. *Right absorption:* Use techniques like those of *raja yoga*.

The early Buddhists had a pantheon that began with the five cosmic elements (*skandhas*): form, sensation, name, conformation, and con-sciousness. Known as the five Dhyani Buddhas, these elements were eventually conceived as the five primordial gods responsible for creation. A sixth Dhyani Buddha, Vajrasattva, is often added to the list, although he is of a rather different order because he serves as a priest to the others.

This system, though somewhat polytheistic, still posited ultimate reality as indivisible, a problem complicated by the fact that wherever Buddhism traveled, it incorporated indigenous religious practices—and along with them, indigenous gods.

Perhaps as a response to the millions of gods in the Hindu tradition against which Gautama Buddha and his followers were reacting, contemporary Buddhism relies more on the teachings of the Buddha than on the action of any particular gods. Moreover, the objects of worship in Buddhism tend to be humans who become divinized as a consequence of their acts during a lifetime, or local gods who are incorporated into the Buddhist tradition are then perceived to be Buddhas themselves.

In Mahayana Buddhism, the school dominant in northern Asia, including China, emphasis is placed on a Buddha's decision to remain a *bodhisattva*, that is, one who qualifies for entrance into Nirvana but chooses to work for the salvation of all beings before doing so. The importance of a *bodhisattva* in popular religion is quite understandable, as such a figure plays a vital intermediary role between the human and the divine worlds, just as Jesus, Mary, and the saints in Christianity, Mohammed in Islam, and the prophets in Judaism help to bridge the chasm between heaven and earth in their respective religions.

In practice, Buddhist religion places emphasis on the "Three Jewels," the Buddha, the **Dharma** and the **Sangha,** the teacher, the teaching, and the organization of followers, respectively. In a core ritual of worship, the faithful Buddhist chants that he or she takes refuge in the Buddha, the Dharma, and the Sangha, thus attempting to transcend this world of suffering and treat others with compassion in order to relieve both their suffering and his or her own.

Judaism

In the twentieth century no religious tradition has lived in isolation. The major living world religious traditions spring from the Indian subcontinent, where Hinduism and Buddhism emerged, and the ancient Middle East (or "West Asia"), where Judaism began and gave birth to the so-called "**Religions of the Book,**" which include Islam and Christianity as well as Judaism itself. The Judeo-Christian tradition became intertwined with Western civilization and was diffused even further as the Europeans conquered the Americas, Africa, and parts of Asia. Islam remained strongest in the Middle East, although it made substantial inroads into Africa and Central Asia.

Unlike Islam and Christianity, Judaism did not seek converts, nor did it syncretize well with other religions, as did Hinduism and Buddhism. As a result Judaism has remained primarily an ethnic religion with strong social boundaries separating Jews from other socioreligious groups. Jews did become widely dispersed geographically, however, and took their religion with them. Moreover, despite its continued identification with a specific social group, Judaism developed a universalistic theology. The impact of the Jewish faith thus goes far beyond its limited social and ethnic boundaries.

The God of Judaism was originally a clan god called **Yahweh,** the God of Abraham, Isaac, and Jacob. Hebrew tradition emerged out of the legendary relationship of two people, the husband and wife Abraham and Sarah, with this clan god. These founders of Judaism were apparently part of a large eighteenth century B.C.E. migration of people around the ancient fertile crescent of the Middle East, from present-day Iraq to what is now Israel. According to Jewish tradition, their migration, or **Exodus,** had a divine sanction:

> Now the Lord said to Abram, "Go from your country and your kindred and your father's house to the land that I will show you. And I will make of you a great nation, and I will bless you, and make your name great, so that you will be a blessing." (Genesis 12:1–3)[8]

This ancient tribal legend contains two elements of universalism: (1) the god is associated with a clan but is not limited to a particular place; and (2) the promise of blessing to Abraham (Abram) will benefit not only his clan, but "all the families of the earth." The movement toward universality is thus part of a decision to migrate, a journey that involves both disengagement from ancestral space and a sense that the protective clan god will travel with them. This mobility of their deity, the bond between a people and a god, and a nascent sense that the god is concerned about others outside their covenant are hallmarks of Judaism that persist through the centuries.

Judaism was institutionalized as a religion only after the Exodus from Egypt, probably in the thirteenth century B.C.E. According to the Hebraic scriptures, the descendants of Abraham and Sarah migrated to Egypt during a period of famine and became slaves of the Egyptians. Moses, a Jew raised in the palace, had a religious vision in which the god of his ancestors instructed him to liberate the slaves from the Pharaoh. In the watershed event of Hebrew history and religion, Moses and his brother Aaron organized the slaves, confronted the Pharaoh, and eventually escaped, after the Egyptians suffered a series of "plagues" because the Pharaoh refused to release them. A final divine punishment befell the land: "At midnight the Lord smote all the first-born in the land of Egypt, from the first-born of Pharaoh who sat on his throne to the first-born of the captive who was in the dungeon, and all the first-born of the cattle" (Exodus 12:29). The only first born who were spared were the Hebrews', because they put the blood of a lamb on the doorposts of their houses so that the destroyer would pass over it.

Released at last by the Pharaoh, the freed slaves wandered in the desert and established a covenant with their God. The **Decalogue** (Ten Commandments) given to Moses at Mt. Sinai established the exclusive relationship of the Hebrew people—a *berith*—with Yahweh, their god— no longer simply a clan god but God of the nation of Israel. In the ensuing years, the Israelites invaded their "Promised Land," conquered the people living there, and established a monarchy. The religious tradition laid down by Moses was dominant among the Israelites, but worship of the indigenous gods of the region was frequent as well, especially Ba'al, the God of Storms, and Anath (or Ashtoreth or Astarte), the Goddess of Love, War, and Fertility. Not surprisingly in an agricultural society, the worship of these gods involved the central issues of sex and fertility; the mating of the rain-vegetation God with the fertility Goddess was reenacted ritually by humans playing their respective roles, much to the dismay of Yahweh's priests (see Deuteronomy 23:17–18).

Ancient Judaism was a primal clan religion whose social organization took the form of a **theocracy,** a fact that put its stamp on the tradition that persists to this day. As a way of life, Judaism insisted on strict ethical standards in all economic enterprise and political activity. Yahweh demanded strict adherence to standards of justice, with special attention to the poor, the orphans, and widows. This concern for the downtrodden reflects the tradition's origins among an oppressed people seeking liberation.

The Hebrew scriptures (known in Christianity as the "Old Testament") were believed to come from God; the first five books (the Pentateuch) were believed written by Moses, an idea modern scholars generally reject. The **Hebrew scriptures** are comprised of (1) the **Pentateuch,** known as the **Torah,** or Law; (2) the **Prophets;** and (3) a vast body of commentaries containing oral and written traditions, including the Mishnah and commentaries on the Mishnah. Because Judaism emphasizes that Yahweh spoke to the Hebrew people through the Torah, this early emphasis on the written word rather than on an oral tradition placed its stamp on Western civilization as well. The rabbinic tradition, especially after the fall of Jerusalem in 70 c.e., cultivated the study of the Torah and later the **Talmud** (the Mishnah, along with collections of rabbinical commentaries); centuries of rabbinical training and Judaism's emphasis on learning, reading, and writing have produced a rich literature.

Much like Buddhism and its Three Jewels, the ideas of the Jewish faith can be summarized in three concepts: God, Torah, and Israel (the deity, God's teachings, and the community—in this case, the holy nation, or chosen people, of Israel). Ritual is more important than doctrine to the Jewish tradition, which except for the most fundamental confession of faith allows a wide latitude in belief. This lack of emphasis on doctrine, and the concomitant stress on ritual and community, is primarily a function of the fact that a Jew is not, for the most part, someone who *believes* in Judaism—that person is either born Jewish, or is not. A Jew is a member of a family, and those few people who convert to the faith are not just members of a religious community but become the "adopted children" of Abraham and Sarah (see Hertzberg 1962: 21).

The fundamental belief of Judaism is expressed as a ritual confession of faith found in the Torah and repeated in the *Shema*, the heart of morning and evening prayers:

> Hear, O Israel: The Lord our God, the Lord is One. Praised be His glorious sovereignty for ever and ever.
>
> You shall love the Lord your God with all your heart, with all your soul, and with all your might. These words which I command you this day shall be in your heart. You shall teach them diligently to your children. You shall talk of them at home and abroad, night and day. You shall bind them as a sign upon your hand; they shall be as frontlets between your eyes, and you shall inscribe them on the doorposts of your homes and upon your gates. (Deut. 6:4–9; trans. from the *Weekday Prayer Book* in Hertzberg 1962: 239)

With its vast literature and formidable richness, the Jewish belief system became the basis for the Christian tradition, a historical fact that resulted in its dissemination far beyond the boundaries of the ancient Hebrew tribes. Of particular importance for Christianity was the Jewish belief that one day the "annointed one," the Messiah, would usher in a messianic age of peace and justice for all humanity. The followers of Jesus insisted that he was that messiah.

Christianity

The religion we know as Christianity was started by a Jewish prophet, Jesus of Nazareth, who now has 1.5 to 2 billion followers (almost one-third of the world's human population); more people now call themselves Christians than identify with any other religious affiliation. *Sociologically,* the reason for Christianity's dominance of the religious landscape has not been a superior theology but its alliance with the power structures of Western civilization, first with the Roman Empire after the conversion of Constantine in the fourth century, and then with the Western European powers through the Middle Ages and into the expansionism of the colonial period. In the nineteenth century, colonial and missionary movements spread in tandem from Europe to other parts of the world, conquering land, economic and political resources, and cultures.

As many countries joined the global community through the colonial system, its political, economic, and intellectual elites were educated by Christian missionaries. Christianity, like other transplanted religions, transformed dramatically as it diffused across cultures and became increasingly cosmopolitan. One characteristic of Christianity, deriving from its multiculturalism, is the tremendous variety of "Christianities" around the world. As the religious movement spread, many of the indigenous religious beliefs and practices of various cultures were grafted onto the basic ideas of the Christian faith. Christian worship often includes pre-Christian religious rituals and takes on the color and many of the features of the indigenous religions it has replaced.

Before it became the official religion of Europe, Christianity was originally a backwater religious movement favoring the poor. Despite the diversity of its participants (see Grant [1963] 1972), the early Christian movement appealed especially to isolated, marginal people in a politically insignificant location rather than to those at the center of power. Because early Christianity was much different from contemporary practice, we have to cut through many layers of culture to understand its primary form (see Loisy [1903] 1976). Christianity was initially a Jewish movement, one of several reform movements at the time, and fell within the tradition of the Jewish prophets with whom Jesus identified himself. The apostles were a group of passionate itinerant preachers who ran into trouble with the authorities wherever they went—a far cry from the contemporary Christian leaders, especially in the West, who are respected members of the community (and usually middle class).

Jesus first joined the movement started by his cousin, John the Baptist, and did not develop his own group of followers until after John's execution. Although Jesus never declared himself to be the head of a new religion and repeatedly affirmed his faithfulness to the Jewish tradition, he did struggle frequently with religious and civil authorities of his day.

From the very beginning, people sought to kill him. In his first sermon, Jesus proclaimed:

> The Spirit of the Lord is upon me
> because he has chosen me
> to give the good news to the poor;
> he has sent me to heal the afflicted in heart,
> to announce freedom to the prisoners
> and give sight to the blind;
> to set free the oppressed,
> to announce the year of grace of the Lord.
>
> (Luke 4:18–19)

Immediately following the sermon (according to Luke 4:28–29), "all those in the synagogue were filled with wrath. And they rose up and put him out of the city, and led him to the brow of the hill on which their city was built, that they might throw him down headlong." This sort of controversy followed him throughout his ministry until he was finally executed by the religious and political authorities.

After Jesus' death, a dramatic occurrence changed the character of this small reform movement: his followers became convinced that he was raised from the dead. The movement itself was dramatically revitalized, becoming a thriving force that gradually spread throughout the ancient Middle East, and eventually into the centers of power, as well as the margins, of society.

One of the most sociologically significant characteristics of Christianity is its universalistic criteria for membership. Unlike other religious belief systems, which are usually closely tied to a specific social grouping, early Christianity was deliberately universal in its recruitment. Judaism is basically an inherited religion: to be a Jew, one essentially has to be born into the community. To be a Christian, in the early church, one had to meet no ethnic or tribal qualifications; one simply had to declare "Jesus is Lord" and go through a rite of passage of baptism to become a member of the community. This radical new nature of Christianity, consistent with Jesus' teachings, was institutionalized by the apostle Paul, who spread the new religious system throughout the ancient Middle East.

This lack of ethnic or tribal membership criteria led to a multicultural religious community very early on. Christianity emphasized belief more than ritual. A persistent central question of the community, "What must I do to be saved?" may sound familiar to many readers of this book, but it is a rare question indeed in the world's religions and in most religions makes no sense at all unless it is reformulated. Christianity thus became highly intellectualized as people began to fight one another over what beliefs were required to be a member in good standing of the community. In most other religious traditions, such issues were simply not central because the matter of membership was not so problematic. Thus the Christian belief system carries an added weight of historical importance as the defining feature of membership in this religion.

It is possible, despite the enormous number of variant Christian communities throughout the world, to isolate some Christian beliefs that are nearly universal among its believers:

1. Jesus Christ is God, and God is Love.
2. One should love God and one's neighbor.
3. God intervenes in history.
4. God's nature and will are revealed in the Bible.

The religious movement of early Christianity was centered around the person of Jesus, believed to be the **messiah,** the savior or liberator sent by God to deliver people from bondage. Gradually, the church came to see Jesus himself as God, along with the Creator (or Father), and the Holy Spirit. The combined divinity and humanity of Jesus—the doctrine of the **incarnation**—is not peculiar to Christianity but is one of its central characteristics. The idea of a "Godhead," similarly, is not altogether unlike the Hindu idea that a single Supreme Soul can be found in three manifestations that are incarnated in various ways. Together, the three elements, or "roles" of the Christian God, known as the **Trinity,** make up one single being, although the way in which they do has been a matter of considerable controversy throughout Christendom. The Christian concept of God incorporates the complementary (or contradictory?) ways in which the divine is experienced—as an originator of life (the Father, in its patriarchal imagery), as a liberator who comes to people's aid (the Son or Messiah, Jesus), and as the sustainer or spiritual energizer of life (the Spirit).

That god who created the universe, became human, and then sustains people as they pass through both the suffering and the joy of life is a god of love. In fact, God is frequently identified with love, providing an important element of the Christian **theodicy,** or theory of suffering and death: no matter how bad things seem to be, one can always be confident that the universe is a friendly one and love will ultimately triumph. The second major belief—that one should love one's neighbor as well as God—derives from Jesus's own teaching and forms the basis of Christian ethics, which we will discuss in more detail in Chapter 4.

Third, because Christians believe that God acts in history, the tradition has an historical perspective on the nature of the world. Ultimately, most Christians believe, God will bring about a dramatic transformation of the universe to fulfill the "Kingdom of God" on Earth as it is in Heaven. This kingdom is generally imagined as a peaceable one in which love and justice reign. Christian **eschatologies** (theories about the end of time) provide two distinct theories of how the kingdom will arrive: (1) A major cataclysmic event will occur, the Apocalypse, in which good people will be rewarded and evil people punished; and (2) a universalistic vision in which all of creation will be united in the Christ when he returns. Members of the early church were convinced that Jesus would return before they died, that the end of the world was imminent, and the Kingdom of God, as portrayed in the parables of Jesus and the teachings of the Christian scriptures, requires a radical commitment to God. People are expected to shed their traditional loyalties—even to their families and jobs—and live a life of love and justice.

Finally, Christianity is known as a religion of the Book; that is, its central beliefs are written and codified in a set of scriptures that are considered especially sacred. Two primary collections of writings comprise the Christian **canon** (the writings declared authoritative for a given tradition): the Hebrew scriptures (known to Christians as the Old Testament) and the New Testament (written between 50 and 140 C.E.), together known as the **Bible.** In practice, however, a smaller section—a "canon within the canon"—identifies portions of the Bible as more significant than others. The four **Gospels** are traditionally given primary importance in the church because they record the life and teachings of Jesus, but in many churches (especially more conservative congregations), the **Letters** (or Epistles) take a more prominent place.

Much contemporary scholarship has focused on the historical development of the Christian scriptures, believed by some to be the literal word of God and by others to have been written and changed over time. As noted in Chapter 1, controversies about inconsistencies in the Bible are as much political as religious, because they raised questions about the reliability of Christian theodicies and other truth claims, and so were used by nineteenth-century pro-democracy forces in Western Europe to attack the church as a basis of the monarchy's legitimacy. Most of the claims about a literal interpretation of the Bible that the Roman Catholic Church made in the heat of the battle have since been withdrawn by Rome, but many Protestant groups continue to believe that such a position is a necessary doctrine for any true Christian.

Islam

In the name of God, the Mercy-giving, the Merciful!

Praise be to God, Lord of the Universe,
the Mercy-giving, the Merciful!
Ruler on the Day of Repayment!
You do we worship and You do we call on for help.
Guide us along the straight Road,
the road of those whom You have favored,
with whom You are not angry,
nor who are lost!

—*The preferatory chapter of the Qur'an*[9]

Judaism, Christianity, and Islam are sometimes called "three strands of a tightly woven rope: the **Abrahamic tradition,**" because they trace their roots to the same Semitic religious heroes, Abraham and Sarah. The particular situation of Islam was to retain the universalistic doctrine of early Christianity while tightening the social boundaries of its faith community.

The Islamic faith is one of the fastest-growing and most misunderstood religions in the world today. Approximately one out of seven people, many of them living in some of the most politically sensitive parts of the world, call themselves Muslims. At the center of Islamic belief is a strict monotheism (the concept of *tawhid,* the unity of Allah) and the belief that God spoke to humans in the **Qur'an,** the Islamic scriptures.

Islam's founder, Muhammad, known as the **Prophet,** was born about 570 c.e. in the Arabian peninsula. Orphaned at a young age, he grew up in his merchant uncle's household and became a well-established and very respected merchant himself. He married a wealthy widow, Khadija, had children (two sons died and four daughters survived), became a respected citizen of Mecca, and then became disenchanted with his comfortable life and the materialistic meaninglessness of his culture. Muhammad experimented with spiritual contemplation in a cave on Mount Hira, just outside of the city, and spent long hours in solitary meditation. One evening in the cave a voice spoke to him, the first of a series of revelations recorded in the Qur'an. He was petrified and ran home to his wife, who was one of the few who stood by him at the beginning of his long and difficult spiritual journey.

Muhammad began relating the revelations he had received to others in Mecca, but he was met with hostility and mounting opposition from religious and business elites there, who considered him a threat. The tribe of Quraysh, which controlled Mecca, first tried to coopt him and then threatened him; local merchants instituted a social and economic boycott against his entire family and then attempted to kill him. Some of the Prophet's converts fled to Ethiopia in 615, and in 622 Muhammad and his followers left Mecca, moving to the nearby city of Medina, where they established their religious community, the *ummah*, the foundation of Islam. The Muslim calendar, in consequence, begins in that year.

The *ummah* grew quickly in Medina, and its influence spread to the surrounding territories. This expansion led to military conflicts between Muhammad's followers and a Quraysh army, among others. Eventually the *ummah* became the dominant religious, military, and political force in the region. In 629, Muhammad and his followers returned triumphantly to Mecca, took control of the city, and established the religious practices and organizational patterns of Islam.

The Islamic faith, which draws extensively from Judaism and to some extent from Christianity, centers first of all around intense commitment to and worship of the One God, Allah, the Creator of the universe; as the Qur'an puts it:

> Your God is God Alone;
> There is no deity except Him,
> the Mercy-giving, the Merciful!
> (2:163)

Second, God's word is found in the Qur'an as revealed to the Prophet Muhammad. Thus the Qur'an is the Word of God for Muslims in the same sense that Jesus is the Word of God for Christians. The Qur'an is written in the Arabic language and, among the strictly orthodox, cannot be translated into any other language; this prohibition is breaking down, however, as Islam becomes more cosmopolitan.

Third, God requires a disciplined, ethical life, as outlined in the Qur'an; and fourth, the tradition is institutionalized within the context of the all-encompassing religious community, the *ummah*. Strict doctrinal and social boundaries are drawn around Islam and the community of believers, although Islamic conquerors have often shown considerable tolerance for others to practice their own religions. The uncompromising monotheism of Islam led to a strong condemnation of "idolatry" and the association of other deities with Allah, sometimes leading to conflict with other religious communities, as in India, where a plethora of gods is sometimes seen as competing with Allah. The disciplined life, Mohammed believed, was essential for believers to cultivate in a natural and social environment hostile to spiritual growth.

Despite Muhammad's prophetic departures from earlier religious practices, Islam remained close to its roots in early Judaism. Muslims believe Islam is merely the latest expression of the Abrahamic tradition, and the language and ethos of their religion is similar to aspects of ancient Judaism. Muhammad is a prophet who stands in the direct line of prophets stretching from Abraham and Moses through the ancient Hebrew prophets Isaiah and Jeremiah. A sophisticated and very diverse tradition today, Islam still retains many elements of a primal religion, in which religious life is ideally coterminous with everyday life. Human conduct should always be oriented to God, according to Islam, so that daily life is sacralized by the religious experience. These ideas are reflected in the so-called **Five Pillars,** the basic ritual practices of the faith, which will be discussed in more detail in Chapter 3.

If the Qur'an is Islam's soul, the family is its body. The family is the basic unit of Islam and is supposed to mirror the ideal society. Religious institutions still regulate the traditional Islamic family, in which there is little blurring of gender roles. Women play an important role, although a complementary rather than egalitarian one; just as God is the head of the human family, the man is the head of the household. This is part of the reason for the strong reaction against the intrusion of Western ideas about the changing role of women, now a major political issue throughout the Islamic world.

The Social Construction of Religious Traditions

Specific religious beliefs provide a coherent worldview for people in a specific cultural and historical situation; they may or may not make sense to people outside the context in which they were created. The social organization of a people, and the religious tradition(s) to which they subscribe, are intimately and dialectically related, molding and shaping each other over time. Religious tradition explains to those within a faith community why the world and its inhabitants are here; why evil, suffering and death exist; and how one should live one's life. These ideas are expressed both through rational discourse and through myths and legends that incorporate the contradictions of life. They are reenacted and reenforced through rituals that solve social problems, identify evil, offer guidelines for action in times of crisis, and legitimate the religious institutions that emerge out of each religious movement that survives. These ideas, rituals, and institutions do not operate only on some abstract plane, they also deeply infuse the daily lives of believers. As people with different traditions are thrown together in the same social space, the changes the new situation precipitates are profound.

Many of the same threads, such as the ethical system that orders everyday life, run through different religions. Distinct cultural styles emerge within separate religious traditions, however, that persist over long periods of time and space; they affect how people love and fight one another and establish a general tone and lifestyle for a people (their ethos). Although enormous variations exist within each broad cultural framework, some general tendencies reach across entire civilizations. We can see these large patterns more clearly when we compare Eastern and Western cultures and religion.

One general *tendency* we find in contemporary Western religions (primarily the various Judaisms, Christianities, and Islams) is the idea of one God who created the universe and regularly intervenes in history. The implicit message to believers is, "Go thou and do likewise"; that is, an active deity who is constantly shaping and creating the world expects worshippers to do the same. God often sends people on missions to do the divine work in the world, and sometimes even everyday economic activity; this is defined as a "calling" from the deity. Consequently, a tendency toward a this-worldly orientation, emphasizing action in the world at the behest of the deity, is evident in most of the Western religions, although each of them possesses an other-worldly theology as well.

Eastern religions, in contrast, tend to worship either many gods, specialized according to different functions, or humans who become deified, such as the Buddha or K'ung Fu tzu (Confucius). Rather than giving commands and intervening in history, these gods seem to prefer simply to explain how the universe works and tell people how to do their best with what they have been allotted in this lifetime. They instruct people to determine their *dharma* (religious obligation/duty) for a particular stage of this lifetime and carry it out to the best of their ability. Because of **karma** (the law of cause and effect that governs the universe), they will either be rewarded because of their faithful commitment to their *dharma* or they will be punished for failing to fulfill it. One's duty is, therefore, not to change the world, as in Western religions, but to follow its rules in order to escape its control. The usual reward, according to Hindu and Buddhist traditions, is a more favorable incarnation for the next lifetime, and the expected punishment is an unfavorable one. Thus, it is not a matter either of being particularly moral or immoral or of doing or not doing what the gods tell one to do or not, but simply whether or not one is harmoniously aligned with the universe.

Each of the five major world religious traditions was forged as a response to the social and existential conflicts of their founders and the social strata that carried them. Hinduism probably emerged out of conflicts between the indigenous Dravidians and Aryan invaders of the Asian subcontinent. Buddhism was formed in the era of changes sweeping Asia during the sixth century B.C.E. and the Buddha's own representative struggle with the tensions between wealth and poverty. Judaism emerged from the context of the migration and enslavement of a clan; Christianity was created in the intercultural conflict of the Roman empire's conquest of the ancient Middle East; and Islam came into being amidst warring Bedouin tribes and the growing materialism of the merchant class. Those varied social contexts and intercultural conflicts provided the soil in which the beliefs, rituals, and institutions of each tradition were cultivated.

3

Beliefs, Rituals, and Institutions

A religious tradition's worldview is outlined in a set of interrelated beliefs that explain the world and guide people in living their lives. These ideas are expressed through narratives (myths and legends) that incorporate the oppositions and contradictions of life. They are reenacted and reenforced through rituals that are sustained by, and in turn provide legitimacy for, the institutions of each religious movement. This interplay among beliefs, rituals, and institutions is the focus of this chapter. The elements of religion we explore will no doubt continue to play a role in human societies however they may evolve in the next centuries. The form and contents of these inherited traditions will persist, although they will also be transformed. When the world changes, so does tradition—even when it is presented as immutable truth. In this chapter we will take a closer look at what Durkheim identified in his classic *The Elementary Forms of the Religious Life* (1915) as the central components of religious life: beliefs, rituals, and institutions. We will undertake a brief overview of many contemporary religious patterns not only in terms of how they function (Durkheim's primary focus) but also how they have changed over time. The change process especially has profound implications for the future of religious life and collective life in the twenty-first century.

Anatomy of a Belief System

Each religious tradition has a set of interdependent beliefs that are woven together in such a way that the integrity of the entire fabric is dependent on each strand. The structure of these cultural systems involves the identification of what is considered sacred and meaningful, a set of theories about how and why the world was created, and an explanation for suffering and death.

Belief systems express a worldview, that is, a culture's "picture of the way things in sheer actuality are, their concept of nature, of self, of society. It contains their most comprehensive ideas of order" (Geertz 1973: 127).

In contrast, Geertz continues, the **ethos** of a people encompasses the culture's "tone, character, quality of life, its moral and aesthetic style and mood; it is the underlying attitude that people have about themselves and the world that life reflects" (Geertz 1973: 173).

Religious myths both reflect and inform the world or, as Geertz (1973) puts it, provide both *models of* and *models for* reality. First, they are models of reality in the sense that they offer information and explanations about the world. As models *for* reality sacred stories also show how the world "really is," in spite of appearances to the contrary. They often highlight the gap between appearance and reality, or between the sacred and the profane. We will now examine each of these elements of a belief system.

Cosmogenies

Most religious systems have a **cosmogeny,** a story about how and why the world was created. These stories tell us a great deal about a religion's most significant ideas. All the world's creation stories fall into a few basic patterns: A god creates the world out of nothing (*ex nihilo*). Life emerges from a cosmic egg. A prechaotic animal pulls mud up out of the water. A mountain rises up. A giant sustains the sky. The world takes shape as a spiral. A god delegates power to a demiurge (minor deity)—and so forth.

These cosmogenies link the people who tell the story with the creation process, because their gods and/or ancestors were involved in giving birth to the world. Most creation stories also have an **anthropogeny** as well—that is, a theory about the creation of humans and how they should think of themselves. Sometimes the gods are bored and want to play; other creation stories provide no clear reason why humans come into existence. Sometimes people are created out of clay, mud, water, or blood; other times, they are chiseled out of stone or a primeval tree trunk or are brought out of a plant. Not everything always goes right in the process of creation, nor are the gods uniformly good or evil. Sometimes the creators are good, other times they are amoral jokers or tricksters. In most cases, however, the events at the beginning of time have special significance for the faith community's present situation. The stories provide a paradigm for all creation, blueprints of necessary accomplishments to prevent evil or the reversion to chaos. A cosmogeny is one of several basic building blocks of the world-constructing process, the means by which a system of beliefs is developed that explains the world and its implications for daily life.

Not all religious traditions posit a clear-cut beginning point for creation. The Vedas, for example, present a vision of vast time and space that involves endless cycles of birth and rebirth. The cosmos has no beginning or end, although the known ages of the world are born and die just as individuals do. Consequently, the Hindu belief system suggests there are strict limitations on what one individual can change about this vast world and even on the given cycle of time in which one now lives. Buddhist cosmogenies present a similar philosophical view of the universe, in which the five cosmic elements (*skandhas*)—form, sensation, name, conformation, and consciousness—participate.

Because a religion's worldview and ethos are closely related, its creation story provides clues into the nature of the culture that religion is linked to. In the Babylonian creation story, a great God made minor gods out of stone, brick, and other materials; because these lesser gods had to do menial tasks, they in turn created humans to do their work. Such a cosmogeny implies that the meaning of human life is to be found in serving God, or perhaps God's representatives. In other religions' creation stories, God created humans in God's own image, thus setting *homo sapiens* apart from the rest of creation. Such a creation story may empower the species to take control of the rest of nature in an effort to force it to serve humans.

People living in modern cultures often deride these so-called "primitive" explanations of the world, believing scientific explanations to be superior. Many of us have difficulty believing, for example, that the Native American rituals designed to bring the sun up every morning actually cause the event as claimed. Yet which of us actually knows what force causes the earth to spin on its axis? We have many good theories—our own scientific cosmogenies—based on considerable evidence about how such things might have happened, but no definitive proof. Even those prominent scientists who have developed the most widely accepted theories about the origins of the universe set limits on their theories in the absence of hard empirical evidence. Religious cosmogenies rely upon different sources of evidence than modern scientific ones do, but the question is always the same: How did we get here? We ask it, in part, because we just want to know, but more profoundly because the answer seems to have implications about why we are here and where we are going.

The Boshongo tribe of central Africa tell the following narrative about the creation of the world. We will use it to illustrate how the tools of sociology can examine a cosmogeny and its implications for a people's sacred canopy.

In the beginning, in the dark, there was nothing but water. And Bumba was alone.

One day Bumba was in terrible pain. He retched and strained and vomited up the sun. After that light spread over everything. The heat of the sun dried up the water until the black edges of the world began to show. Black sandbanks and reefs could be seen. But there were no living things.

Bumba vomited up the moon and then the stars, and after that the night had its light also.

Still Bumba was in pain. He strained again and nine living creatures came forth; the leopard named Koy Bumba, and Pongo Bumba the crested eagle, the crocodile, Ganda Bumba, and one little fish named Yo; next, old Kono Bumba, the tortoise, and Tsetse, the lightning, swift, deadly, beautiful like the leopard, then the white heron, Nyanyi Bumba, also one beetle, and the goat named Budi.

Last of all came forth men. There were many men, but only one was white like Bumba. His name was Loko Yima.

The creatures themselves then created all the creatures. The heron created all the birds of the air except the kite. . . . The crocodile made serpents and the iguana. The goat produced every beast with horns. Yo, the small fish, brought forth all the fish of all the seas and waters. The beetle created insects.

Then the serpents in their turn made grasshoppers, and the iguana made the creatures without horns.

Then the three sons of Bumba said they would finish the world. The first, Nyonye Ngana, made the white ants; but he was not equal to the task, and died of it. The ants, however, thankful for life and being, went searching for black earth in the depths of the world and covered the barren sands to bury and honor their creator.

Chonganda, the second son, brought forth a marvellous living plant from which all the trees and grasses and flowers and plants in the world have sprung. The third son, Chedi Bumba, wanted something different, but for all his trying made only the bird called the kite.

Of all the creatures, Tsetse, lightning, was the only trouble-maker. She stirred up so much trouble that Bumba chased her into the sky. Then mankind was without fire until Bumba showed the people how to draw fire out of trees. "There is fire in every tree," he told them, and showed them how to make the firedrill and liberate it. Sometimes today Tsetse still leaps down and strikes the earth and causes damage.

When at last the work of creation was finished, Bumba walked through the peaceful villages and said to the people, "Behold these wonders. They belong to you." Thus from Bumba, the Creator, the First Ancestor, came forth all the wonders that we see and hold and use, and all the brotherhood of beasts and man.[10]

In its cosmogenies, a religious tradition provides a vast array of "information" about various levels of existence and the meaning of life: the natural and social world, and the self; the family and tribal or ethnic group; the past and the present. The Boshongo cosmogeny retold here expresses the fundamentally social nature of the religious enterprise in its linking of the present with the past and the Creator, who is an ancestor. It describes how one is to understand the nature of the world and one's place in it.

A sociologist approaches the Boshongo cosmogeny with an eye toward the narrative's social elements. First, we might wonder about the theodicy implicit in the story. According to this belief system, something positive comes out of the process of suffering: the initial creation of the world is itself an outcome of Bumba's pain. Through his vomiting its various elements emerge, from the sun to the first living creatures, who then complete the creation. Although Nyonye Ngana dies in the process of creating the white ants, the ants find black earth to bury and honor their creator. The Boshongo might learn from this story that suffering is natural and will result in a positive outcome. Suffering should therefore be endured with joy, even when one is dying.

A second striking feature of the story is the social hierarchy it implies, notably along gender and racial lines. Only one female is highlighted in the story: Tsetse, the lightning. It is no accident that she is depicted as a troublemaker (just as Eve precipitates the fall of humanity in the Jewish cosmogeny). This detail in the story no doubt both reflects and legitimates a patriarchal social hierarchy: the inferior status of women in a society is said to be a natural consequence of primordial events in which they were proven untrustworthy.

Finally, one narrative element that may be sociologically significant is mentioned only in passing: Bumba, the Creator, is white; the story says that Loko Yima was the only man who was white "like Bumba." A sociologist wants to know more about this story's sociocultural context: Did it change after the region was conquered by Europeans? What is the status of Loko Yima in Boshongo history? Is this story told often? Is it widely known, or is it just something that the Boshongo pulled out for a visiting anthropologist? Is it acted out ritually or celebrated in some regular fashion?

These questions could be part of a larger sociological investigation that would try to identify linkages between beliefs as expressed in myths and social organization. The story would offer many clues about what the observer would look for: the animals mentioned, for example, might play a special role in Boshongo life. Whites may be considered superior, and women may be labeled as troublemakers in order to subordinate them. These ideas may be ritualized in the community's life and have implications for ethical values, such as respect for ancestors and burial rites. Finally, certain ambiguities and paradoxes of life—such as the dual presence of life and death, joy and suffering—are resolved at an abstract level in the narrative; persistent health problems such as gastrointestinal illness are seen as less significant because they were also experienced by the creator god.

Let us move to another religion's cosmogeny. The Jewish understanding of the nature of the cosmos begins with the Jews' own sacred history and their special relationship with the creator. The same god who sacralized Abraham and Sarah's migration freed the Hebrews from slavery under the Egyptians and led them to the Promised Land, created the world. Moreover, at the end of the process, God created humanity in God's own image and gave this last creature dominion over the rest of creation. Herein lies the creative tension of Judaism, which can lead to remarkable dedication to the causes of justice and peace as proclaimed by the ancient Hebrews, but also to the exploitation of power by those who proclaim themselves to be specially chosen by God. It is precisely this potential for abuse of power that was denounced by the ancient Hebrew prophets and was the source of the prophetic tradition and activist orientation within Western culture, a fountain of the West's strength as well as its weakness.

The creation story in the Hebrew scripture known as **Genesis** is a major piece of literature in Western culture and reveals a great deal about that civilization's worldviews. The Christian and Islamic cosmogenies are borrowed from that of their parent religion, Judaism, and expressed in the creation stories of Genesis, in which the one God, Yahweh, created the universe. First, this story states that although creation was declared good by its creator, humans disobeyed God and thus were expelled from the paradise in which there was no pain or suffering. Second, humans were given control over the rest of the natural world: "and God blessed them, and God said to them, "Be fruitful and multiply, and fill the earth and subdue it; and have dominion over the fish of the sea and over the birds of the air, and over every living thing that moves upon the earth" (Genesis 1:28). This feature of the Judaic cosmogeny lays the groundwork for the activist approach toward the world in general, and the scientific-technological revolutions of the modern West in particular.

Third, the patriarchal strains in the creation story are significant and are often used to legitimate male dominance. Eve is said to have initiated eating the forbidden fruit, which led to the so-called "Fall," so the blame for the expulsion of humans from Paradise is often assigned to the female. There are, however, two separate Hebrew creation stories, probably coming from two distinct sources. According to the first version, "So God created man in his own image, in the image of God he created him; male and female he created them" (Genesis 1:27). In the second version, God creates Adam and then decides: "It is not good that the man should be alone; I will make him a helper fit for him" (Genesis 2:18). Then God makes all of the beasts and birds and finally causes the man to sleep, takes a rib from his side, and uses it to create the woman. In the first version, the two genders are created simultaneously as equals. In the second version, the female is created as a helper to the male, implying her inferiority.

Finally, competing themes of freedom and domination are woven into the Hebrew creation narrative. On one hand, humans are created in the image of God and thus have a wide range of freedom; on the other, they are disobedient and therefore in need of authoritative social institutions that keep them from engaging in immoral behavior. Contradictory worldviews are an important aspect of religious myths and are found in a wide range of examples: opposing ideas are woven into a narrative, which then often becomes a focus for cultural conflict.

Theodicies

Theodicies are the explanations a religion offers for the presence of evil, suffering, and death in the world, a perennial concern of religious traditions. What causes these events, how can they be alleviated or transcended, and why should the righteous suffer? Each tradition has a theory about suffering. It may be interpreted, for example, as a punishment for an individual's sinful behavior or as a consequence of a battle between good and evil forces. Because suffering and death are such obviously universal and mysterious elements of the human experience, a tradition's theodicy plays an important role not only in religious traditions but in social relations as well. Though we are not usually conscious of it on a daily basis, the everpresent fact of death affects the way in which we organize our lives (see Dunne 1965). And a theodicy that explains suffering primarily as punishment for wrongdoing, for example, can lead to a justification of social oppression of those who suffer.

One significant element of most theodicies is the **social construction of evil,** that is, identifying the sources of evil in the world. This framing of evil often has a profound impact on collective life because it affects the nature and intensity of social boundaries; as a social construct, it encourages certain kinds of conflict and discourages others. The most potent construction of evil occurs when a social group's enemies are defined as a deity's enemies so that the latter's destruction or subordination is seen as divine retribution. Sometimes the same god is claimed by both sides, of course, as in the Iran-Iraq War of the 1980s or in World War II, when Allies and Germans alike claimed a Christian God on their side.

Evil may be of divine or human origin, although the two are often intertwined, especially in the heat of conflict. **Dualistic theodicies** connote a struggle between the powers of light (good) and those of darkness (evil). Suffering is thus caused by the evil forces as part of the ongoing battle for control of the universe. Dualistic theories, most highly developed in Zoroastrianism, Mandaeism, Gnosticism, and Manichaeism but also found in other religious traditions including Christianity, often lead to contentious political views. Enemies are identified with evil cosmic forces, making peaceful coexistence difficult and affecting the style and tone of interpersonal and intergroup relations as well as cross-cultural and international conflicts.

Eastern religions do not delineate good and evil as clearly as Western religions do because they tend to claim that the cosmos is unified and that such distinctions are mere illusions. On another level, however, Eastern sacred texts (especially Hindu) are richly populated with demonic figures who battle with heroes. Even the worst characters have some element of good in them and the gods themselves can cause pain and suffering, so that evil can still be seen as something independent of persons or even the gods themselves. This characterization of evil as an independent entity, as we will see later, was emphasized by Mohandas Gandhi in his effort to promote the idea of struggling against ideas and systems rather than other people.

One of the most troubling realities for a religion to explain is why the righteous suffer. Because most theodicies offer a way out of suffering through ethical behavior, the fact that the righteous do suffer presents a difficult anomaly. The major religions prefer to suggest that suffering is simply embedded in the nature of the universe and leaves no one, including the righteous, untouched.

This tension between admonitions to live an ethical life and the apparent lack of immediate reward for doing so has inspired theodicies that promote the idea of reward or release from suffering in another world. Those who fulfill their religious duties can sometimes escape suffering by leaving this existence altogether, either in the Hindu-Buddhist effort to liberate themselves from the cycle of rebirths or in some sort of heaven or other-worldly plane, as in Christianity or Islam. A second major solution to the problem of the suffering of the righteous is to hope for some positive result to come out of the struggle itself—the "no pain, no gain" belief that pervades many theodicies. A third solution is to recognize that one's current woes are not as bad as they could be; suffering is thus reframed and placed in another context.

Suffering is viewed as a natural process in animistic theodicies that explain death as part of the cycles of nature. Similarly, some theories of suffering minimize individual pain by putting it in a broad cosmic context, as in the cycles of rebirth in which the process of dying is analogous to changing one's clothes. In the primal religions of pre-agricultural (hunting and gathering) societies, suffering and death are framed as part of the natural rhythms of the universe. No sharp boundaries divide the individual and society, or even human society and the rest of nature, so continuity is provided from generation to generation as part of the ongoing rhythm of life. Death does not signal the end of the vital force embodied in a person; as in transmigration, the force is simply transferred to another plane of existence. Moreover, the ancestor spirits are part of the ongoing life of the community: the "living dead" continue to participate, in a modified way, and are honored by their descendants with periodic gifts. The only potential danger for the individual in such a system is in becoming disengaged from the community, which does not occur at death, but rather when that person transgresses social boundaries and violates sacred taboos—a much more dangerous act than the natural process of death.

The explanation for suffering and death in Hinduism is related to the ultimate goal of existence—that is, to become liberated from the world by uniting the individual soul or spirit known as the **atman**, with the *Brahman*, or Universal Soul, that encompasses the entire universe. That goal is not easily reached, however, and is accomplished only by struggling through successive lifetimes during which one must fulfill one's *dharma*. This worldview results in a highly rational theodicy in which suffering is explained on the basis of one's *karma*, or actions from previous lifetimes. Each individual soul goes through a cycle of rebirths, known as **samsara** or the wheel of life, the endless round of deaths and rebirths: when a person dies, the soul leaves its body and transmigrates to another. The nature of the next **reincarnation** is determined by the person's *karma*, that is, the collective consequences of all individual actions. The gods do not punish or reward; negative actions bring their own dire consequences, and positive actions bring their own rewards. The law of *karma*, or action, is a basic notion of cause and effect: "As we sow, so shall we reap" is the saying one Hindu author uses to explain the law (Jagannathan 1984: 54), which has a status in Asian thought similar to the law of gravity in Western science. All elements of the cosmos are interdependent, constituting a self-contained cosmos of ethical retribution, which does not require the intervention of gods to punish or reward. Encounters with the gods are primarily for educational purposes so that people can learn how to be rewarded, rather than punished, for their actions.

In this system death is not to be feared or mourned; it is simply another passage. The soul leaves one body and enters another in the same way that a person changes clothes. The broad cosmology of the Hindu tradition allows the individual to look somewhat philosophically upon the transitory pain of present existence. Even if life seems intolerable, a person can work diligently to do the best with his or her current lot and thereby look forward to a better life in the future.

The *karma-samsara* concept contains a deterministic element that sometimes convinces people to accept their fate and not try to change their immediate life circumstances, which amount to rewards and punishments for actions in a previous life. Some *karma* (*praradbha karma*), such as family or environment, is beyond our control. The *karma-samsara* theory is supposed to facilitate the individual's transcendence of the profane life by endowing it with religious duty. The system leads to remarkable abuse when exploited, however, by providing a powerful rationale for the ruling classes and legitimating a false consciousness among the poor, who are taught that their poverty is punishment for their deeds in a previous lifetime. This is ideal rationale for what sociologists call "blaming the victim" (Ryan 1976; Piven and Cloward 1971).

The idea of *karma* is not entirely deterministic, however. First, two of the three stages of karma are amenable to change. The accumulated *karma* of all previous births (*samchita karma*), and actions in the present life determine a person's future (*agami karma*). The impact of the habits of previous lifetimes can be altered by cultivating new habits and ridding oneself of evil thoughts and desires. Finally, a better life in the future can be constructed through attention to present life duties. Moreover, we have the freedom to choose whether or not to live according to our *dharma*— that is, the duty appropriate to the state produced by individual *karma*— just as we can decide to ignore gravity if we are willing to face the consequences. Finally, even though we should not strive to change one's own life situation, we should attempt to improve others', an idea promulgated both by Hindu activist Mohandas Gandhi and the current Tibetan Buddhist leader, the 14th Dalai Lama (1990).

In the Asian religions, then, suffering is seen as integral to the very fabric of existence, as we experience it. It enters into human consciousness when people develop desires for worldly or material objects and become excessively attached. The solution to the problem of suffering is *moksha* (liberation) in Hinduism, or the attainment of *Enlightenment* or *Nirvana* (that is, supreme bliss) in Buddhism, which allows one to escape the "wheel of *karma-samsara*." In Hinduism, the paths of yoga cultivate detachment of the self from dependence on this world, allowing one to escape it. Similarly, in Buddhism, following the Eightfold Path prescribed by the Buddha allows us to reach Enlightenment, or Nirvana.

Death in Hinduism is sometimes a means of liberation, and a believer does not even have to wait for its natural occurrence. A widow may jump onto her husband's burning funeral pyre, or a devout Hindu can become a *sanyasi,* who renounces the world and lives a life of isolation and self-denial. The *sanyasi* "dies" to his own life; funeral rites are celebrated and the person's inheritance is passed on as if he were dead. The Hindu theodicy is most fully developed, however, in the legends of the god Shiva, who is simultaneously destructive and life giving, representing death but also the recreation of life, as in the cycles of death and rebirth in nature. This close connection with the natural world reveals the primal origins of Hindu beliefs. Although many Indians live highly urbanized lifestyles, the country is still based on its villages, and popular religion is intimately tied to the struggle to survive in a relatively hostile natural environment in which resources are scarce and months of drought are followed by violent monsoons in which millions are annually left homeless or killed.

The Hindu concepts of *dharma* and transmigration explain the deprivations of individual existence in a highly rational manner, at the same time giving hope for a better lifetime in the future. They provide a source of comfort at times of death as well, because the end of this life is merely a passage into the next one. One's fate in each successive lifetime is self-determined, within the boundaries of the law of *karma,* so that one can earn a better life in the next incarnation and hope for ultimate release from the struggle. Although this theodicy solves many problems on both psychological and social levels, it has also been exploited to maintain a strict social hierarchy that has come under attack in contemporary Hinduism.

Whereas the Eastern religions tend to explain suffering and death on the basis of long-term continuity and cycles of history, Western religions usually rely upon a theory of suffering caused by dramatic changes in history. The Judeo-Christian-Islamic tradition posits that humans once lived in paradise, the Garden of Eden, where suffering and death did not exist. By disobeying God—eating the forbidden fruit of the knowledge of good and evil—humans became estranged from God and were expelled from paradise, ushering in both suffering and death.

The Genesis account of the "Fall" also suggests that God was somehow threatened by the possibility of human immortality, and that is at least partly why Adam and Eve were expelled from the Garden (Genesis 3:22–23). Because suffering and death are caused by separation from God, the solution is to return to God. The usual paths in Judaism, Christianity, and Islam are conversion and/or repentance, turning back to God and restoring the lost relationship with the deity, a process facilitated by the rituals and actions of the faith community. In Christianity, one confesses and loves God and neighbor. In Islam, one relies upon the Five Pillars: affirming one's belief in the One God, performing ritual prayers, sharing one's wealth (*Zakat*), celebrating Ramadan (the month of fasting), and undertaking a pilgrimage to Mecca. In Judaism, the community must engage in repentance and a restoration of the covenant, to do justice and walk with God.

Jewish theodicies reflect the social nature of Judaism and the ancient Hebrews' covenant with their God. The "Fall" in the Garden of Eden identifies the emergence of evil in the world as a result of alienation from God. Suffering and death themselves are consequences of Adam and Eve's disobedience, which in turn resulted in their separation from the Creator, in the same sense that a child feels pain when separated from the parent. Suffering can be overcome through individual conversion and/or repentance, in order to return to God. This theory of suffering remains a constant reminder throughout Jewish history that—as in the Eastern law of *karma*—the person who causes suffering or breaks the covenant with God will somehow suffer, sometimes even at God's hands.

It appears, however, that the just also suffer, a problem discussed eloquently throughout Jewish literature, in part because of the great suffering which Jews have experienced as a people over the centuries—from that expressed in the ancient book of Job to the literature of the Holocaust. A popular contemporary Jewish exploration of the problem of suffering is Rabbi Harold Kushner's (1981) *When Bad Things Happen to Good People*, in which he contends that a satisfactory explanation for the suffering is possible only when people forfeit the idea of God as omnipotent or all powerful.

Christian theodicies borrowed from Judaism are also based primarily upon the theory that separation from God—the creator and source of all good—causes evil, suffering, and death. They are **eschatological**, asserting that the problem of suffering will be resolved at the end of time, and they tend to be **messianic.** Christians believe that a messiah or liberator—Jesus Christ—has already come, and will come again to reunite creation with God. Most Christians are also **millenarian:** they believe that an ideal society will come; some are convinced that the transformation will take place in this world, although others believe that the change will happen in the next world.

There are two major differences between Christian cosmologies and theodicies and those of the Jewish parent religion: (1) The Christian church's emphasis on "right belief" evolved as a consequence of its universalistic criteria of membership (belonging was a matter of believing); and (2) Christianity, especially Protestantism, places a stronger emphasis on individual responsibility. Once more the sociological reason for this shift in emphasis lies in the nature of the tradition: whereas Judaism has defined suffering as something the community experiences collectively, Christianity has placed more emphasis on individual choice and its consequences.

With their similar origins in the creation story of Genesis, Muslim theodicies, like Christian and Jewish ones, focus on the idea of separation from God as the source of suffering and death. The creator aspect of Allah is highly significant to Muslims, who place a strong emphasis on a transcendent God who is nonetheless compassionate and merciful despite his exalted position. The pain of the separation from the creator is a central theme among the **Sufis,** the mystical branch of the Muslims. Sufis seek an intimacy with God through devotion and prayer, like that the Prophet obtained through his long hours of solitary worship. Sufis sometimes use the metaphor of the reed to explain suffering and death. The reed is fashioned into a flute that laments being separated from its source, the reed bed, and yearns to be reunited. The human separated from his or her creator is brought back to God through the rituals of the Islamic community.

Although not traditionally classified as a messianic religion by social scientists, Buddhism has a strong messianic element as well in the concept of the *bodhisattva*—that is, those individuals who obtain Enlightenment but return to aid others rather than entering into Nirvana or eternal bliss. **Avalokitesvarais,** the most widely revered *bodhisattva* in East Asia, appears in several forms, as a Buddha, an *arhat* (enlightened human), and an animal, and in many spheres (heavens and hells) in order to free all creatures from suffering and lead them to the Pure Land of Amita. Thus this *bodhisattva* is known for compassion and mercy and is celebrated in the Lotus Sutra, in which he appears in thirty-three transformations in order to meet the needs of each audience to whom he addresses his teachings.

The female manifestation of this *bodhisattva* is Avalokitesvara, the Goddess of Mercy, one of the most popular images represented in Chinese popular culture. As such, she serves a function similar to the widely popular Virgin Mary in Christianity, especially appealing to the poor and women because of her approachability and merciful demeanor. According to legend, she vowed to serve the Buddha and fled to a nunnery over the objections of her father. His agents pursued her and set fire to a temple where she had sought sanctuary, resulting in her death but also in the reward of immortality. According to the story, her father was blinded as punishment, but Avalokitesvara plucked out her own eyes to restore her father's sight, thus earning her title as Goddess of Mercy.

Avalokitsvarais and Avalokitsvara are not just ancient or mythical figures. They play a very real role in contemporary world politics, incarnated as the Tibetan Dalai Lama, now living in exile in India. The current Dalai Lama, fourteenth in the line of succession, has become a popular figure worldwide, especially after winning the Nobel Peace Prize in 1989 for his championing the nonviolent struggle for Tibetan independence from China.

The Sacred and the Profane

Emile Durkheim believed that the entire world of human experience could be divided into two categories: the **sacred,** what is of ultimate concern, and the **profane,** what is considered ordinary and mundane. The fact that Durkheim was the son of a Jewish rabbi may have influenced his theoretical model because the division of the world into these conceptual categories is central to Judaic thought and ritual. Durkheim's distinction became central to the academic study of religion even though some religious traditions insist that all of life, not simply one sector, is sacred. To understand most of the world's religions, however, we must grasp this fundamental distinction.

The two categories of sacred and profane actually lie on a continuum. Some things are considered more sacred than others and are ranked according to their sacrality. What constitutes the sacred varies from culture to culture and changes over time. The sacred may be recognized (or "manifest itself") in the form of a stone or tree, a flag or mountain, or even an idea. Scholars use the term **hierophany** to identify the process in which people encounter and experience the sacred. Sometimes two phenomena defined as sacred may come into conflict, and people must choose which is more sacred than the other.

For the religious, specific times and places are identified as sacred. Most societies designate holidays ("holy days") and sacred sites (Eliade 1959). A certain location—a temple, mosque, or cathedral; a war memorial or cemetery; the birthplace or grave of a famous person—often affords an encounter with the sacred. Crossing from profane to sacred space often requires certain actions, dress, or attitudes: taking off shoes, genuflecting in front of the cross, bowing in respect, refraining from loud talk, and so on.

Religions also traditionally divide time into the sacred and the profane. Religious festivals and rituals involve the **reactualization** of sacred events that took place "in the beginning," or during some significant hierophany; the sacred elements of time are thus transformed and shifted to the present moment. Belief systems of the various religious traditions are almost always systematized and disseminated by a select group of religious elites, but also in the everyday speech and rhythms of everyday life; for most people, their faith is encountered not in the subtle theologies or massive writings of their tradition, but in its rituals, that is, the regularly repeated behaviors that symbolize the values of their belief system. Ritual behavior, as Durkheim (1915) observed, provides the occasion for an encounter with the sacred, and it is socially organized in such a way as to reenforce the values and authority of the community.

Faith communities preserve their religious beliefs in often contradictory narratives united at an abstract level by the structure of the stories themselves (Kurtz 1979). Life and death, good and evil, the divine and the human, all exist side by side within the narrative. The world gets created twice in every culture: first, in the material sense, the world comes into being. Then it gets recreated through sacred stories or mythologies (or by means of scientific theories) in a cosmogeny that links the present with the past. Some sacred events are more significant than their frequency would suggest (like religious visions, death and sexual intercourse).[11] Conversely, they may even be statistically insignificant but still have a profound impact on our lives.

Religious Rituals

Ritual, a regularly repeated, traditional, and carefully prescribed set of behaviors that symbolizes a value or belief, plays a central role in all the world's religions. Rituals come in a wide variety of forms; some help people to show devotion to the gods, as in corporate worship and certain modes of communicating with the gods, such as prayers, chanting, singing, and dancing. Others, such as meditations and mantras, facilitate the process of life organization, on both personal and collective levels. Rituals help to frame daily life by regulating such matters as hygiene, diet, and sex; rites of passage surround major transitions such as birth, puberty, marriage, and death; and still other rituals, such as seasonal festivals, processions, and holidays, help people cope with the cycles of nature.

Rituals are not only limited to religious practice, however. All social institutions rely on ritual behavior to sustain their values and participants' consciousness of their authority. Rituals solve problems of the collective life in a time-tested way by identifying evil, marking social and ideological boundaries, and reenforcing the institutions that sponsor them. Religious rituals in particular link the experience of ordinary life with the sacred and place both trauma and joy within the context of a worldview that orders a people's life and provides them with meaning.

Although rituals often preserve a social order and sustain old habits, they are crucial to cultural innovation and change as well. Victor Turner (1967) observes that religious rituals often signify a special or **liminal period** set apart from ordinary reality. During the liminal period, which involves a separation from, or marginalization of, ordinary reality, participants leave ordinary time and space and enter a sacred region in which the problematic aspects of everyday life—filled with suffering and injustice—are solved, or perhaps denied. Thus rituals fall "betwixt and between" different worlds: the world of everyday life, and the sacred time set apart from mundane reality. During the ritual normal rules of interaction and social structure no longer apply or are inverted.

Some religious rituals are designed to assure people that death is not final because it is followed by rebirth and that social change is not ultimately destructive; the person who stays in the folds of the community is never alone in times of crisis. Thus the world is renewed annually through the cycles of the seasons and the rituals that mark them, such as Mardi Gras, Divali, and the Chinese New Year. These rituals signal the paradigmatic nature of time; life is regenerated through a return to the time of the origins. This liminal period is filled with inversions and transformations (see Turner 1967; Babcock 1978). During those moments of ritual time (e.g., when the crucifixion of Jesus is relived at Easter), the mundane characteristics of life are reshaped: the children and the Princess of Spring run Old King Winter off of his throne at Mardi Gras; the god is taken out of his or her temple and paraded through the streets. The births, deaths, and sometimes resurrections of the gods are celebrated with a renewed emphasis on the things that, contrary to the appearances of earthly, everyday life, "really matter": family, justice, love, order.

Rituals as a social form share a number of common structural characteristics, no matter what their content: (1) they provide solutions to problems; (2) they are rooted in experience; (3) they involve the demarcation of boundaries and the identification of evil; and (4) they reenforce, or reify, social processes. Let's examine these characteristics in turn.

First, how do rituals solve a variety of human problems? This is a key to the important role of religion in human life: on the abstract level, religious rituals bind a social order together, linking it to the culture's worldview and ethos. On a practical level, rituals provide a proven repertoire for social action, especially at times of crisis. When people are confronted with suffering or death, go through major passages in their life cycle, or experience rapid change, religious rituals may guide them through the crisis. Rituals provide socially approved responses, preestablished scripts, and social support for those who have suffered a loss.

Perhaps the best example of religious ritual as problem solver is the funeral rite: a death creates a crisis among the living that must be acknowledged as such and acted upon. The funeral ceremony provides a sense of closure on that stage of the grieving process and places the death within the broader worldview of the tradition. As long as the sacred canopy is in place and retains its legitimacy, the scripts provide a modicum of relief for sufferers. People surrounding the bereaved are familiar with the rituals, and specialized institutions and ritual experts usually guide the victims of the crisis. A ritual package for the ceremony includes a repertoire of appropriate comments for the bereaved and their social networks, some general in character ("It was God's will that he go at this time"), others tailored to a specific situation ("At least she's out of pain now"). A major feature of ritual problem solving is the provision that allows the bereaved to focus their energies on arranging details of the rituals. By accomplishing the detail work surrounding ritual, the individuals involved feel as though they have accomplished something in the midst of a crisis that would otherwise make them feel impotent; taking care of the deceased's needs after death can address lingering unresolved tensions.

Second, how are ritual practices rooted in experience? Because rituals were constructed in the past, they have the authority of time-tested formulas: as Weber (1968: 226–227) puts it, rituals are "believed in by virtue of the sanctity of age-old rules and powers." People wiser than us, confronted in the past with a similar situation, created this solution. Evidence confirming that ritual brings about the desired effect is essentially anecdotal, passed on in mythical stories that contain the underlying principle: "We've always done it that way, and it's always worked." The elders recall a time, long ago, when a drought brought disaster to the village. A rain dance was performed, the rain gods were pleased, the clouds rolled in, rain fell like a monsoon, and the village was saved. The efficacy of rituals is in the eye of their performers—they appear verifiable to those who believe in them, if not always to outsiders. Similarly, evidence calling a ritual into question can be discounted by pointing to flaws in the *performance* rather than the ritual itself. If any ritual performance is scrutinized closely enough, mistakes can be identified that could have been responsible for the ritual's failure. The reason for failure may be attributed to sabotage by an outsider, such as an enemy who performed a more powerful counterritual.

The fact that rituals ensure continuity and reliability is both a blessing and a curse. Because the world is constantly changing, the conditions for which a specific ritual was created may alter to such an extent that the ritual is no longer appropriate. Yet the change may be unnoticed or may be considered unimportant by its advocates, who continue to perform it anyway. This is the phenomenon known as **cultural lag** (Ogburn 1922). Rituals are valuable because people can rely upon a known procedure to maintain the social order, but they resist changing procedures when conditions change, thereby rendering the ritual behavior counterproductive. A ritual designed to protect people from drought may not be useful to a tribe moving from the desert to a rainforest.

We usually need to identify a problem's cause in order to solve it, and most rituals contain a theory about the origin of the problems they are designed to alleviate; in short, they contain a theory of evil. Rituals mark boundaries between good and bad ideas, between "us" and "them." An "evil" force, situation, or group is identified as the source of the difficulty, opening the way to a solution. Ritual behavior is thus an integral part of the social construction of evil by which an image of the enemy is created and then spread throughout the culture by media, folktales, and jokes. Evil is often attached to enemies outside the belief system or to those within the system who can be labeled as heretics (see Kurtz 1986). Many religious traditions personify evil in a particular figure, such as a monster or humanlike creature, who needs to be defeated in battle, making the evil appear more manageable.

Whether the figure deemed responsible for evil is personified in a devil or mythical figure or identified in a human enemy, rituals identify it and give people something concrete to do about mastering it. Sometimes the simple act of naming an evil and denouncing it is useful; at other times, the evil is physically punished or ridiculed, or exiled from the social order. Some will engage in exorcisms to drive away evil spirits, others will repeatedly denounce a group of people for a misdeed. Psychologically, this process of ritual identification of evil can sometimes be helpful in the short run, but destructive in the long run if we simply project evil onto another person or group (like the Nazis did to the Jews during the Holocaust). Such naive projections distort our view of reality: "The enemy appears as the embodiment of all evil because all evil that I feel in myself is projected onto him. Logically, after this has happened, I consider myself as the embodiment of all good since the evil has been transferred to the other side" (Fromm 1961:22).

Finally, rituals have social as well as psychological consequences, one of which is the reification of social processes. **Reification** means the treatment of an abstraction as a concrete material object.

Ritual "Packages"

Religious belief systems integrate different kinds of rituals into sets of interdependent practices by which people can engage in showing devotion to the gods while organizing their individual and collective lives. These sets of "packaged" rituals, though containing diverse practices, fit together neatly as a whole. Two "packages" of rituals, yoga in the Hindu tradition and the Five Pillars in Islam, deserve a closer look.

Yoga and the Three Paths to Enlightenment. **Yoga** (literally, to yoke or unite) is the Hindu ritual for uniting the soul with God through meditation and certain ethical practices. Hindu rituals are extremely well developed, spelled out in rich complexity and elaborate detail in ancient ritual manuals.[12] At the most abstract level, Hindu rituals solve the threat of chaos. Discord is held at bay by the gods, who in turn require gifts (especially signs of deference and food) in order to do their work. Thus, it is the obligation of each Hindu to carry out the rituals of the faith as an individual contribution to maintaining the cosmic order.

Because of the syncretic and flexible nature of Hinduism, a number of paths to Enlightenment are possible. All, however, involve disciplined self-transcendence to overcome excessive attachments to this world. Hinduism identifies three main paths, with a different yogic discipline to facilitate progress along each route:

1. The Path of Wisdom or Knowledge, *jnana yoga* (for reflective persons)
2. The Path of Action, *karma yoga* (for active persons)
3. The Path of Devotion, *bhakti yoga* (the most popular path)

Jnana yoga, the quickest but therefore steepest and most difficult path to Enlightenment, is rarely chosen; it requires not only cognitive but intuitive knowledge, gained from a disciplined reading of the Vedas, the Upanishads, the Bhagavad-Gita, and other works, then the guidance of a guru who helps one to reflect upon the readings and engage in deep meditation on the Absolute.

Karma yoga, also relatively rare, focuses on selfless acts or service, so that action—even in one's work—becomes a form of worshipping God. The key to liberation through *karma yoga* is doing a task for its own sake rather than for any reward. Consequently, the process contains a paradoxical element: if practiced only for one's own liberation, it will not work because it will not be selfless action at all.

Finally, **bhakti yoga,** the broadest and most popular path, consists of acts of devotional worship and requires daily *poojas,*[13] expressions of respect toward a representation of God in one's home, a temple, or one of the small shrines that dot the Indian landscape. The aim of these rituals of personal worship in *bhakti yoga* is to become consumed with love for God and therefore to be intoxicated by a divine vision.

Choosing the path most suitable to personal inclinations and abilities, the believer strives to transcend selfish desires and the routine of profane life through disciplined practice of the appropriate rituals. Such practices may be as elaborate as a sustained pilgrimage to a holy place or as simple as chanting the Lord's name in the privacy of one's home. For every devout Hindu, however, power accumulates in the performance of rituals so that the use of ritual packages sustains them in daily life and at times of crisis.

The Five Pillars of Islam. Islamic rituals center around the Five Pillars, rules that reenforce the religious and social boundaries of the *ummah,* draw people into the community, and provide an important redistribution of wealth:

1. *Shahada,* or profession of faith
2. *Ritual prayers* as part of communal and individual life cycles
3. *Zakat,* the sharing or giving of alms from a proportion of one's wealth
4. *Ramadan,* a month of fasting from daybreak to sundown to cultivate spiritual, physical, and moral discipline
5. *Hajj,* a pilgrimage to the sacred places in and around Mecca

The first pillar, the *shahada,* is the profession of faith: "There is no God but Allah, and Muhammad is His messenger." The *shahada* is affirmed at all key events in one's life cycle (especially at births and deaths) and is included in daily prayers. To embrace Islam, one must simply make this declaration before witnesses.

The second pillar consists of making personal prayers along with the formal ritual prayer (*salat*) that is repeated several times daily, normally at dawn, noon, afternoon, sunset, and late evening. The *salat* is used to frame the entire day, reminding believers that God should be at the center of their lives. The equality of all before God is underlined as the devout of all social classes worship together; the entire Muslim world faces Mecca and prays, turning to neighbors at the end of the prayer with the traditional greeting, "Salaam" (peace).

The third pillar, *zakat*, requires Muslims to give a portion of their wealth to the poor and others needing assistance. This ritual giving includes the important practice of hospitality and provides a mechanism for sustaining the social order by redistributing wealth and addressing social needs. The term literally means "purification," suggesting that wealth is defiling unless shared with others. This practice, stemming from Muhammad's vision of justice and condemnation of the materialism of his own time, now requires an annual donation of 2.5 percent of a believer's wealth.

The fourth pillar of Islam is Ramadan, a month of fasting from daybreak to sundown to cultivate spiritual, physical, and moral discipline. Besides abstaining from food, drink, and sex during the daylight hours, Muslims are enjoined to focus on the core values and practices of their faith during that period. After sunset, the fast is broken, followed by prayers and shared meals with family and friends. After the last day of the month, Muslims celebrate *'Id al Fitr,* one of the major festivals of the Muslim year.

Finally, at least once the believer must participate in the fifth pillar, *hajj,* the pilgrimage to the sacred places in and around Mecca. Although not required if it is a financial burden, this pilgrimage is a highlight in the lives of the faithful as they retrace the steps of generations of their predecessors. Mecca is the axis of the Muslim world, toward which all face in prayer; it is the holy center where humans encounter the sacred. By making their own pilgrimage to Mecca, the believers trace their spiritual roots back through the centuries: they reenact the founding of Islam with Muhammad and finally join Abraham and Ishmael in encountering the god who created the world and is gracious and merciful to all who will follow.

The ritual package known as Five Pillars reminds Muslims on a daily basis that religion is not part of the structure of Islamic society—it *is* the structure; that Islam is not part of the daily life of a Muslim—it *is* his or her life. The rituals associated with the Five Pillars are designed to draw believers constantly back to Allah. Performed publicly, they mark Muslims as believers wherever they may be. A religious tradition that is not compartmentalized but diffused throughout a believer's life is undifferentiated and primal in character, makes more demands on its adherents, and is less tolerant of other belief systems and lifestyles than more cosmopolitan religions. However, it is also more effective in providing believers with religious purpose and guiding their lives, so many practitioners understandably resist efforts to "modernize" their beliefs and secularize the other spheres of their lives.

Acts of Devotion

Let us continue our inventory of contemporary religious practices by examining different types of rituals found across religious traditions. Religious practices are often designed to draw a people closer to the ideals of the faith by reminding them of the gods, values, and principles of their faith as well as important events and figures of their shared history. Religious rituals thus involve many forms of communication with the gods, or with saints, boddhisattvas, and other heroic figures, as well as occasions for collective worship in public gatherings of the believers.

Communication with the gods. A central aspect of religious practice is the set of rituals designed to facilitate communication with the gods, such as prayer, chanting, singing, dancing, reading from the scriptures, and offering sacrifices. From a sociological point of view, it should be noted that messages designed for communication with the gods are also ways of communicating with oneself and with others, especially those within the religious community.

Most Buddhist rituals, for example, involve efforts to obtain merit of some sort, either for oneself or for someone else, thereby transcending one's current state through the performance of the ritual. The foundation of Buddhist ritual consists of *dana* (giving), *sila* (precepts), and *kamma* (karma). Keeping the precepts includes conscious acts of service to others and paying respect to them. All of these ritual acts are rooted in the concept of *karma*, which is conceived in much the same way as it is in Hinduism: because every act has a consequence, if one engages in meditations, chanting, and service and keeps the precepts, merit will accrue to oneself and to others.

A central Buddhist ritual is the chanting of refuge that a believer takes in the Three Jewels: the Buddha, the Dharma, and the Sangha. This chant is a prelude to the performance of Buddhist rituals throughout Asia, which incorporate many ancient rites and a variety of indigenous practices. The metaphor of crossing the river helps to explain the meaning of these sacred symbols: An explorer—the Buddha—makes the trip first, proving that it is possible. He comes back to show us the way. The Dharma, or teachings of Buddhism, is the vehicle of transport, the boat or raft we will use in our journey; and the Sangha, the organization of followers, is the boat's crew, in whom we can have confidence because of their training and discipline. Chanting that one is taking refuge in the Three Jewels helps a believer to recenter and focus attention on the path to liberation from this world of suffering:

> Veneration to the Blessed One, the Enlightened One,
> The Perfectly Enlightened One:
>
> To the Buddha, the [chosen] resort, I go.
> To [the] Dhamma, the [chosen] resort, I go.
> To [the] Sangha, the [chosen] resort, I go.
>
> —*Ti-ratana* in the Pali text[14]

Chanting is very common throughout Buddhism—especially chanting the *paritta*, the protection discourses. Chants are most significant at times of crisis or change: death, illness, possession, danger, embarking upon a new activity, entering a new house, etc. (see Cousins 1984: 310).

Formal worship varies widely in the Buddhist tradition, in part because the religion has been grafted onto local traditions so is often practiced according to ancient indigenous customs. Followers often worship relics with offerings (food, water, clothing, incense, candles, etc.), bowing or prostrating, cleaning or adorning the relic, and chanting verses. Worship can also be carried out at home, although a temple or pagoda facilitates the worshippers' gain of merit, sometimes through ingenious methods. The Ten Thousand Buddhas Temple, located in Taichung, Taiwan, contains 10,000 images of the Buddha, all of whom can be worshipped in a single visit, and hundreds of whom can be venerated with one bow or prostration.

In other religions the devotee's relationship with the deity is sometimes highly personal, especially in popular traditions. Protestant Christianity often emphasizes the believer's personal relationship with Jesus, who is perceived as a friend or a brother, and with Mary who, although not formally a goddess, is considered endowed with great power and yet empathetic, especially with the plight of poor women.

The notion of sacrifice to the deity also lies at the heart of many religious rituals, sometimes including acts of considerable violence to humans and animals. In the earliest rituals, the totem animal, usually protected from harm, is sometimes killed and devoured in an orgiastic frenzy (see Girard 1977). In ancient Judaism, sacrifices to the deity were performed in the same way as in other religions of the region: burnt offerings were made, including animal sacrifices, along with other offerings representing the first fruits of the harvest, tithes, and taxes. Human sacrifices may have been part of the original set of ritual practices, but if so, the tradition was rejected in early Judaism, as shown in the story of Abraham's sacrificing a ram in place of his son Isaac (Genesis 22). The relative merit of animal and vegetable sacrifices, as in the story of the conflict between the brothers Cain and Abel, probably reflects an early conflict between people growing crops and those raising animals. Many religions shifted from human to animal to purely symbolic sacrifices over time; ritual practices became increasingly abstract as personalistic ferociousness declined in public behavior (see Collins 1974).

Collective rites of worship. Many religious rituals are performed in identical fashion at home by believers and in temples by priests and laity alike. The temple is usually the "home" of a deity, represented by an image that takes on the power of the god who resides in it. In Hinduism, the *puraris,* or temple priests, follow a prescribed daily pattern in which the deity is awakened, bathed, fed, visited and honored, anointed, decorated, and retired for the night. Sometimes worship is carried out collectively, especially in *bhakti yoga,* with chanting or hymn singing. The combination of the congregational members' mutually reenforcing attitudes, the presence of the gods, and the stimulation of all senses through music, incense, touching of the god or offerings given to God, sometimes produces trances in zealous devotees.

In the Abrahamic religions, collective worship centers on the Sabbath, a ritual that recreates the primal creation myth in which God rested on the seventh day after bringing the world into being. As Abraham Heschel notes, the celebration of the Sabbath reflects the significance placed on sacred *time,* as opposed to place, in the historically oriented, geographically mobile Jewish tradition: "Judaism teaches us to be attached to holiness in time, to be attached to sacred events. . . . The Sabbaths are our great cathedrals; and our Holy of Holies is a shrine that neither the Romans nor the Germans were able to burn (Hertzberg 1962: 119). In this tradition place is not as important as time: work ceases on the Sabbath, which is observed in both home and synagogue, and the sacred interval is marked by the lighting of candles, the recitation of prayers, the drinking of wine, and the eating of bread.

The two central rituals of the Christian faith, the **Eucharist** (communion) and **baptism,** involve communication with God in the context of collective worship. Ironically, these rituals were borrowed from the Jewish tradition and adapted by the church to denote distinctive Christian identity. Even though they are explicitly designed for communication with God, both rituals address the sociological problem of membership in the community. Because the early church broke so radically with the religious context it grew out of by denying ethnic or tribal requirements for membership, the issue was an important one. Controversies about circumcision and kosher laws recorded in the New Testament reflect the difficulties of this new form of socioreligious organization no longer rooted in ethnicity. Baptism thus became a rite of passage into the community, and the Eucharist was designed to bring members together in the body of Christ.

Several layers of symbolic meaning can be found in the Eucharist or communion service, the eating of bread and drinking of wine: first, the ritual involves a reenactment of the "Last Supper" Jesus had with his disciples before his crucifixion. Second, it also recalls the ancient Hebraic Passover meal, the ritual occasion for which Jesus and his disciples had assembled. The Hebrew rite commemorated the delivery of the slaves from Egypt and the night of the "Passover," when the Egyptian sons were slaughtered but the Hebrew children were spared. (Behind both of those rituals, it should be noted, hovers the much more ancient idea of a hierophany involving human and animal sacrifices. In some ancient traditions, the god, or the animal in which the god resides, is killed and eaten, allowing participants literally to partake of the god and incorporate it into their very being.)

Because the early Christian church saw itself as the resurrected body of Christ, the Eucharist was at the center of worship life as a way of reinforcing the internalization of Jesus into the members of the community. As they ate the body and blood, their "incorporation" in the church, the body of Jesus, was reconfirmed (Matthew 26:26–28). As Christianity was removed from its primal roots, in which the natural and symbolic worlds are one, the relationship between the blood and body of Jesus to the wine and bread was rendered increasingly abstract. At the Council of Trent (1545–1563), the Roman Church countered the Protestant Reformation by insisting that the bread and wine actually became, through the mystery of the Eucharist ritual, the body and blood of Christ (the doctrine of *substantiation*). In the modern world, the literalness of the Eucharist has been stripped away; ironically, those contemporary Christian communities that insist most vociferously on a literal interpretation (fundamentalist Protestants) are often the most symbolic in their interpretation of the ritual. In some churches, a further abstraction is made by introducing grape juice as a symbol for the wine that represents the blood.

Ritual Organization of Life

Religious rituals link daily life routines with the broader order, allowing individuals and groups alike to place life's crises within a broader religious frame. A variety of rituals organize a person's personal and collective lives: (1) rituals that regulate daily life from hygiene and diet to sexual practices link that daily life to the broader worldview; (2) rites of passage routinize life cycle changes at birth, puberty, marriage, and death; and (3) seasonal festivals and processions bring self, society, and nature into harmony by linking human activity to the seasonal cycles of the natural environment. We will look briefly at each of these rites.

Daily life. Most traditions advocate a practice of regular meditation, prayer, and chanting that provides moments for introspection. Daily devotional rituals sacralize the profane existence of a worshipper's life, giving it larger meaning and purpose and framing it within the ongoing processes of the cosmos. Every Hindu devotee—especially Brahmans— is expected to engage in daily *poojas* and ritual washings. Buddhists can frame their day by chanting *Om*, the fundamental sound of the one undivided universe. St. Paul told the early Christians that they should "pray without ceasing," and devout Muslims traditionally stop whatever they are doing five times daily, bow toward Mecca, and pray to Allah.

Many daily activities such as eating become acts of faith that reflect a worldview and/or link the individual in a special way with the religious community. The act of sharing a meal together is frequently used as a ritual for the creation of group solidarity, as in the Jewish Passover meal (*seder*) or potluck dinners in American Protestant churches. Membership in a religious community is sometimes expressed through dietary restrictions; in India, for example, most Muslims eat meat and most Hindus do not. The vegetarian diet of many Hindus and Buddhists reflects a worldview in which all creatures are of equal importance and none should be harmed.

Jewish **kosher laws,** a complex set of regulations about food selection, preparation, and eating according to ancient Hebrew rituals, provide an interesting case of religious rituals that link routine social life with the broader goals of the tradition. Such dietary restrictions serve the obvious purpose of providing norms for approved eating practices, important in primal societies in which religious and social regulation were not clearly differentiated. As well as forbidding the eating of certain kinds of animals, kosher laws prohibit mixing meat and dairy foods, which must not even be prepared or served by the same utensils. Finally, the Talmud and later works define the exact manner in which food must be prepared and eaten: animals must be killed in a prescribed procedure, all meat must be free of surface blood before being eaten, and so on. These boundaries of food preparation and eating were no doubt constructed as a practical measure in early days to protect the population from disease and other hazards. Many of the regulations may not sound immediately logical within the context of twentieth-century theories of health and nutrition but reflect ancient public health practices and perhaps even historically specific problems that were encountered by the Hebrew community. A related concern is a humanitarian one for the animals themselves. Some of the preparatory regulations, such as instructions for how an animal is to be killed, mitigate the extent to which it suffers.

Anthropologist Mary Douglas suggests that the logic of the kosher laws lies in the principle of classification itself. Establishing boundaries between purity and danger is a direct way of ordering the world. Categories of forbidden food include types of animals that do not neatly fall into one category or another in the threefold Hebrew classification of the universe as the Earth, the waters, and the firmament: "Any class of creatures which is not equipped for the right kind of locomotion in its element is contrary to holiness" (Douglas 1966: 55). Through this complex set of dietary laws, orthodox Jews are reminded with every meal and in every encounter with the natural world of the link between the people and their god, the boundaries between Hebrews and other tribes. In this sense, then, the *medium* is the message. What is important is not which foods are taboo, or even which criteria are used, but that the laws have a logic to the people who follow them and that the boundaries around food consumption reinforce boundaries around religious, and hence social, identities.

Ritual sometimes transforms the profane into the sacred, thus inverting the normal order of things. In this framework eating becomes not just a way of gaining nourishment for the body but an act of worship that makes a material action spiritual. One of the most striking examples of the effort to sacralize bodily activity is the use of sexual acts and imageries as part of worship rituals. One of the most well developed of the sexual rituals is *tantra yoga*, a spiritual discipline that opens a permissible avenue of sensuality in a sexually repressed society. As Sinha and Sinha (1978: 142) explain:

Rites of Tantra affirm the need for intelligent and organized fulfillment of natural instinctual desires. . . . The essential element underlying the Tantric practices is the belief that these rites cleanse or purify mundane or profane acts and in the process sacralize the acts themselves by superimposing certain constraints on them. Hence Maithuna [participation in a sexual act] for a Tantric Yogi is a rite and not a profane act; since the partners are no longer human beings, but "detached" like gods, sexual union is elevated to the cosmic plane. (Eliade [1958] 1970)

Paradoxically, then, the transformation of the sexual act into a sacred one results not in condemnation, but salvation. The tantric texts themselves are conscious of this paradox, and comment frequently: "By the same acts that cause some men to burn in hell for thousands of years, the Yogi gains his eternal salvation" (Eliade [1958] 1970: 263; Sinha and Sinha 1978: 143).

Rites of passage. Religions provide rituals for all major life passages; these rites sanctify each transition of an individual's life (see Weightman 1984: 216ff). Within the Hindu tradition, at the occasion of a new birth horoscopes are drawn up, a name-giving ceremony is performed on the sixth or twelfth day, the house is purified, and restrictions on the new mother are relaxed. On the first birthday the baby's head will often be shaved (sometimes at a temple or festival) as a sign of thanks for his or her health.

The ritual of baptism in Christianity serves, in some congregations, as a birth ritual as well as a public expression of belief for converts. Baptism, as we have noted—borrowed from ancient Judaism and used by Jesus—was extremely significant in the early church as a rite of passage into the religious community because of the absence of social boundaries around the church. The literalness of the earlier practice gave way to a more symbolic interpretation in which the death and resurrection of Jesus are celebrated by immersion in water followed by a rebirth, as if the believer first died and then emerged from the womb a second time.

Most religious traditions have a rite for the passage from childhood to adulthood, such as the *bar mitzvah* for boys and *bat mitzvah* for girls in the Jewish faith. In some Protestant Christian congregations, baptism comes at puberty rather than at birth. In orthodox Brahman families, an initiation ceremony occurs when the child enters the *brahmachari*, or student, stage of life. A sacred thread is put around the neck of the child, who is taught a *mantra* for worship and begins school or training with a guru or religious teacher. Only male children now receive the thread, which is to be worn for life, but ancient temple sculptures showing women wearing the thread may suggest that the practice was formerly universal. Some reformers advocate introducing the ceremony for both boys and girls of all classes and sects (Jagannathan 1984: 63).

The ritual climax of the Hindu life cycle is the marriage ceremony, in which the couple are treated as gods in the sacred interval when bride and groom and (just as importantly) their two families are united. A priest chants appropriate scriptural passages for several hours while the wedding party engages in an elaborate procession through the streets and then feasts. In this way the union is sacralized and made a part of the universal order; the bride and groom enter another stage of their life cycle and thus obtain a new *dharma*, which they must identify and fulfill.

One of the most significant rituals in most religious traditions is the funeral, and the process of dying is often full of religious significance as a passage from one world to another. The problem-solving character of rituals can be seen in the way that they frame the end of a human life. Typically the lifestyles, values, and social structures of an entire culture are reproduced in funeral ceremonies. Filial piety and honoring the dead, for example, are important aspects of Chinese culture. The departed's son traditionally goes to a stream to offer his parent wine and "ghost money." For seven days he offers sacrifices before the coffin, supplemented by Taoist exorcisms and Buddhist prayers for the dead. The funeral procession includes music, exploding firecrackers, and banners and tablets inscribed with the services the deceased performed during life. Elaborate provisions are made for the departed's needs in the next life, including paper money, clothing, bedding, and even models of houses and cars, easing the grief of those left behind because the unknown world after death is rendered more familiar and the departed are well-provisioned for their next life.

The final ritual ceremony of a Hindu's life is the *antyeshti samskara*, in which the body is cremated on a pyre lit by the deceased's eldest son, if possible, followed by a period of restrictions placed on the relatives, and then offerings to the departed soul. Traditionally, a wife would join her husband in the passage by throwing herself on the funeral pyre, a practice called *setee*, which is still relatively common but widely denounced and no longer expected.

Cycles of nature. The more spectacular ritual events are often pilgrimages and festivals, usually associated with seasonal cycles of nature or milestones in a tradition's sacred history. Virtually every religious tradition acknowledges the importance of special times and places during which, and at which, the sacred is experienced. Pilgrimages to places where the gods were born or engaged in heroic encounters with each other or humans hold special promise to believers for their own experience with God. Often a pilgrimage site offers a specialized benefit, such as healing or the prospect of a son. Similarly, the annual cycle of festivals provides regular occasions for lavish ritual practice. Many are related to the seasons and have ancient roots in the cycles of nature; others are associated with specific gods, such as Krishna, Shiva, Ram, Lakshmi, Durga, Ganesha, and Hanuman in popular Hinduism, various *boddhisattvas* in Buddhism, and saints in the Christian calendar. Often modern believers who participate in ancient festivals rooted in natural cycles, such as the winter and spring rituals now associated with Christmas and Easter, have lost touch with their original meaning.

On significant festival days for each god in many religions, the god is brought out of his or her resting place in the temple, anointed and dressed, and paraded through the streets with much ceremony. People crowd around to greet the god and pay homage, and (depending on the powers of the specific god) special benefits are received by those who participate. This process serves to remind people of the ideas and moral implications of their faith and reinforces the status of the temple and its personnel. Through regular cycles of *poojas*, prayers, pilgrimages and festivals, the sacred canopy remains intact over the millions of Hindus on the Asian subcontinent.

Buddhist practices are often connected with the agricultural year or the significant dates of local heroes or gods. From the Chinese New Year to the end of the rainy season, Buddhist festivals are celebrated, usually with much fanfare and often with fireworks, lights, and processions. These religious festivals are also social occasions that get people together, uniting families, friends, and members of the community. Seasonal festivals are often cultural residues from agricultural times or even earlier, when people's lives were more closely linked to the cycles of nature and people were more appreciative of the "help of the gods" in coping with lifestyle changes from one season to another.

The major festivals of the Jewish year reflect this religion's agricultural roots and recall significant events in the history of Israel. Three autumn festivals include **Rosh Hashanah** (New Year), **Yom Kippur** (Day of Atonement), and the **Sukkoth** (the Feast of Booths, a harvest festival commemorating the wilderness wandering following the Exodus). **Pesach,** or Passover, in the spring celebrates God's liberating activity in history, portrayed symbolically in the *seder* meal. The ritual serves as a reminder of social history: the Jews' liberation from slavery and their hope for a messiah. It is sustained by the ethnic religious community but is couched in universalistic terms for the benefit of all humanity: just as God worked through Moses to liberate the Hebrew slaves, Jews today are reminded of their duty to work for the liberation of all who are oppressed.

The Diffusion and Transformation of Rituals

Because rituals establish the link between a people and their worldview, social transformations and ritual changes are mutually interactive. The move toward universalism is common in religious traditions that shift from being locally oriented to more cosmopolitan. When religions diffuse across different cultures, or when the territory in which they are based is invaded by traders or conquering armies, religious practices are almost inevitably modified. When Buddhism moved into China and the rest of east Asia, the indigenous festivals and gods of the various cultures became part of the overall Buddhist practice, or lived side by side in the same ceremonies and temples.

The most widely diffused religious tradition, Christianity, has a long history of transformation from its Jewish roots. Although the central rituals of the faith have considerable continuity, they have also been diversified and modified through contact with other cultures as Christianity was carried by various empires and colonizers. Let us look briefly at this process, which hints at what may happen in the contemporary globalization of society and culture.

Because of its detachment from social criteria for membership, Christianity was syncretistic from the beginning. Its earliest advocates picked up on the universalism of the founder's teachings and took the movement from the core to the periphery of the ancient Roman Empire. Along the way, it became infused first with Greek philosophy (as in the Gospel of John), and later with a wide variety of other religious and philosophical perspectives. During the Western colonial period, Christianity became transnational and global and its practices grew exceedingly diverse. Although the colonial church eradicated many indigenous local practices in an effort to carry out its perceived mission of spreading an exclusivist religious truth, Christianity itself was dramatically changed by its encounters with various traditions. In the West, especially in New World Protestant denominations, it took on features that would seem foreign to the Christians of ancient Palestine. Elsewhere, Christian belief and practice melded with local practices in a way that most Americans would find astonishing. Although the most general sets of symbols and core beliefs remain intact, they are interpreted in quite different ways around the world, expressed in rituals and ideas that reflect the indigenous religions which Christianity replaced or with which it coexists.

One of the most striking examples of this process is in India, which is predominantly Hindu but has a Christian tradition claiming roots in the first century c.e. from the apostle Thomas, who reportedly first took the Christian gospel to the Asian subcontinent. In traditional Indian culture, the gods each have their special festival days when they are brought out of their temple and paraded through the streets on a chariot borne or pulled by believers. Over the centuries, the Indian Christian church has adopted many of the practices of the indigenous folk religions, including these processions. In Kodaikanal, in the mountains of South India, the statue of Mary is annually removed from her resting place at St. Mary's cathedral, put on a "chariot," and reverently pulled through the streets of the town in a day-long procession. Thousands of people come on foot, and by bus, oxcart, and car, to participate. The streets blaze with lights, and as Mary works her way through the crowds babies are lifted up to the statue for her blessing. Vendors hawk their wares: everything from religious artifacts and worship aids to food, clothing, and toys for the kids. A carnival atmosphere prevails, and people gather to talk, renew acquaintances, and enjoy the holiday. Through the process of this festival honoring Mary, life in Kodaikanal is also honored and their collective life is celebrated, even in the midst of much poverty and disease.

Another example of syncretism between Christian and indigenous Indian practices can be seen in a Catholic orphanage outside of Madurai in South India, where a statue of Mary adorns the central courtyard. That the sisters who run the orphanage would make Mary the visual focal point of their establishment is not surprising . . . except that she is standing atop a lotus flower.

Although religious traditions sometimes appear fixed and immutable, they are in fact dynamic phenomena that grow out of specific social circumstances in specific natural environments and are then transformed as the conditions in which they flourish change. This tension between continuity and change is characteristic of all human institutions, including religion.

Religious Institutions

Religious traditions do not exist in isolation but are institutionalized and often highly bureaucratized. The institutional nature of religious practice is one of its most sociologically significant aspects and has changed substantially over time despite its seemingly immutable nature. The most significant development is the shift from local to cosmopolitan religious institutions, a transformation that each of the major religions has undergone and intensified in the twentieth century as institutions in every social sphere become linked to global processes.

Religious institutions create a base from which religious beliefs and practices can have regularity over time. Indeed, the provision of continuity is the very essence of institutionalization. As social organization changes over time, however, so too does the organization of religious life. This perception of permanence in the midst of change is one of the most interesting aspects of institutional life. What we now know as established religious traditions were once small religious movements, often sustained only by the charismatic authority of a religious figure—Moses, Jesus, Muhammad, the Buddha—and a small group of devoted followers. If a movement is successful, the initial period is followed by a process Max Weber calls the "routinization of charisma" in which the mobilizing energy of founder and followers becomes routinized and "crystallized" in a social organization that sustains the beliefs and sponsors the founder's practices.

Religious institutions tend to reflect the more general types of social organization in a given society. Wallace (1966: 84–88) suggests the following categories of religious organization:

1. *Individualistic cult institutions,* that tend to be "magical"—that is, they sponsor ritual acts to implore or coerce forces into meeting specific needs, either general "luck" or for guardian spirits or success in economic or travelling ventures.

2. *Shamanic cult institutions,* an early and persistent form of specialization in religious practice, because the shaman (either full or part time) is a specialist, a private entrepreneur who aids clients in ritual matters.

3. *Communal cults,* which are not led by specialists but meet the needs of a particular community, such as that found in a family, kinship, or locality group, and other social groupings that have a common membership characteristic such as age or sex.

4. *Ecclesiastical institutions,* which have religious professionals organized into a bureaucracy along the same lines as other nonreligious organizations in the culture as well as a clear-cut division of labor between the professionals (or clergy) and the laity.

The first three types are found in the primal religions of pre-agricultural (i.e., primarily hunting and gathering) cultures and contemporary folk religion, including what Redfield (1957) calls the "little tradition" variants of the more well-known "great traditions." In primal cultures, as we saw in Chapter 2, religious practices and beliefs are generally more integrated into the broader social organization of the environment than in modern cultures, and their institutions are not as highly specialized.

That is not to say that these primal institutions—or elements of them—haven't persisted into the late twentieth century. Shamanism still represents a large proportion of the world's religious practice, although it is usually associated with primal cultures. The **shaman** is an individual thought to have special powers for performing beneficial religious rites and may even be "possessed" by one or more spirits, thus enabling others to come into contact with these forces, or at least to use their services (see Wach 1944). Even postmodern societies have shamanic roles, such as that of medium or faith healer. Hargrove (1989: 94) suggests that televangelists and media celebrities function much like shamans do. Ironically, television has also made it possible for this ancient cultural artifact to become highly developed and institutionalized, sometimes in the form of multimillion-dollar corporations.

As religious traditions become part of complex societies, their institutional forms become highly embellished and specialized, as we see in the case of the shaman-evangelist who represents something of a mixed type, with the personal charisma of the leader supported by an elaborate institutional framework. Every religious movement, but especially in the global village, experiences the pressure to become increasingly institutionalized. The structural form ultimately adopted is related both to the social context in which the movement is born and takes shape and to the organizational preferences of the group that is the new religion's carrier.

Today all the major religious traditions are what Wallace calls **ecclesiastical,** because they have a highly developed institutional structure run at least in part by professionals. Each tradition also has elements of the other four types of institutional structure as well, sometimes as a residue of earlier organizational forms that persist and sometimes as a revival responding to particular needs of the time or abilities of particular leaders or groups. Examples of revivalism include the shaman-evangelist already mentioned, communal cults of protest movements, or individualistic cult institutions like the Reverend Gene Ewing's "Church by Mail" that provide people with specific "religious services" for tasks that promise spiritual and financial blessings to those who participate in their program.

Considerable variation has emerged even within the ecclesiastical institutions of the major traditions, which we shall now examine briefly. Of particular interest sociologically, and also because of the democratic ethos associated with the global village, is the elective affinity between particular traditions and certain types of institutional forms. Although this is not an inevitable outcome, religious institutions that encompass a diverse population and a pluralistic religious worldview may tend to be decentralized in their authority structures; monotheistic religious traditions and those with more homogeneous populations and belief systems, in contrast, may tend toward more centralized structures. There is no strict relationship, it should be noted, between degree of centralization and the extent to which an institution is formally democratized, although a decentralized system may be more lenient toward local deviations than a centralized one. Moreover, a system that is nonhierarchical across a broad geographical area (such as the Southern Baptist Church in the United States) can have local branches that are extremely hierarchical.

The broad variation within each religious tradition makes it difficult to generalize about differences among them, but some further general statements may be useful. Whereas Hinduism and Buddhism tend to be less centralized and hierarchical, Christian churches have often become more formalized as a response to the universalism of their membership. Judaism, despite its highly rational tone, has until very recently retained a more tribal, less differentiated social organization, in part as an attempt to retain the sacred canopy over a specific ethnic identity that has been reinforced by persecution and adversity as well as sharp exclusionary boundaries. We will now examine each of these institutional structures.

Decentralized Structures in Hinduism and Buddhism

Hindu institutions and their priests do not have the same authority as priests in the traditional Roman Catholic Church, for example. In traditional Catholicism (especially before the Second Vatican Council substantially democratized the church in the 1960s), priests were appointed by the bishop and people were expected to defer to them no matter how competent or incapable they were. This was an "authority of the office" rather than of the person. The Hindu system rather resembles American Protestant churches, in which the authority of a religious leader or institution is based primarily on charismatic qualities such as the ability to perform and deliver in a way that satisfies people in a congregation. The authority of the ancient texts persists in popular Indian culture, as does, therefore, the importance of their interpreters, the **pandits.** Hindus believe that answers to any question can be found in these writings, and the pandits can interpret their advice on everything from the origins and purpose of the cosmos to the meaning of an individual's own life, from ethical dilemmas to important decisions such as a choice of occupation or marriage partner.

Eastern religious traditions have never had strong, centralized institutions as in the West, and there is no central authority like a pope or patriarch. This fact both reflects and shapes the nature of the beliefs and practices of the faith, which are thus more decentralized and flexible. Moreover, Hindu worship takes place in households as well as in temples, so that a wide range of authority structures sponsors religious practices and the family remains a religious institution as well (as in the primal religions) despite specialized institutions and a priesthood. Since people can pick and choose their gods and gurus, the religious pluralism of India cultivates a diffusion of authority. This might give us a clue about the nature of religion in the global village, in which a large variety of religious institutions exist side by side and people have considerable latitude in choosing from the sacred marketplace (see Warner 1993; Lee 1992; Robertson 1992b; Iannaccone 1990).

Two broad branches of Hinduism center around two of the most important gods, the **Vaishnavites** (or Vaisnavas) who worship Vishnu, and the **Shaivites** (Saivas), or followers of Shiva, and each branch has its own temples, although people can choose freely to go to more than one. A third significant group, the **Saktas,** are usually treated as a subdivision of the Shaivites. Temple priests, called *pujaris,* serve the deity in each temple, treating the god's representation as an honored guest. Being responsible for the god's maintenance, the priest has considerable authority that is linked to the god's reputation. Hinduism is, of course, replete with famous teachers who claim to become enlightened, gather a body of disciples, and become known as a **guru,** whose authority is essentially of the charismatic variety, confirmed by the testimony of his or her followers but sometimes routinized into a more formal movement.

Some of the most sacred sites in Hinduism, such as the locations of encounters with God, or **dharshans,** are given special authority because of the traditions and stories of miracles, serving as places of pilgrimage for believers. Consequently, those in charge of the famous temples built at those spots have a particular authority. Of particular importance are the five Shankaracharyas, that is, *acharyas* (teachers) who succeeded the famous eighth-century Shankara who systematized Hinduism, traveled by foot throughout India, and established a monastic order with *matams* or *ashrams* (dwelling places for the monks) in each part of the country. A Shankaracharya governs the *matams* of the order in each of five locations around the country, and often manages the major temples in his respective region. These leaders are not appointed or self-appointed but are "found" through a series of signs and clues given by the gods.

The Hindu solution to questions of ordering the collective life of a highly diverse population is reflected in this religion's theology and its organization, which in turn help to shape the nature of Hindu society. Respect for authority in general is highly regarded and internalized; Hindus are expected to be submissive to legitimated authorities. Any claim to authority must be proven, though, and a variety of options are available, some specific to particular social functions, allowing believers to choose gods and teachers whom they find most appropriate for their needs. The fact that charismatic authority is highly regarded prevents the excessive rigidity of institutional forms. Moreover, the criteria for authority are somewhat functional—that is, any prospective god or guru must bring benefits to his or her followers or suffer from neglect.

Buddhist ideas were spread from the beginning primarily by highly disciplined monks, members of the **sangha** who lived communally and developed a collective, nonhierarchical authority structure. The sangha remains central to the organization of Buddhist life today, although it does not have an authority comparable, for example, to the clergy in Christianity. Lay Buddhist societies are also important and relatively independent from the monks. Much as with its sibling religion Hinduism, theological tolerance and institutional flexibility go hand in hand in Buddhism. Religious practices are by no means the monopoly of monks and may be conducted in the home as well as the temple. The authority of the monks and other holy figures derives more from their knowledge and demonstrated abilities than from any official authority.

The most significant aspect, sociologically, of the organization of Buddhist religion is the differences that emerged over time as the religion's ideas and practices were diffused throughout Asia, picking up elements from indigenous cultures in different regions. The **Theravada** ("Doctrine of the Elders") branch is dominant in southern Asia, especially Sri Lanka, Burma, Cambodia, Laos, and Thailand as well as parts of Vietnam, Bangladesh, India, and various immigrant communities (especially in the United States). The larger branch, **Mahayana** ("The Great Vehicle"), is practiced in China, Japan, Korea, Vietnam, and elsewhere. A third branch, found primarily in Tibet, Mongolia, the Himalayas, and in parts of China and the former Soviet Union, is significantly smaller than the two main branches and remains much closer to classical Indian Buddhism. Another popular variant is Ch'an Buddhism, which took root in Japan, where it is known as **Zen.**

Huston Smith (1965) observes how the image of crossing the river also distinguishes the different branches of Buddhism and their respective approaches to the search for Enlightenment. The Theravada tradition says we should make ourselves a little raft and shove off across the water. The Mahayana tradition says we seek out a ferry and rely on the ferryman to take us across safely. Before the crossing, the world on the other side is scarcely visible: it is a mere line on the horizon, misty and unsubstantial. After the crossing, the shore that is left behind—which was once tangible and real—is now just as unsubstantial as the shore on which we now find ourselves. Zen Buddhism says that once we have reached the shore of Enlightenment we no longer need the raft. We no longer need the doctrines or the *dharma*, the Four Noble Truths, the Eightfold Path, or even the Buddha himself: hence the rather shocking Zen saying, "If you meet the Buddha on the road, kill him."

Christian Hierarchy and Rebellion

Christianity's social organization, the most formalized of all the major religious traditions, is a direct response to the universalism of its theology, which encouraged efforts to convert all nonbelievers to the faith. Whereas many traditions can draw on the social organization of the culture in which they are carried, the deliberate break made by the early Christian movement with the Jewish socioreligious order precipitated the construction of cultural and ideological, rather than ethnic or tribal, boundaries to shape the new religious movement. Such a radical break with social organization is inherently destabilizing, however, so that the history of the Christian church becomes a story of continual efforts to attach the ideas of the faith and the interests of its institutions to particular social orders.

Reading between the lines of the New Testament, we can detect many religious conflicts emerging from this universalistic experiment in social organization as the early Christian community fought to establish its identity. First came the division between the ethnically Jewish church in Jerusalem, headed by the local leader Peter and the non-Jewish congregations founded or nurtured by the more cosmopolitan Roman citizen Paul, who was dramatically converted to the movement and later transformed it (hence the Christian saying, "robbing Peter to pay Paul"). Many of Paul's letters address the relationship between what it means to be a Christian on one hand and whether or not this excludes non-Jews on the other; whether one needs to be kosher or circumcised or otherwise connected to the ethnic roots of the faith in Judaic culture. Time and again, the early community, especially under Paul's charismatic leadership, came down on the side of universalism.

These early battles were waged over and over again as Christianity diffused and became entangled in social and political alliances, finally resulting in institutional divisions of the church that were more political than theological. The church councils of the early centuries, meetings of high church officials from the far-flung corners of "Christendom," were called to settle doctrinal disputes that had political or societal bases. The Roman church attempted to monopolize the tradition, tracing the authority of the pope back to Peter, who, according to tradition, was anointed by Jesus to succeed him. When the church split between the Roman and Eastern Orthodox branches in 1054 C.E., it was because the Holy Roman Empire itself had divided into Eastern and Western branches. Similarly, the Protestant Reformation of the sixteenth century reflected not only legitimate religious disputes over the need for reform in a religious hierarchy that had become infatuated with power, but also the struggle between Roman ecclesiastical authorities and German political elites (see Bainton 1950). Along with the **Roman Catholic** and **Eastern Orthodox** branches, the Reformation created a third major branch of the church, **Protestantism,** but the Protestant branch subsequently subdivided into an extremely large number of sects that later grew into **denominations** in their own right, setting the stage for further reformations.

The history of the Christian church is one of continual rebellion and recrystallization in conjunction with related historical social and political developments. As the church attempted to compensate institutionally for its lack of a social organizational base, it became increasingly rigid and hierarchical in sharp contrast to the egalitarian nature of the early Christian community. The vast complex of the institutional order of Christianity at the end of the twentieth century reflects the tremendous diversity of cultural styles, sociological and political alliances, and theological differences within the church. This institutional diversity runs across denominational boundaries, but it is internally marked as well and has been radically challenged by Christianity's confrontation first with a myriad of indigenous cultures and recently with the democratic ethos of the modern world. The Roman Catholic church, with its strict chain of command developed over the centuries, has taken much of the brunt of the modern rebellion against authority, but other branches of the church have been similarly shaken by populist and democratic movements as well.

The shape of modern democracy was influenced positively by people demanding political freedoms as a vehicle for religious freedom. Important structural innovations were developed by the founders of the American republic, for example, and models of democratic participation were created by such Christian sects as the Society of Friends, also known as the Quakers. The Quakers rebelled in the mid-seventeenth century against the formalism of ecclesiastical institutions and practices even within the reformed Protestant churches. Rejecting even the sacramental rituals of the Eucharist and baptism, the Friends (as they called themselves) emphasized the four principles of equality, peace, simplicity, and community and cultivated a radically democratic institution. One arm of the Friends, in an effort to purge the community of empty ritualism, resorted to silent worship, interrupted only when any participant felt "moved by the spirit" to speak. Gradually, however, although they continued to emphasize simplicity in their interactions and forms of worship, even the Quakers developed their own distinctive rituals and specialized language that help to solve the problems of collective life and to create the boundaries not provided by a common ethnicity.

Tribal Continuities in Judaism and Islam

Whereas Christianity broke with the ethnic identities of its roots, both Judaism and Islam struggled to retain elements of their tribal organization in which religious and social organization were not clearly divided. The ancient Hebrews built an ark in which to keep the tablets with the Decalogue, or Ten Commandments, that Moses received at Mt. Sinai, and they carried it to Jerusalem, where a temple was built to house it. The religious specialists who maintained this temple prefigured the **rabbis**— the teachers—who became especially prominent in Jewish life after its destruction. In the Rabbinic period, which dates from about the beginning of the Common Era, the two institutions of modern Judaism were clearly established: the **Temple** and the **Torah.** The Temple in Jerusalem was rebuilt after the Babylonian Captivity, but the rabbis helped to shift the focus of Jewish practice from the Temple to the Torah, especially after its destruction by the Romans in 70 c.e. following a period of Jewish revolts against Rome. The Torah itself, the written scriptures of the faith, became something of a portable institution; it was believed to contain the presence of God and served to facilitate the rituals of worship much like the Temple, but it could be transported when members of the community were forced to migrate to other parts of the world.

The shift from an emphasis on the Temple to the Torah was significant historically as Judaism became somewhat disengaged from sacred locations, less local, and more cosmopolitan. Jerusalem retained sacred significance because of its historical importance, but Israel's God could be encountered wherever the rituals of the faith were performed. Gradually, all of Israel, not just the priests, could perform every ritual practice required by the tradition. No matter where they were in the world, Jews could act in their homes and their daily lives as if they were priests in the Temple (although some rituals require a minimum of ten Jews, a *minion*, to be properly conducted). A major reason for the decentralization of Jewish institutions was the mobility and dispersion of the community. After the Babylonian Captivity in the sixth century B.C.E. and again following the destruction of Jerusalem and the temple by the Romans in 70 C.E., Jews were scattered all over the world and carried their religious traditions with them, constituting what is called the **Diaspora.**

Because ritual is more important than belief in traditional Judaism and the religion is rooted in an ethnic identity reenforced by ritual, the rabbis became ritual experts more than theologians. The emphasis on the written revelation from God in the Hebrew scriptures, however, means that the rabbis also became experts in the written tradition, especially the Torah, and were the intellectual leaders of the community as well. The authority of the Jewish rabbis is similar to the pragmatic authority of the priests, monks, and *pandits* of Hinduism and Buddhism; it comes from effectively demonstrating their knowledge of the scriptures and the rituals of the faith. The rituals must be perceived as bringing benefit to worshippers, although it is more for the collectivity than the individual.

Just as the mosque forms the center of the Muslim city from which all life emanates, so Islam and its institutions lie at the center of individual and collective life. Initially a relatively small, homogeneous religious movement, Islam developed institutions that were identical to the general social organization of Islam. The **Shari'a**, or law, provided a comprehensive judicial system but also defined the Muslim state and the responsibilities of the **caliphs,** the heads of the Muslim *ummah* (the community of believers). The Shari'a, also called the "Way," grew out of efforts to develop systematic instructions for all aspects of individual and collective life as prescribed by the Qur'an, and is found in a collection of books initiated in the first centuries of the faith, such as the *Hadith*, records of early Islam comparable to the New Testament of Christianity, and less authoritative collections within various branches of the Islamic community. Because "early Islam made no distinction between law and religion," the word Shari'a is itself a later development (Williams 1962: 92). As the community grew after the death of Muhammad, first Uthman and then Ali (Muhammad's son-in-law and cousin) became caliphs, but internal divisions erupted into deep and long-lasting conflicts and finally civil war. The group of Muslims that supported Ali came to be known as the **Shia** ("followers") or Shiites and created an institution called the *imamah* (from *imam*, meaning "leader") in which each leader appointed his successor to be the *imam*, whom the Shias believe is divinely inspired and can provide both religious and secular leadership. When Ali was assassinated in 661, his eldest son Hasan succeeded him, followed by a younger son Husayn, who was massacred along with his family by troops supporting his rival, Yazid.

The other major branch of Islam, the **Sunnis,** became the majority Muslim group, deriving their name from an emphasis on the *sunnah*, the custom or practice of the Prophet. The Sunnis developed an elaborate set of means for interpreting the Shari'a that relied upon the use of consensus and analogy by the scholars who specialized in the study of Islamic law. Not surprisingly, some broad differences of opinion in how to interpret the Shari'a led to the creation of four schools of law in Sunni Islam, each named after the scholar most responsible for its creation: Shafi'i, Maliki, Hanbali, and Hanafi. Each school has its own distinctive characteristics but recognizes the others' right to their differing views (e.g., on whether the Qu'ran had been created by God or is eternal), thus allowing for a considerable level of tolerance and autonomy while recognizing a common membership in the Islamic community.

In both Judaism and Islam, the solidarity of socioethnic ties of the community diffused authority and gave religious elites socially derived authority rather than the formal authority of a religious institution. Divisions within each tradition emerged mostly along social cleavages and have become somewhat more complicated as the tradition was diffused around the world and its body of adherents became more heterogenous.

Diffusion and Change in Religious Traditions

Every major religion has undergone substantial change over time as its social context changed, especially as each diffused geographically and encountered other indigenous traditions. We may summarize the major modes of religious adaptation to these new situations as follows:

1. *Cooptation and syncretism* of indigenous traditions, as in Hinduism and Buddhism, which developed a loose federation of organizations affording considerable autonomy to local units and knitting institutional and belief systems together into new forms.

2. *Conversion* of people in alternative traditions, as in Christianity's alliance with western European colonialism, using more or less coercive tactics in different situations depending a variety of factors.

3. *Segregation* of the traditions, as in Judaism, through strict rules prohibiting interfaith marriage and excessive interactions with outsiders.

4. *Integration* of religious communities, as in Islam and some sectors of established Christianity, which allowed people from other religious groups to participate as minority groups in the society with some measure of religious freedom.

In actual practice, of course, sectors of every religious tradition have engaged in some combination of each of these adaptation strategies, although the cultural style of a tradition often shows affinity with a single option.

Hindu and Buddhist syncretism and cooptation. The cooptation and syncretism modes of adaptation can best be seen in the Buddhist diffusion into China over a period of several centuries. Because Buddhism flourished in China and the rest of Asia rather than in its founder's native India, the way in which this religion was transformed and in turn affected other religious traditions is instructive of the syncretism process through which all the major faith traditions have undergone. Eventually, the worldview and ethos of Buddhism became profoundly intertwined with that of Asian culture generally and consequently grew extraordinarily diverse. Different schools of Buddhism emerged as adaptations to indigenous cultures, forming separate sects.

Emperor Ming Ti, after dreaming in 62 C.E. of a golden image from the West, sent representatives to India, who returned with Buddhist teachers, images, and texts. Reliable records from the first century C.E. of vegetarian feasts may reflect a Buddhist influence, given the prohibition against taking life found in Buddhist, but not Chinese, teachings. Many Chinese at first resisted Buddhist practices, especially because the 4,000-year-old practice of honoring ancestors was undermined by the Buddhist monks, who eschewed family ties to join the *sangha*, took vows of celibacy, and failed to "keep the ancestral fires lighted," thereby endangering the ancestors' status and raising the specter of their becoming "hungry ghosts" (Bush 1988: 138–139). Buddhism was not fully embraced in China until the early fourth century C.E., when much of the country was conquered by the Hsiung-nu, a non-Chinese tribe from Central Asia. The Hsiung-nu adopted Buddhism because there was already some popular basis for it, but also because this religion was not totally Chinese and advocated a universalistic ethic that encouraged intercultural tolerance. The conquerors coopted the monks, giving them legitimacy but forcing them into service projects such as managing official charities and building the country's infrastructure.

Religious belief and practice in China now consists of an amalgamation of three religious traditions: Confucianism, Taoism, and Buddhism. **Taoism** is a set of indigenous religious practices, sometimes primal, that are closely related to the natural world and loosely linked to the teachings of its apparent founder **Lao tzu,** who may have lived during the fourth century B.C.E. Confucianism is an official ethos and a system of ethics for public life, as first formulated by the Chinese philosopher **K'ung Fu tzu,** known in the West as **Confucius,** who lived in the sixth century B.C.E. Confucianism emphasizes filial piety (*hsiao*), respect for one's parents and ancestors. K'ung Fu tzu was himself more oriented toward this world than the spiritual realm, but his teachings had a clear affinity with the notion of ancestor worship. Living in a tumultuous time in which warfare was common and corruption thrived, K'ung Fu tzu emphasized the importance of order in human relationships, based on respect, benevolence, and reciprocity. He valued learning, ritual, and discipline as vehicles through which to overcome the ignorance and chaos of his time. Taoists offered an alternative, less hierarchical perspective on the world and often ridiculed the formal hierarchism of K'ung Fu tzu's philosophies.

Both Buddhism and Taoism were considered heterodox by Confucian officials, but over time these religions were incorporated into popular Chinese culture, perhaps *because* they were somewhat at odds with the official culture. The Buddhist emphasis on respect for all life, its general tolerance for all religious perspectives, and its ability to incorporate other traditions in its teaching helped this religion to establish deep roots in China by the first century C.E. Over the centuries Buddhism coexisted alongside Taoism and Confucianism with Confucianism remaining the official state cult until the twentieth century and the two other religions pervading folk culture.

When Buddhist texts were translated into Chinese, translators used the idioms of Taoism to express the ideas and rituals of the new religion. Over the centuries, consequently, many elements of Taoism and Buddhism became so closely intertwined that it is often difficult to separate the two traditions. Not only did Buddhism rely upon Taoist language, but Taoism in turn borrowed from Buddhist stories and concepts, especially as the Taoists began to have access to the rich collection of Buddhist texts coming from India from the fifth century on. As Ch'en ([1964] 1972: 474) notes, sometimes Lao tzu's name was simply substituted for the Buddha's and texts were incorporated wholesale. Other times the copyist simply forgot to change the names, as in the Taoist passage that proclaims: "Of all the teachings in the world, the Buddha's teaching is the foremost." [15]

Christianity's conversion strategy. The distinction between religious belief on one hand and social and ethnic status on the other in early Christianity resulted in a conversion-oriented faith that shaped institutional practices. From the time of the early church, Christians felt compelled to convert nonbelievers of all national and ethnic groups to their faith. On the ideal level, it was an effort to "share the good news" with others. As a practical matter, the conversion strategy became a tool of various social forces to conquer others, from the Roman emperors to the Western European colonialists.

The Roman emperor Constantine converted to Christianity in 312 c.e. immediately before a decisive battle in which he painted the Christian cross on the shields of his soldiers, won the battle, and became convinced that the Christian God was a great war deity who could advance his imperial ambitions. Constantine's entire army was forced to convert and the Empire and Christianity spread simultaneously over broad areas of the ancient Middle East into Europe, Asia, and Africa, converting people from their indigenous religions to Christianity as they went from region to region. Christianity was also changed substantially through the process, shifting from a radical oppositional community, pacifist and egalitarian in nature, to a hierarchical, establishment-oriented institution that facilitated imperial military conquest. The beliefs and rituals of the faith were transformed as well by Greek philosophy and indigenous beliefs and practices throughout the ancient world. Although the central ideas remained mostly intact in the process and local religious leaders and masses of people were sometimes forced to convert formally to the Christian faith, the link between the church and the power elite of Western civilization together with the encounter with diverse beliefs and practices created a tradition so radically different that the earliest followers of Jesus might not have recognized it.

A similar process occurred in the eighteenth and nineteenth centuries as the European colonists conquered vast regions of the world in search of trade and profit, accompanied by the Christian missionaries. The missionary movement did not always legitimate the colonial conquerors, but it often did, providing the rationale for the subjugation of populations throughout the Americas, Africa, and Asia. Local gods and spirits became identified with the saints of Christianity; indigenous festivals were grafted onto celebrations in the Christian calendar; and the dominant population of the church became not white Europeans and North Americans but people of color in the so-called Third World. As the anticolonial movement took hold following World War II, people in the former colonies that gained their political independence demanded independent religious institutions as well, and much of the control over religious institutions exercised by Europeans and Americans was turned over to indigenous leaders. The newly independent nations, often run by people trained in Christian missionary schools, asserted their own authority in their local arenas but also became part of the decision-making process at the core. Italian and other white bishops and cardinals were challenged at the Vatican in Rome, and people of color sent delegations of their own leaders to church centers in New York and elsewhere. After the mid-twentieth century, the shape of the Christian institutions was altered along with the ethnic and racial composition of international gatherings and legislative bodies. The global village had reached Christianity.

Judaism's universalistic belief and exclusivistic practice. Where Christians and Muslims tried to convert nonbelievers to their respective religions, the Jewish community took a very different approach. For the most part, Judaism has deliberately segregated itself from its host cultures as it diffused around the world, making no effort to impose the tradition or to convert others to join, but focusing instead on coexistence with its neighbors whenever Jews left the Middle Eastern homeland.

   This institutional path has an elective affinity with the needs and interests of the Jewish community, which has its roots in a nomadic tribal culture and has experienced substantial geographical mobility over the centuries. As a primal religion, ancient Judaism was simply a tribal variant of existing religions in the regions where Abraham and Sarah lived before they migrated to the region now known as Palestine. It was probably only when Moses was leading the Israelites out of Egypt and back to that region, many centuries after Abraham and Sarah, that the earliest institutions of ancient Judaism began to emerge. The first notable event was when the priesthood of the Levites sided with Moses during a conflict among religions at the time that Moses received the Decalogue at Mt. Sinai.

   The division of modern Judaism into three main branches—the Orthodox, Conservative, and Reformed—reflects the modern transformation of the segregation strategy and especially the emigration of large number of Jews to the United States, where they have become more assimilated into mainstream culture than in most of Judaism's long history. The Reform movement was first initiated in the nineteenth century, primarily among German Jews who immigrated in large numbers to escape waves of persecution starting in Germany in the mid-1850s. They were joined by Eastern European Jews fleeing the pogroms of Eastern Europe in the late nineteenth and early twentieth centuries. The Reform Jews wanted to retain their traditional faith and many of its rituals but felt it necessary to respond to changing social conditions with new forms of religious practice. The Conservative movement emerged as an American Jewish response to these reforms, growing out of a concern by some that the Reform movement had given up too much of the tradition; it advocated not a return to Orthodox Judaism's more rigid order, but a more flexible approach that retained the spirit of the ancient tradition. Moreover, high rates of interfaith marriages further undermined the traditional segregation strategies of the Jewish tradition, a situation exacerbated by ongoing changes in Jewish social organization around the world with the establishment of the state of Israel in 1947 and the recent lifting of restrictions on Jewish emigration from the former Soviet Union.

Segregation and integration in Islam and established Christianity. A final mode of adaptation to intercultural conflicts is this interplay between attempts at segregation and efforts to integrate all religious groups under a broader sociopolitical order without swallowing up minority religions in the dominant faith. The structural situation created by the linking of a religious tradition with a sociopolitical order results in an unresolved tension between efforts to segregate the established and minority faith communities, while at the same time attempting to integrate them into the civil society. Sometimes this uneasy alliance results in a flexibility and tolerance for diversity; at other times it promotes a rigidity that results in the persecution of minorities and/or splits within the dominant religious community.

This dynamic is best found in the established faiths of Islam and Christianity in those contexts where they are the official religion of a sociopolitical order and forge an alliance with the state. In the established versions of Christianity and Islam, elites from the official religion set moral and religious standards as they attempt to stretch the sacred canopy of their faith across the entire society. The reign of Christendom in medieval Europe is the clearest example of this union between church and state, though similar alliances were forged elsewhere, and it was precisely this institutional arrangement—more than anything inherent in

Christian beliefs or rituals—that precipitated the intense conflict surrounding the advent of modernism in the West, as we will see in Chapter
5. The Islamic community, especially in the West, has often shown some
intolerance to nonbelievers, but a tradition of hospitality to strangers and
a sensitivity to the need for peaceful coexistence among many Muslims
has resulted in the extension of tolerance to believers from other faith
traditions as long as other religions do not restrict the religious freedom
of Muslims. While the Christian church was tormenting Jews during the
Inquisition in seventeenth-century Europe, for example, the Muslims allowed Jewish communities substantial religious and social freedoms
within predominantly Muslim territories.

The Elementary Forms of Religious Life

This brief overview of religious beliefs, rituals, and institutions has focused on a number of characteristics relevant to an assessment of religious life at the end of the twentieth century. First, religious traditions are
dynamic, particularly when they encounter one another—as they are
with increasing frequency in the emerging global village. Usually presented as immutable truth passed down intact over the generations, religions have changed dramatically over time as the social conditions
around them have transformed. Always the norm, change within the
globalization process has become a tradition. There are no "pure" religious traditions preserved intact over the centuries. Orthodoxy is as
much the result of a political battle within a religious institution, or between the institution and forces outside it, as an inherent feature of the
belief system.

It is, in part, the tension between continuity and change that makes
religious traditions such a powerful force in social life: religions often
preserve ancient wisdom, allowing a culture to recover lost knowledge
and insights that may disappear from view within the ruling conceptual
paradigms of any given age. These preserved traditions, even as they
strive to conserve, then become the source of change. "Conservative"
ideas of harmony between humanity and the rest of the natural world,
for example, sometimes provide the basis for a radical critique of contemporary practices that are destructive to the environment and a call for
change within the society.

Because of the dynamic nature of religious life, we can expect dramatic social and religious changes in the next decades as the various

regions of the world community become increasingly interdependent. The relatively autonomous sacred canopy may be an artifact of the past. Far from disappearing, however, religious beliefs, rituals, and institutions are emerging in new forms from among which people can choose in a global marketplace of religious ideas and practices. Although religion is so embedded in social practice that people do not switch lightly from one religion to another, conversions do occur from time to time. Perhaps more important is the transformation of religious traditions themselves that is growing out of the increased contact among the faith communities, especially at the top. Ancient religious institutional forms persist in the contemporary world, but religious bureaucracies have taken their place alongside other multinational corporations. Religious elites continue to play an important role in social and political life and often provide an alternative voice emphasizing values that sometimes collide with the utilitarian rationality of modern corporate and political elites.

A second salient feature of religious life is the diversity that persists even in the face of an expanding world system and, ironically, may be enhanced by the unification process. As we will see in Chapter 6, efforts to unify culture on a global level have been countered by the revival of more localized practices in the form of religious fundamentalist and other protest movements. The revitalization of specific religious traditions, ethnic identities, and other countersystem movements has created an intensity of the complex interplay between increased unity and diversity that Durkheim (1893) noted at the end of the nineteenth century.

Many people will object to religious diversity and make exclusivist claims to the truth for their own religious perspective, but this very insistence on the value of a single religion ironically adds to the strengthened diversity of religious life on the planet. Competing religious traditions are enhanced by arguments against religion in general or the formulations of specific traditions. Some of the most eloquent statements in defense of religious beliefs have been responses to strong attacks, and some of the most important truths of religion have been revitalized by atheists when the religious institutions that formerly promoted them have long ignored them.

Could it be that religious life, like natural life in the ecosphere, thrives on a system based on the interdependence of a wide variety of distinct species that serve a specific function within the larger dynamic environment? When a rainforest is cleared to make way for a single crop, the fragile ecology of the region is destroyed and even that crop—valuable as it may be—cannot readily thrive. Whether the same is true of cultures and religious communities is an open question, but the fact that global unification is being met with such strong resistance in so many ways around the world suggests that the question is important.

A third important aspect of religious life is the systemic character of beliefs, rituals, and institutions. Every element of a set of religious beliefs and practices is interdependent on a number of levels. At the most abstract level, beliefs within a single tradition are interdependent and reinforce one another. These beliefs are, in turn, intricately intertwined with the rituals and institutions of their tradition, each acting on the other and thus giving shape to the daily observance of the religion.

The sacred canopy metaphor has shown us that each thread of a tradition is woven together with the others and that the unraveling of one part threatens the integrity of the entire fabric. The problem with the canopy metaphor in the global village is that it may be too static an image to represent reality. A religious tradition may be, in fact, more like an energy field than a piece of fabric. Although an energy field has definition and its effects can be seen and felt, it is still made of a dynamic interplay of ever-moving forces. Perhaps we should simply say that the fabric of the sacred canopy is not static, either; at the subatomic level, it too is comprised of dynamic energy fields that are in constant motion despite the canopy's deceptive appearance of solidity to the human eye.

A final characteristic of religious life is its dialectical nature. Religion is something that grows out of, and yet also acts back upon, the social context in which it is born and persists; the elective affinities between certain religious ideas and the interests of social forces that promote them are mutually reinforcing. The canopy (or energy field) of any given religion is socially constructed out of the life experience of a group of people in a particular environment. The principal cause of the diversity across and within religious communities is the diversity of human life situations on the planet. The primary source of their similarities is the universality of human experience regardless of social and natural environments: every individual and community appears to be living in a world that is full of joy as well as suffering and death, and the worldview that each community constructs has implications for how people can make the best of the lives they have been given.

Rather than replacing religion, as Durkheim predicted, science has become another major means for obtaining knowledge about the world in which humans live, and a tool for interpreting it. Science itself is not monolithic, of course; it remains embedded in the process of dynamic changes in its beliefs, rituals, and institutions as well and takes its place in the ecology of human affairs. Rather than destroying religious life, science has in many ways revitalized and reformulated it, forcing people of faith to rethink their ideas and practices and to reapply their religious perspectives to the changing conditions of a postmodern world.

Durkheim's treatise on religious life a century ago was a major contribution to our understanding of how knowledge itself is constructed and the relevance of that knowledge to our collective life. The various theories about the world and its meaning embodied in religious traditions show an elective affinity with diverse social forces attempting to shape the nature of the emerging social order. The knowledge and values of one age as preserved by religious tradition often provide the critique of the next, just as an emphasis on justice for the oppressed among the ancient Hebrews serving as slaves under the pharaoh became the basis for scathing critiques by the prophets of King David's monarchy. This tension between sustaining and critiquing, legitimating and challenging the status quo has characterized religious traditions throughout the centuries and persists in our time, becoming a major element of ethos construction for the global village that we will explore in the next chapter.

4

The Religious Ethos

The future of the global human community depends in large measure on the ability of humanity to forge a common ethos out of current competing traditions. The major religious traditions continue to provide guidelines for the way most people believe they should live their lives—the ethical bases for both the individual and the collective life of a society. Every social order must produce a set of ethical standards that facilitates coexistence, and the emerging global village is no exception. To understand the complex issues surrounding this ethos construction, we will explore the way in which it is carried out in contemporary societies as well as the ethical inheritance provided by the major religious traditions.

Constructing a Religious Ethos

A people's **ethos**, or lifestyle that grows out of their worldview, serves three social functions. An ethos (1) facilitates the process of identity construction; (2) shapes and legitimates or challenges the stratification system of the social order; and (3) identifies taboo lines and lays out the ethical guidelines implied in a given worldview.

This chapter will examine how this process of ethos production occurs in contemporary religious practice and its implications for the question of peaceful coexistence among diverse populations and religious communities. We begin by looking at the process of individual identity construction in each tradition, noting ways in which a people's understandings of the personal and the social are guided by their definitions of the sacred. The ethical implications of a worldview are built into the individual's sense of identity, the lifestyles of particular status groups and subcultures, and ultimately a culture's understanding of how people are ideally to act in the context of its various institutions.

When identities are linked to religion, class, ethnicity, nationality, gen-

TABLE 4.1

Ethical Teachings and Treatment of Those Who Violate Them

Founder	Key Ethical Teachings	Treatment of "Sinners"
Buddha	Silver Rule: Don't do unto others Ten immoral actions, five precepts	If you really repent, then it's okay (e.g., King Ajatasattu)
Jesus	Golden Rule: Do unto others Love God and neighbor	Let the one without sin cast the first stone (adultery story)
Moses	Decalogue: Ten commandments Love God and follow the law	Pleads with God for mercy but destroys those who refuse to follow
Muhammad	Love God, follow the law Hospitality, strict discipline	Compassionate with repentant sinners; ruthless with those who won't repent

der, and other potential social cleavages, the intensity of conflicts may increase, especially if conflicts of interests fall along the same lines. Each of the world's major religious traditions contains the potential for promoting chaos or community in the world order even though their worldviews and styles of life may differ. The fundamental ethical teachings of all the major traditions, in fact, are very similar: they tend to start with a basic compassion or respect for others, such as the Golden Rule from Jesus ("Do unto others as you would have them do unto you") or the Silver Rule from the Buddha ("Do not do to others what you would not have them do unto you"). The ethical standards of each religion, and the way in which its major leader deals with violations of these precepts are listed in Table 4.1.

Most traditions allow for a mitigation of the consequences of an ethical violation through a confession of guilt by the violator. Acknowledging the infraction is the key in every tradition to changing the negative consequences of one's actions. In the East, the law of *karma* simply explains the natural outcome of one's actions rather than declaring a god's specific judgment. Even here, however, confession seems to make a difference, as illustrated by the story of King Ajatasattu, who approached the Buddha with remorse over killing his father in order to usurp the throne. The Buddha, known for his compassion, assured the king that he could reverse the negative consequences of the horrible deed by admitting his mistake and changing his life.

Similarly, Moses and Muhammad both insist on repentance as a condition for escaping dire consequences; they are ready to forgive the repentant sinner but are extremely harsh with those who do not repent. Moses intercedes with God on behalf of those who have sinned, however, and argues with Yahweh about sparing their lives. Yahweh agrees, but those who refuse to admit their mistakes and reaffirm their faithfulness to God are destroyed. In the Christian ethos Jesus also calls on people to repent but shows a compassion similar to the Buddha's in dealing with sinners and insists that people not pass moral judgment on each other (Matthew 7:1–6). Moreover, he makes it quite clear that punishment for sin should be left to God, as demonstrated by the story of an adulterer caught in the act. By law she was to be stoned to death, but Jesus challenged the crowd by saying that the person without sin should cast the first stone. Gradually the crowd, recognizing their own guilt in other areas, dispersed without harming her.

Ironically, although Jesus may have had a remarkable compassion toward violators of ethical standards, Christian institutions have sponsored some of the most intolerant practices in human history, from the Crusades and the Inquisition to witch hunts and excommunications. Such a paradoxical intolerance of the institution coupled with the tolerance of the founder often leads to contradictory behaviors among people within the tradition, an issue we will take up again in Chapter 7. The central issues here are significant for life in the global village. First, the human community must find a way to create an ethos that permits peaceful coexistence, and the basis for that lies at the foundation of every religious tradition: respect and compassion for others is a central obligation. Less consensus exists on how violations of the ethical standards should be treated.

The religious ethos is not a simple list of acceptable and taboo behaviors, however; ethical standards do not exist in isolation but as part of a complex set of elements associated with individual and collective identities, the legitimacy of the social order, and the taboo lines and ethical standards for all spheres of life. In most life situations, conflicts emerge between abstract ethical ideas and the interests of religious elites and various social strata.

Despite both the similarities and the internal diversities of the major religious traditions, each has a distinctive ethos. The ethos of the Hindu worldview, based on the laws of *karma*, is rooted in the conviction that one must find one's *dharma*, or duty for one's station in the universe and position in one's life cycle, and fulfill it to the best of one's ability. Each individual is responsible for maintaining the order of the cosmos within his or her own sphere, and must therefore carry out his or her duty, show respect for elders and superiors, and avoid harming living creatures. Buddhism shares with Hinduism an emphasis on explaining the nature of the world (the law of *karma*) and expecting individuals to determine their own duty within broad general guidelines. One is then punished or rewarded in the form of reincarnation at higher or lower statuses or in being released from the cycles of rebirth altogether. The Buddhist ethos focuses on the expression of compassion for all creatures as a way of building "good *karma*."

The Jewish ethos, rooted in the tribal identity of the ancient Hebrew tradition, takes an activist stance toward the universe within Yahweh's principles such as justice; the "Chosen People" remain faithful to God and perform acts of kindness. According to rabbinic tradition (see Hertzberg 1962: 186), each person should clothe the naked (as God did for Adam and Eve), visit the sick (as God did Abraham), and comfort the mourners (as God did Isaac after his father Abraham's death).

Because Islam is intended to be all encompassing, its ethos is designed to embrace all elements of Muslim society and the daily life of its participants. The difficulty of maintaining the intensity of that commitment to God, which is shown in the internal and external struggle (*jihad*) of believers, pervades Muslim lifestyles and culture. An all-embracing religious ethos is frankly somewhat difficult to maintain in a multicultural society.

Despite the common symbols and cultural roots its various branches share, the diversity of forms Christianity has taken renders impossible efforts to describe a coherent ethos for this religion. Members of the various Christian communities, especially the elites, increasingly interact with one another, however, and substantial cross-fertilization is taking place. Moreover, many elements of the Judeo-Christian tradition now play an important role in efforts to construct a contemporary global ethos because of the powerful position Christian cultures and institutions hold in an emerging world order that is dominated by Western elites. Although the ethos of contemporary Western culture differs dramatically from the ethos of the early Christian church (it is often a religion of the rich rather than the poor), the impact of Christianity on Western norms and values, and hence on the rest of the global village, is formidable.

Let us begin our exploration of religious ethos by looking at the relationship between religious traditions and the process of identity construction.

Religion and Identity Construction

At least five aspects of the identity-building process are related to religious traditions:

1. *Standards or models.* A belief system may provide the standards and models for personal and collective identity construction, especially heroic and demonic models of behavior and the criteria for evaluating good and evil. On a more subtle level, even the tone of a culture—and by implication, personalities valued or disparaged within it—may be highly influenced by a religious tradition. A religious group or subculture may encourage certain traits in the socialization process and discourage others (aggressiveness or passivity, diligence or submissiveness), because the gods approve or disapprove of certain kinds of people. Similarly, the same tradition may promote one personality type among males and another among females; one among lighter-skinned and another among darker-skinned people.

2. *Religious social networks as reference groups.* Religious institutions often provide individuals a social network, a significant reference group of people who shape self-concept. An individual turns to his or her most significant others for positive or negative reinforcement in the identity-construction process. The religious reference group may not only include those who are immediately present in a congregation or social network, but also significant others who are geographically distant (e.g., important religious personages) or even the dead (e.g., the saints and ancestors). As Assimeng notes in discussing religion in Ghana, "the living believe that they are also dialectically linked in some metaphysical oneness with the ancestors of the community 'who have lived before and gone beyond'" (1978: 99). Specific advice, or the general tone of personality development, may thus be related to ongoing interactions, not only with living members of one's community, but—through prayer, mediums, and now mass media—with persons physically present and absent, living and dead.

3. *Interaction with a deity.* The process of engaging in religious rituals, and thereby actually interacting with the gods, may have an impact on one's sense of identity. Whether the interaction—or even the deity itself—is real or imagined is not important here, nor is it sociologically ascertainable. As W. I. Thomas (1966) observed, situations defined as real are real in their consequences; what is significant is the *perception* that one is interacting with God or the gods. When people believe that they are acting on behalf of a deity, for example,

they may consider themselves (individually or collectively) as "chosen" and therefore subject to different norms and standards than others. This phenomenon cuts more than one way, of course, since the person acting under "God's instructions" may be either a Gandhi or a mass murderer. Ellison (1993a) and Pollner (1989) observe that the role-taking process in religious rituals may involve assuming the role of the "divine other" in much the same way that people engage in interaction with concrete social others. Thus, an individual may define his or her own life with reference to religious figures and heroes in their tradition and may even "begin to interpret their situations from the point of view of the 'God-role' (i.e., what God would expect and want)" (Ellison 1993a: 5–6). Routine devotional practices may also instill certain values with reference to one's identity—for example, in a Christian context, that each individual is special and that God hates sin, not sinners; or in a Hindu context, that showing compassion to others is meritorious. In its more developed forms, devotional activities like prayer, study of the scriptures, rituals of obeisance, and the consumption of religious media may play a vital role in forming a sense of self (see Ellison 1993a).

4. *Mechanisms for sustaining identity changes.* Religious traditions play an important role in the process of changes in identity, whether in terms of dramatic events such as conversion or the standard changes in one's life cycle. Rites of passage, for example, offer people a repertoire of thoughts and actions for difficult times of identity change. The frequency of religious behavior is often closely linked with the life cycle of individuals, in large part because of the rituals that sustain life changes. In the United States, for example, many young people raised in a religious family will stop participating in their churches, synagogues, or mosques when they first leave home and go out on their own to work or college. After they have their own children, they may return to regular religious observance because participation in religious rituals is part of the process of raising children, according to their own experience.

Similarly, religion often plays a role in dramatic cases of what Jones (1978) calls *identity alteration*, that is, the "disentanglement from one particular pattern of identity and the process involved in the adoption of another," which we call by a number of terms such as conversion, brainwashing, or alternation, often perceived as a consequence of a hierophany. Cases of dramatic identity change are often associated with religion because they are difficult to achieve without the powerful legitimation of a new identity that comes from religious communities.

Most people may not have exceptional religious experiences or visions—nor are the life changes of those who have them always permanent—but human history is full of such stories. Conversion tales are the stock in trade of many forms of religious enterprise, such as Christian evangelists on streetcorners or on some television stations. The great divide between the former life and the new one is dramatized in order to show others that there is a way out of their current misery and a better life is just around the corner.

5. *A system of meaning and security.* Finally, a religion's nomos provides a "shield against terror," say Berger and Luckmann (1967); a belief system helps people feel secure, especially at society's margins, and most notably in times of crisis and death. "Every nomos is an area of meaning carved out of a vast mass of meaninglessness, a small clearing of lucidity in a formless, dark, ominous jungle" (Berger 1969: 23). This nomos becomes a tradition that, as Tevye puts it in *The Fiddler on the Roof,* helps us keep our balance. When life seems to be falling apart, we can rely upon socially constructed images of the world and what is true and appropriate to help us keep our wits about us. In a homogeneous society the tradition is usually given and taken for granted, but in a multicultural society individuals and groups of people "shop" for a nomos from a variety of available options, making it more difficult to create a common set of values. A gap between theory and reality as it is experienced can, of course, undermine a religion's believability, and the escalation of competing worldviews in the religious marketplace of the global village does pose a special threat to every belief system, as we will see in Chapters 5 and 6.

Variations in Identity Construction

Although every religious tradition plays a major role in its adherents' identity construction, the nature of the process varies substantially. Let us briefly examine some of the major similarities and differences among and within the traditions. The great divide on this issue is between those religious communities that root the individual's identity within the community itself—especially in Judaism, Islam, and some branches of Christianity—and those that emphasize more individual autonomy, at least in spiritual and ethical matters—such as Protestant Christianity, major branches of Hinduism and Buddhism, and the modern marketplace of religious affiliation. Admittedly, this divide is somewhat arbitrary, but the differences in emphasis are real and have substantial consequences for the ways in which people live their lives.

Community-based identities. Jewish identity over the centuries has been linked to membership in the socioreligious community, underscored by the rituals of family and community life that emphasize the special character of one's heritage and one's responsibilities to God and neighbor. Strict regulations of interaction—especially restricting marriage across the boundaries of the community—reinforce the socialization process by which Jews are meant to see themselves first and foremost as Jews. This ethnic consciousness has been enhanced by bitter persecution over the centuries, and a Jewish sense of identity has often thrived in the sense of adversity.

The adaptability of the Jewish ethos to the world of modern society has been both a blessing and a curse to Judaism. Many of the traits valued and cultivated by centuries of Jewish socialization—such as advanced education, critical rational thinking, adaptability to new environments, egalitarianism, and the pragmatic rootedness of Jewish ethics—have facilitated Jewish involvement in societies in which they have been allowed to participate, notably the multicultural North American setting. Their entry into the mainstream has placed tremendous strains on the tradition, however, as many of the boundaries between Jews and non-Jews have broken down, and Jewish identity has become undermined in the same way as other ethnically bound religious and cultural constructs.

Muslims construct their religious identities much like Jews, in form at least if not in content, and especially with regard to the deep roots of religion in the community. The Five Pillars of Islam provide a visible and regular reminder of the believer's duty to uphold God and the *ummah* at the center of his or her life. Signs of the ever-present religious community—such as the punctuation of daily life by prayer and religiously prescribed modes of dress, especially for women—have high visibility in public life. The Islamic family and the *ummah* provide the context from which one's meaning in life and protection from its dangers are to come. Ultimate security comes, of course, from Allah, who watches over the community. Forged in a context of raiding Bedouin tribal life, Islam paid close attention to matters of security in both belief and practice. The traditional Islamic home was a minifortress and life occurred—especially for the women—within the confines of an enclosed courtyard. By means of a system called *purdah*, women were segregated physically from the male society outside the household. On those rare occasions when they ven-

tured forth from the security of their homes, women brought their forti-
fication with them in the form of their traditional dress and veil. This
effort to divide the male and female worlds completely is the subject of
considerable controversy in contemporary Islam.

In a traditional Islamic society, it is difficult to have an identity other
than the religiously centered construction provided within the family and
mosque. In this sense, Islam retains a large element of its primal character
from the days of its founding. Daily life experience with other family
members and society at large constantly reinforces the values and concepts of Islam. In a multicultural society, however, an individual's religious identity is often challenged and sometimes ridiculed, providing
tremendous pressures especially for young people, and most definitely
for young women, to look beyond the traditional religious community
for new role models and values.

Early Christianity, like Judaism and Islam, had a strong community
orientation, and its participants probably perceived of themselves first
and foremost as members of the church. The strong **individualism** of
contemporary Protestantism is a recent historical development, a product
first of the rebellion against the official church during the Protestant Reformation, and then in the individualization of Western culture associated
with the Enlightenment and the industrial revolution. Ideas long present
in Western culture that emphasized the value of individual freedom and
independence were elaborated during the social transformation to modern society. Individualism had an affinity with industrialization, because
it encouraged people to break free from bonds of kinship and feudalism,
and with Protestantism, which constituted a rebellion against feudal
Christianity.

Christian traditions around the world substantially influence personal
and social identities, although in different ways because of the wide
range of groups drawing upon the general tradition. First, major personages and heroes of the faith provide the role models on which to base
personal identity: a host of "ancestral" figures from the scriptures—especially Mary—and a large collection of saints (although their role has been
mitigated in Protestantism), as well as local heroes and models. Christian
identities are also shaped by the process of interaction with the deity,
facilitated by the representation of Jesus as one element of the Christian
Trinity. Routine devotional practices and prayer traditionally provide individuals not only with a quiet time for reflection, but also a specific
relationship with the deity. The content and impact of that relationship
are not simple, however; apparently it can range from the confidence (or,
in some cases, arrogance) provided by the perception of an intimate rela-

tionship with the creator, or it can instill a strong sense of guilt and shame if one becomes too aware of the gap between one's own life and that expected by the deity. (The comedian Emo once suggested that the most universal prayer is to ask God to disregard the laws of the universe for our own personal convenience.)

Across the variety of Christian communities, the person of Jesus remains a focal point of religious belief and practice, and thus a central node for the meaning system of believers. According to the tradition, God's purpose in taking on human form was to speak to humans in such a way that they could understand more fully the substance of God and how they should order their lives. Thus, it is no accident that the image of Jesus in Christian subcultures around the world may say more about the cultural context of the image than it does about the historical Jesus or the god he is intended to communicate. In many parts of the world the image of Jesus tends to mirror the indigenous culture. To some individualistic Americans, Jesus is a friend who will aid the believer in solving personal problems; to impoverished peasants in Solentiname, Nicaragua, he is a poor revolutionary who will mobilize the people to stand up to the establishment. To a Christian paleontologist like Pierre Teilhard Chardin he is a cosmic force toward whom all creation will eventually be drawn. To those who find even Jesus too distant to identify with, many versions of the faith encourage a relationship with his mother Mary or one of the saints who seems more approachable.

Individualistic identities. Even the strongly communal early Christianity probably seemed individualistic to Jewish observers of the time because individuals could break loose from their ethnic and clan groups and join the new religious movement independently. The Protestant Reformation of the sixteenth century extended the individualistic potential of the faith substantially by removing the institutional guarantees of salvation and putting the responsibility for religious belief and decisions squarely in the hands of the individual. This notion of the relatively autonomous individual in Protestant Christianity, combined with the notion of the "calling" in the Puritan branch of the church, cultivated elements of modern individualism, perhaps even—as Weber argued—helping to lay the groundwork for the modern capitalist order.

The Protestant emphasis on a personal relationship with God independent of the institutional structure of the church did not eliminate the communal element of Christianity. In fact, the idea that the individual was responsible for his or her own personal relationship with God sometimes resulted in a vulnerability to social pressures, especially within small homogeneous religious communities in which little deviation from the norm was tolerated. Marx anticipated this sort of dynamic when he observed of the Reformation,

> Luther, without question, overcame servitude through devotion but only by substituting servitude through conviction. He shattered the faith in authority by restoring the authority of faith. He transformed the priests into laymen by turning laymen into priests. He liberated man from external religiosity by making religiosity the innermost essence of man. He liberated the body from its chains because he fettered the heart with chains. (Marx [1843] 1972: 18)

Ironically, some Protestant sects, with their emphasis on personal salvation, constitute a tight social organization with a control over its members that the Vatican never dreamed of having, in large part because participants internalize the norms, values, and rituals of the community.

Moreover, Ellison (1993a: 4) notes identity creation within the religious community in the United States is related to interaction within networks from the religious community:

> Like other social institutions, religious groups are network-driven (Paris 1982; Taylor and Chatters 1988; Williams 1974). Participation in church-related activities brings individuals together with others who have similar status characteristics as well as common religious beliefs. For church members, regular interaction with these like-minded others may reinforce basic role identities and role expectations. Through formal and informal involvement in their church communities, these persons may gain affirmation that their personal conduct and emotions with regard to daily events, experiences, and community affairs are reasonable and appropriate.

Although most Asian societies place individuals in a tightly knit social organization, spiritual matters in both Hinduism and Buddhism have a strong individualistic element that is related to theories of *karma* and *dharma* in which each individual is responsible for his or her own actions and the consequences they produce. As S. Gopalan contends, "the *dharma* of an individual is, in its psychological sense, his innate nature—the law of his being and development" (1978: 128–129). A person who discovers and acts according to his or her actual being is also therefore ethical. But, Gopalan continues, "it cannot be the same for all people . . . or the same for one individual all the time." Thus, one has to continue searching, taking one's cues from family and religious networks and above all from *pandits* and gurus, seeking the path appropriate to one's natural inclinations and abilities in this lifetime.

Religious rituals play a role in the Hindu identity construction process by providing patterns of behavior upon which individuals and groups draw from the larger culture. The techniques of yoga, for example, aid people in the process of "identity consolidation or self-integration," according to Sinha and Sinha (1978: 134). The "basic assumption of Yoga," they contend, "is that an integrated self is essentially sacred. The purpose of Yogic techniques is to unify the spirit." Once individuals discover their *dharma* and develop the spiritual and physical discipline to act on it to their best ability, they bring themselves into syncronicity with the universe, according to the Hindu ethos. Hindu culture therefore relies a great deal upon traditional practices, even in the most modern circles. Horoscopes are drawn to position the individual within the larger cycles of the universe; marriages are still arranged by families in most cases, and the vedas can be consulted (through a *pandit*) for key life decisions as well as for minor ones. Traditional patterns of life and gender- and family-based interaction networks guide an individual from infancy to the grave in a well-established trajectory that continues to reinforce ancient habits of the heart as well as systems of stratification.

Buddhists find meaning in life and, as in Hinduism, construct an individual identity within the broad framework of *dharma* and *karma*. The striking difference between the ethical systems of these two closely related religions lies in the Buddha's rejection of the Hindu caste system of his time. Consequently, Buddhism (along with Christianity) has been an attractive alternative to many of the lower-caste and outcast groups in India. Given the assault on the caste concept in modern Hinduism, it is thus likely that over time the two traditions will become increasingly similar in this respect.

Discussion of caste and class lead us to the next arena of identity construction, namely, social stratification. Whether a religious tradition emphasizes collective or individualistic elements of identity, finally, an individual's sense of self is never fully autonomous and is always linked to the social order in which it is constructed. Out of the many aspects of the social order that could be examined, we will focus briefly on the types of stratification systems legitimated by various religious traditions because a tradition generally puts a strong stamp on the cultural style and thus social organization of societies in which it is dominant. Moreover, religious ideas are strongly influenced by the type of social organization dominant in a specific era and region, so that the ethos of a religion and the forms of social organization in the society in which it is dominant are two sides of the same coin.

Religion and Stratification

The tension between authoritarianism and egalitarianism can be found in every tradition, though each religious community tends to develop an affinity for one or another. The shift from isolated societies each with a single dominant sacred canopy to an increasingly cosmopolitan global religious marketplace since the advent of the modern era has produced contradictory trends within religious traditions. First, individualizing and egalitarian values, which tend to go hand in hand, have become a dominant modern motif infusing every tradition. Each tradition has its own version of these values, although in some religions they are more dominant than in others and they come in a variety of forms. Some traditions may emphasize equality within the community but also the superiority of insiders when compared to outsiders, for example. Second, authoritarianism may emerge in response to the egalitarian motif; such a response is an almost automatic reaction to an attack on the community. When they are not currently under attack, religious elites sometimes invent enemies in order to justify the institution's authoritarian structure.

The authoritarian motif in religious traditions is usually defended with the argument that the structure of inequality within a society is a reflection of inequality in the cosmos as a whole. In general, this position supports a status quo attitude toward the ruling powers unless, of course, they are radically democratic or opposed to the religious tradition. Statements of support or opposition to a particular regime cannot be taken at face value by sociologists because they are sometimes explicitly designed to bring about a change. It is intriguing, for example, that St. Paul exhorted members of the early Christian church to obey the political authorities because they were given their power by God, but he often did so from the jail cells in which those same authorities put him on charges of sedition. Two extreme examples of the support of religious traditions for hierarchical social systems are in the Hindu caste system and the medieval class system legitimated by Christianity, each of which we will now examine briefly.

The Hindu Caste System

Vociferously criticized in the modern, democratic ethos of India, the caste (or *varna*) system has been a fundamental element in Hindu theology and theodicy. In tone and outcome very like to the idea of a "calling" in Christian Puritanism, the notion of caste divisions gives religious justification to a social hierarchy and legitimates a given social order by locating an individual's *dharma* within the strict parameters of the caste into which he or she is born.

In one sense, this system is simply good sociological analysis: it suggests that the social context into which one is born will determine one's life chances and, to some extent, educational and occupational opportunities, social networks, marriage possibilities, and so on. The caste system is an attempt to explain the universe as it appears to be and to help people to make the best of their apparent fate. In another sense, this kind of analysis becomes a sort of self-fulfilling prophecy as people assume that the status quo is the only alternative and simply adjust their aspirations to their situations, producing a kind of fatalism that makes social change seem fruitless and legitimates the worst kind of exploitation. It is a model *of* and *for* social life.

Gandhi attacked the caste system and made his campaign against it—particularly the notion of "untouchability"—an integral part of his Freedom Movement. Gandhi's general condemnation of the system was institutionalized in the independent state of India, established in 1948, where caste divisions were thereafter forbidden by law. Ancient principles of social organization die hard, however, and caste divisions are about as absent from India today as racial discrimination is in the post–civil rights era of the United States.

The traditional system identifies four castes:

1. *Brahman*: priests, teachers, and political advisors
2. *Kshatryia*: rulers and warriors
3. *Vaishya*: merchants, agriculturalists, traders
4. *Shudra*: servants of the other three, manual laborers, but also gardeners, musicians, and artisans

Besides these four castes, there are a wide range of subcastes, the *jatis* or sects, which are largely occupational and clan oriented and often serve as guilds, protecting the interests of their members and prohibiting unwanted outsiders from joining the occupations.

Finally, outside the four castes are the streetsweepers, scavengers, and leatherworkers, the "untouchables" or "outcastes." When Gandhi attacked the system, he renamed this group the *Harijans*, or "Children of God," to object to their religiously sanctioned pariah status. So denigrated were the untouchables, at least in recent times, that their very presence was considered polluting. In some circumstances, as when sweeping the streets or going to clean latrines, they were required to cry out to warn others that they were approaching. Some contemporary Vedic scholars claim that the ancient scriptures were referring not to social castes that should be observed in this way, but to the mental states for which people were prepared as a consequence of their actions.[16]

What is remarkable is not that such a system exists, but the extent to which it functioned consistently over the centuries, essentially providing a system of slavery, with no major rebellions undertaken by the lower castes against the upper ones until the system's moral and legal underpinnings were removed in the mid-twentieth century. Reinforced and legitimated by the theory of transmigration of souls, the social system remained stable since punishments for revolt were believed to be incurred not only in this life, but also in the next. The theological basis for the caste system was dealt a fatal blow by the Indian Freedom Movement, however. As Indians argued for their freedom from the British as a god-given right, subordinates in the caste system made the same claim for themselves and Hindu authorities withdrew their support, for the most part, from the caste system as a type of social order.

Christianity and Western Power Elites

The teachings of Jesus have a strong egalitarian flavor, but the church as an institution has been ambivalent about the distribution of authority and resources, with competing themes of egalitarianism and authoritarianism. During the long history of its alliance with Western power elites, virtually every branch of the church has legitimated status quo systems around the world. After the conversion of the Emperor Constantine in the fourth century c.e., Christianity became intertwined with the Roman empire, then with the power structures from the tsars in Russia to the aristocracy of Western Europe throughout the Middle Ages. The church then legitimated European colonialism, providing a theological justification for conquest by brute force and superior technology and an altruistic account for a process motivated by greed. At the same time, however, Christianity as a belief system and an institution has played a major role in contemporary efforts to reform or revolutionize hierarchical systems from Latin America to Asia, Africa, and Eastern Europe.

Although Jesus empowered women in a number of ways that challenged the gender hierarchy of his day and Paul declared that Christians should not have divisions within their community on the basis of gender, Christianity contains a strong patriarchal motif that has been used to legitimate various forms of gender stratification throughout the centuries. This dual standard was present from the beginning; although women played an important role in the early church, there is no record of their presence in the inner circle or in Jesus' private moments with his close followers, such as the Last Supper. It is possible that their presence was simply not noted by the male chroniclers of the events, however.

Moreover, the authoritarian structure of the church itself as it developed over the centuries seems to contradict claims of an egalitarian Christian ethos. The charismatic early movement was formalized into institutional structures that solidified after Christianity became the official religion of the Roman empire, and although various reform movements have resulted in some models of democracy governance and lay empowerment, considerable tension between clergy and laity persists and much of the leadership in many branches of the church has no democratic pretenses or aspirations. Although at times the social control of the laity by the clergy is blatant and overt, at other times it is more subtle, as in the years of silence on the part of parishioners who were sexually molested by clergy.

Egalitarianism in the World's Religions

It is not surprising that the dominant motif in the world's major religions has been a hierarchical one—the ruling powers of most societies understandably promote authoritarian religious ideologies and suppress the egalitarian beliefs. Early Chinese culture, for example, had two competing traditions: that of K'ung Fu tzu, which emphasized the need for strict social hierarchy and respect for elders and political authorities, and that of Mo ti, who promoted an egalitarian ideology and ridiculed the followers of K'ung Fu tzu for their "exaggerated" emphasis on authority. The first tradition was institutionalized as Confucianism and became the official state religion of the emperors, whereas the second precipitated a relatively unstable popular movement that has been almost lost over the centuries.

Surprisingly, religious traditions have also provided the basis for movements toward equality, primarily because of the ethical dimension of religious beliefs that could overcome efforts by ruling elites to completely suppress the subordinate equality motifs. One of the most significant teachings about equality is that emanating from the Christian tradition, as discussed earlier, which persisted through the centuries despite the tendency toward authoritarianism favored by the political and economic elites aligned with church authorities first in the Roman Catholic and Orthodox churches, and then with the various branches of Protestantism. The Christian emphasis on equality has its roots in the parent religion of ancient Judaism which was distinctive in its time for its consistent emphasis on justice. The apparent equality of the early Christian community, which encouraged membership by all social classes and ethnicities, remained an element of the tradition that laid the groundwork for contemporary democratic theory despite efforts to stamp it out over the centuries.

The Emerging Egalitarianism of Ancient Judaism

Judaic systems of stratification, though rooted in their ancient understanding of Yahweh as a God of justice and community, seem very modern. The early Hebrews developed an image of their deity that shares a number of traits with other high gods in the ancient Near Eastern pantheons: individuated and elevated; active in the world; conceived by natural and human analogies; powerful, just and merciful; in bond with a people or a region; and interpreted by human representatives (see Gottwald 1979: 676ff; cf. Smith 1952, 1973).

Yahweh also has distinctive characteristics, however, not shared by other gods of the ancient Near East, "just as Israel's egalitarian intertribal order is unlike the other ancient Near Eastern social systems" (Gottwald 1979: 693). This uniqueness is sociological: "Yahweh forbids other gods in Israel as Israel forbids other systems of communal organization within its intertribal order. The social-organizational exclusionary principle in Israel finds its counterpart in a symbolic-ideological exclusionary principle in the imagery of deity" (1979: 693).

The idea of Israel as a nation of chosen people only makes sense sociologically, Gottwald argues; otherwise, it is either "irrelevant supernaturalism or exclusivist racism, or both together" (1979: 693). That is to say, the ancient Hebrews perceived of Israel as different because it *was* different, primarily as an egalitarian social system surrounded by stratified societies. Although Gottwald's assessment may be somewhat idealistic given the extreme patriarchy of ancient Judaism, it is nonetheless fair to say that ancient Hebrew society was relatively egalitarian considering its sociohistorical context.

The Separate But Equal Policy of Islam

The social ramifications of Islam, like those of the world's other major religious traditions, are extraordinarily complicated by layers of contradictory ancient and contemporary practice. Highly egalitarian in many aspects, the Qur'an emphasizes justice and attention to the widowed and orphaned, an ethical outlook that derived from the parent Hebrew religion and was adapted to the harsh conditions of the pre-Islamic Arabic world. As noted earlier, the religious institutions of Islam are not rigidly hierarchical, and all classes worship together as equals in the mosque. There is no priesthood per se in Islam, but the *ulama* ("the learned") and the *fuqaha'* ("lawyers"), the scholars and custodians of the law, have acquired an informal authority within the community that is comparable to the status held by professionals in other Western religions.

Because Islam regards all people as children of the same God, an undercurrent of egalitarianism pervades the religion's entire ethos. It is clear that the Prophet Muhammad and his earlier followers—notably his own wife, Khadija—made tremendous advances in protecting the rights of women in a manner that was highly radical at the time. Most of those protections centered on family life in a context of exploitative polygamy and female infanticide, practices that were abolished by the Muslim community. Women were further protected in the event of divorce and were allowed to inherit their husband's property.

Difficult questions arise, however, especially in the twentieth century, concerning the role of women, who essentially have a "separate but equal" status in Islamic society. According to traditional Islam, however, women's place is clearly in the home and they are not afforded the same equality in other spheres, simply because it was not a question at the time of the Prophet. Consequently, a number of people—especially women—have rebeled against efforts to segregate the genders outside the courtyards of traditional Muslim houses.

Religious Taboo Lines and Ethical Systems

Let us now turn to explore the ethical systems of each of the five major religious traditions, with some attention to the way in which those religious ethics shape and are shaped by social organization and action in various spheres of daily life, economics, and politics. Perhaps the most significant aspect of religious traditions for purposes of this survey is their guidelines for the nature of collective life and the ethical standards that facilitate peaceful coexistence among peoples. Every tradition has an ethical system, often growing out of the relationship with a deity, that emphasizes social relations, with regulations about treating one another with compassion and justice, at least within the community, and often across social boundaries as well.

Hindu Ethics

The Hindu ethical system centers on the concept of *dharma*, identifying and carrying out one's appropriate duties. In addition to religious duties, individuals must learn to discipline themselves to transcend the profane aspects of life. Various acts are not judged to be moral or immoral in and of themselves, but appropriate or inappropriate, given one's *dharma*.

A more general code of ethics for all believers stresses the importance of engaging in religious rituals, honoring one's status superiors, giving charity to the poor, avoiding harmful acts against others, not lying, and the like. Because the consequences of engaging in unethical behavior are built into the structure of the universe, one reaps what one sows. According to one rendering of the ancient scriptures, for example, if a non-Brahman kills a Brahman, the penalty is reincarnation as a worm in one's own feces for 10,000 reincarnations. This seems like a stiff penalty, and it raises a number of difficult empirical questions for believer and observer alike: Does such a threat actually deter the killing of Brahmans by non-Brahmans? Certainly such acts have taken place, but perhaps more would have occurred if the threat were not in place. Second, is the punishment really inflicted? (This question is even more difficult to answer.)

An element of Hindu ethics that deserves special attention is sexual behavior. The relationship between religion and sex has been particularly significant in India, where the entire range of activity, from "full indulgence to ascetic denial," has played a central role in the search for the sacred (see Parrinder 1980). On one hand, intense religious practice and everyday morality have long valued *brahmacharya*, sexual abstinence, as a technique for achieving karmic merit. On the other hand, the oldest and most persistent image of the gods themselves are of the *lingam* fixed within a *yoni*, the representations of the phallus and vagina respectively, a coupling found both in contemporary temples and in 1500 B.C.E. Indus plains archaeological sites.

Hindu mythology and art over the centuries is replete with stories about the exploits of Shiva, a god of both sexual virility and asceticism (see O'Flaherty 1973). One popular tale has the gods visiting Shiva and Parvati only to find them engaged in intercourse. They continued despite the presence of their divine visitors; Vishnu laughed, but others became angry and cursed the couple, causing them to die in that position. Shiva declared that the *lingam* would be his new shape, which men must model and worship, and the *yoni* would be Parvati, and this was the origin of all things (Parrinder 1980: 8). In the temples dedicated to Shiva, it is no accident that the *lingam*, still erect in the *yoni*, is covered by devotees with plain white yoghurt and ghee (clarified butter). At the same time, however, women and men are forbidden to touch one another or show affection to members of the opposite sex in public.

The Indian example is instructive because it shows the ambivalence and apparent contradictions of religious teaching. Religion plays an important part in regulating sexual behavior because sex is such a central, pervasive force in human life. Collective life requires sexual activity for the continued survival of the species, the society, and the family, but unregulated sexual activity usually undermines a given social order and the authority of elites to control social processes. Religious legitimations of the guidelines established in any given culture gives those rules a powerful authority, especially if violations of the taboos are believed to result in long-lasting or cosmic negative consequences.

In addition to positive statements about what one should do, act, and think, religions also identify **taboos**, or interdictions against what should not be done. One of the most significant functions of a religious ethos in everyday life is to define taboo lines between ethical and unethical behavior. As Freud (1950) points out, however, taboos do not prohibit things people do *not* wish to do; the list of taboos in a culture provides a catalog of its social problems. Sometimes religious taboos appear antiquated or misguided—and sometimes, in fact, they are. But what often appears illogical from outside a belief system or society may be entirely sensible when viewed from within. Such is the case of the sacred cow in India, which wanders the streets protected by religious taboos, even in the busiest cities. To most visitors these cows appear bizarre or inconvenient at best, and a scandal at worst, that they may not be slaughtered for sustenance, given the fact that so many people are malnourished in the same cities and villages. Moreover, cow worship by Hindus has sparked off riots between Hindus and Muslims, who prefer to eat cows than revere them.

Anthropologist Marvin Harris (1974) finds an explanation for this phenomenon in the small-scale, low-energy economic system of traditional India, based as it has been for centuries on animals. Cows and oxen still provide low-energy substitutes for tractors; for example, large mowers are pulled around by a team of bulls until a considerable section of grass has been cut. The grass is then raked into a pile and consumed by the cow, who converts it into energy for mowing another section. Moreover, India's cattle annually excrete about 700 million tons of recoverable manure, about half of which is used as fertilizer and the remainder as cooking fuel or household flooring and siding. Wandering cows scour the environment for waste products and stubble unfit for human consumption, which they then convert into milk, energy, and other useful products. These ubiquitous cows are not wild animals who wander aimlessly; they are actually owned and tended by individuals who can identify them. Periodic droughts and famine in India threaten the livelihood of nearly everyone, but the Zebu cattle have energy-storing humps on their backs, are efficient, and are capable of existing for long periods of time with little food or water. They provide labor, dung, and, of course, milk and calves (a source of cash for a poor family). During crisis periods, a farmer may be tempted to kill or sell livestock, which might make immediate sense but would be disastrous in the long term. Religious taboos against killing cattle thus help to protect against irrational decisions in difficult times. Compare this rational protection of the cow in India, Harris suggests, to the irrationality of U.S. culture, where the beef industry feeds two-thirds of the country's grain to cattle while people go hungry.

Despite its explicitly spiritual rationale, the religious tradition of protecting cows thus has a concrete economic function. This lesson cannot be lost in efforts to construct an ethos for the global village and it is also the conclusion of Weber's ([1904] 1958) *Protestant Ethic and the Spirit of Capitalism*: rationality is always drawn from a single viewpoint and what is irrational from one perspective may be rational from another. Before we condemn any religious beliefs as irrational, we need to explore their hidden logic and benefits, not only from a limited viewpoint, but from multiple perspectives.

Buddhist Ethics

The moral code of the tradition, summarized in the Buddha's Five Precepts of right behavior, provides a means for escaping suffering: live in such a way as to transcend one's fate and avoid inflicting suffering on others; engage in acts of compassion toward other creatures; rejoice in their good fortune. The Buddha thus advocates an ethical system that is a mirror image of Western utilitarianism: in Buddhism one's own interests are served by serving others while in Western utilitarianism everyone's interests are enhanced by pursuing one's own interests. The Five Precepts are:

1. Do not kill.
2. Do not steal.
3. Do not lie.
4. Do not be unchaste [with different meanings for monks and laity].
5. Do not drink intoxicants.

Buddhist monks are bound by an extensive set of rules, but the observance only of four (taken from the Five Precepts) is necessary to avoid
expulsion from the community: the prohibitions against sexual intercourse, theft, taking human life, and making dishonest claims to spiritual
attainment.[17] Laity are expected to (1) follow most of the same rules as
monks, (2) provide the monks with food when they make their morning
rounds with their begging bowls, and (3) socialize their children into the
Buddha's teachings. Traditionally, some instruction was received by all
Buddhists at the monasteries during daily and life cycle rituals, and from
storytellers, since until recently most of the population was illiterate. Contemporary Buddhists, when they are allowed to, provide copies of the
Buddha's teachings in public places such as restaurants as well as in the
temples.

Buddhism has a highly practical side as well, as shown in the folk
religions that became associated with Buddhist religion. The gods are
considered responsible not only for physical security, but also for providing guidance for everyday life in the community. In Jordan's (1985) account of Taiwanese religion, a village is guarded at all four corners by
supernatural protectors who ward off evil. If the guardians are not properly worshipped, evil may enter the village and special rites are invoked
to exorcize it. In the village of Bao-an a child drowned in the pond, having
been "pulled in by a ghost." The dead child's maligned ghost lingered in
the pond and could not be permitted to stay, so two altar tables containing
small "divination chairs" for the gods were placed in front of the temple.
The god came and advised that people should stop speaking bad words
to one another, since the death had disrupted the harmony of the village.
Second, he suggested that people should keep children away from the
pond.

In Bao-an as elsewhere, religious rituals and the ethos of a religious
tradition provide concrete, as well as general, guidance for a culture's
lifestyles. Just as kosher laws directly or indirectly keep Jews from con-
tracting trichomonis from bad pork, the Bao-an gods' words bring harmony to the village by stopping harsh words and thus maintaining order

in the community. Other children would be saved from drowning by the divine injunction to keep them away from the pool.

The rituals themselves may appear nonrational to people outside the belief system, but they seem to provide a sense of security and in some ways actually helped to protect the people of Bao-an. Is it mere illusion, mere false consciousness? In traditional Chinese folk religion, those who die are always still present in the form of gods and ghosts; they continue to have needs in the next world and so are given gifts regularly. One's fate in the next world is thus related to how well one's descendants provide for one after death. But one's status in the next world is also determined by the merit accumulated in a terrestrial life. As one villager put it,

> When we men are good, we have a good report; and when we are bad, we have a bad report. The idea is always the same. Gods are those who have done good deeds as men, those who love virtue and study the ways of the buddhas and after death join the buddhas. . . .
> Men of a good nature become gods; men of virtue become gods, and those without it become ghosts. (quoted in Jordan 1985: 35–37)

It is not clear, at least in Jordan's account, how much of one's fate is determined by one's own merit and how heavily one's descendants' actions count, but the rational calculus is not important. Because gaining one's own merit and honoring one's ancestors are essential components of the ethical system, both are connected logically to one's fate in the afterlife.

Jewish Ethics

According to rabbinic tradition,

> A heathen once came to Shammai and said, "I will become a proselyte on the condition that you teach me the entire Torah while I stand on one foot." Shammai chased him away with a builder's measuring stick. When he appeared before Hillel with the same request, Hillel said, "Whatever is hateful to you, do not do to your neighbor. That is the entire Torah. The rest is commentary; go and learn it." (Shabbat 31a in Hertzberg 1962: 109)

This parable summarizes the core of Jewish teaching in several ways: (1) Judaism consistently emphasizes social ethics, guidelines for interacting with others; (2) the tradition honors its teachers (rabbis) but also challenges them to think clearly; (3) all necessary knowledge is in the Torah, but the process of understanding it involves continuous revelation, debate, and interpretation; and (4) though religion is to be taken seriously, a good sense of humor can help a person understand the sacred.

The foundation for Jewish ethics is the Decalogue, or the Ten Commandments, traditionally believed to have been given to the ancient Hebrews by God shortly after their escape from slavery in Egypt (ca. 1300 B.C.E.). In the third month after their escape from the Egyptians, the Hebrews camped before Mount Sinai. Considerable social unrest emerged at the time, perhaps because of the difficult existence the Jews experienced as refugees, after the relative security of their slavery. At this key moment, according to Jewish tradition, Moses went up onto Mount Sinai and received a set of stone tablets from Yahweh, on which were inscribed the laws that will regulate the community's life. The commandments are:

1. Thou shalt have no other gods before me (Exodus 20:3).
2. Thou shalt not make unto them any graven image, or any likeness of any thing that is in heaven above, or that is in the earth beneath, or that is in the water under the earth (20:4).
3. Thou shalt not take the name of the Lord thy God in vain . . . (20:7).
4. Remember the Sabbath day, to keep it holy (20:8).
5. Honor thy father and thy mother: that thy days may be long upon the land which the Lord thy God giveth thee (20:12).
6. Thou shalt not kill (20:13).
7. Thou shalt not commit adultery (20:14).
8. Thou shalt not steal (20:15).
9. Thou shalt not bear false witness against thy neighbor (20:16).
10. Thou shalt not covet thy neighbor's house, thou shalt not covet thy neighbor's wife, nor his manservant, nor his maidservant, nor his ox, nor his ass, nor any thing that is thy neighbor's (20:17).[18]

Note that eight of the ten commandments are expressed in the form of taboos, or injunctions; only two are positive (remember the Sabbath and honor your parents). Most of them (commandments 4 through 10) concern social relations rather than direct relations with the deity. This religious tradition did not intend simply to mediate between the people and their deity; it provided a foundation for their collective life.

The events surrounding the introduction of the Decalogue are full of social drama and are equally instructive. After a preparatory period in their camp at Mount Sinai, Moses established boundaries beyond which only he, his brother Aaron, and later selected leaders from the community, could go. The people were not even to touch the border of the mountain where Moses was to talk with Yahweh or, they were warned, they would be put to death. The delegation was allowed to see Yahweh (which was usually taboo), but not to climb to the summit with Moses, who stayed there for forty days. The people left behind became restless, made a golden calf out of their jewelry,[19] and began to dance in front of it, turning from the worship of Yahweh to the indigenous religious practices of the region. Both Moses and their God were furious; Moses shattered the tablets containing the Law, and Yahweh threatened to destroy the Hebrews. When Moses asked them to choose sides, the Levites went with Moses, who reported Yahweh's instructions to his followers:

> Thus says the Lord God of Israel, "Put every man his sword on his side, and go to and fro from gate to gate throughout the camp, and slay every man his brother and every man his companion, and every man his neighbor."
> And the sons of Levi did according to the word of Moses; and there fell of the people that day about three thousand men. (Exodus 32:27–28)

Moses gave the Levites a blessing and intervened with Yahweh on the people's behalf. Yahweh decided not to destroy the survivors and provided Moses with new tablets. At that point Moses and the Levites, having eliminated all opposition forces, became priests in full control of their society.

Contained in the story of the ancient Hebraic ethical code is thus also a lesson about the nature of their God (who insists on loyalty and justice, subject to negotiation), the ruthlessness of their leaders' control, and an explanation for the Levites' special authority among the ancient Hebrews. The remarkable violence of the story, which stands in sharp contrast with the taboo in the Decalogue against killing, is almost lost in the narrative because attention is focused on the shame of the people who have disobeyed. Thus inherent contradictions are taken for granted as the reader is swept along by the story.

In the third period of what Judaism considered its "salvation history," the prophetic movement (which may have begun as early as 1050 B.C.E.) took the establishment to task for not keeping the covenant with Yahweh. Instead of polytheism or idolatry, the prophets exposed injustice and the general faithlessness of the people as well as the emptiness of their religious rituals. As the prophet Amos (c. 750 B.C.E.) put it, Yahweh complained that the people "trample upon the needy, and bring the poor of the land to an end" (Amos 8:4). Consequently, their rituals of worship were no longer pleasing to the deity:

> I hate, I despise your feasts,
>   and I take no delight in your solemn assemblies
> Even though you offer me your

> burnt offerings and cereal offerings,
> I will not accept them. . . .
> Take away from me the noise of your songs;
> to the melody of your harps I will
> not listen
> But let justice roll down like waters,
> and righteousness like an
> ever flowing stream.
>
> *(Amos 5:21–24)*

Because the Israelites had broken the covenant with Yahweh, Amos said, God would destroy them—a sentiment echoed by other prophets such as Hosea, Micah, and Isaiah. Yahweh was no longer perceived as a god who favored only a particular clan or nation, but one who insisted on justice for all people and would punish violators of these principles even if they had a special relationship with their deity. This development signaled a significant break with the particularism of both clan and national religious expressions and exhibited a universalism similar to that found in Buddhism. Such a decoupling of the belief system from a particular social structure enabled the system's survival. In 721 B.C.E. the north fell to the Babylonians, and in 586, more decisively, Jerusalem was crushed. The Temple was destroyed, and much of the nation's elite was carried off into exile in Babylon. Ironically, not only did Judaism survive this debacle, it was even strengthened by the suffering of this "Exilic" period.

Three consequences of the Exilic period were:

1. A clear monotheism was established that had only been hinted at in early Judaism (e.g., the Decalogue declares that the other gods are not to be worshipped before Yahweh); because monotheism seemed the only plausible explanation for the defeat by the Babylonians: Yahweh was not weaker than the Babylonian god, but was punishing the Hebrews for their sins.

2. The Torah was finally written down, probably for the first time, and the community ceased to rely on oral tradition. The theological and ethical ideas of the Exilic and Post-Exilic tradition were then written back into the earlier history of the people, who reconstructed a sacred past.

3. The very notion of Israel was constructed after the northern and southern kingdoms were destroyed. When the religious identity of the Jews became problematic, it was more clearly defined. By the time the exiles returned (when the Persians defeated the Babylonians in 539 B.C.E.), they had defined precisely who they were: mem-

bers of the nation of Israel had a bloodline from their ancestors and they worshipped the One God, Yahweh, whose word was revealed in the Torah.

Thus, the conflicts precipitated by dramatic (in some cases quite violent) conflict between Judaism and other socioreligious orders resulted not in the destruction of the tradition but in the re-creation of the faith. Out of these conflicts the notion of monotheism was forged, the scriptures were written down, and Judaism became less bound to specific geographic locations. Over time, the stories of this history held the Jewish community together through centuries of adversity and dispersion throughout the world.

The example of Judaism demonstrates how it is possible to see the way in which religious traditions are constructed to meet sociological and psychological needs. In this sense the classical theorists such as Freud, Marx, Comte, and Durkheim were right in regarding religious beliefs and practices as projections of human psychological needs; these theological explanations for the crises of life put a cosmic frame on personal troubles. Just because belief systems are constructed by humans to answer human needs and explain human perceptions does not mean, however—as the earlier theorists claimed—that the referents of religion do not exist. It simply means that if the gods do exist, they are perceived by humans in a human way.

Because of its ethnic-tribal basis, ancient Judaism was closely linked with the economic life of the socioreligious community. The Jewish ethos places its distinctive stamp on economic activity in three ways: (1) Economic activity, like all elements of life, should be conducted on a highly ethical basis, with special attention to problems of injustice within the community. Everyone should be cared for and all should be treated fairly, even those outside the community. (2) Because the earth is a gift from God, humanity is given stewardship over it and should be thankful. Success in business is somehow related to God's grace, and a portion of the profits should be given as an offering. (3) Finally, the emphasis on rational thought and a disciplined life in the Jewish ethos has cultivated an entrepreneurial spirit that has served the community well over the centuries. Ironically, some of the entrepreneurial skills cultivated within the community were an inadvertent consequence of prohibitions against Jews owning land in many parts of Europe until well into the modern era. Anti-Semitic groups over the centuries have exploited these historical circumstances for their own purposes by making unfounded claims about Jewish financial acumen.

Christian Ethics

At the center of the Christian ethical system is the proposition that God is love. In its more radical forms, the Christian ethic requires one also to love one's enemy, a concept we will explore more fully in the discussion of religion and social conflict in Chapter 7. This emphasis on loving others comes from Jesus' teachings as recorded in the New Testament. When asked what constituted the greatest commandment, Jesus responded:

> You shall love the Lord your God with all your heart, and with all your soul, and with all your mind. This is the first and great commandment. And a second is like it, You shall love your neighbor as yourself. On these two commandments depend all the law and the prophets. (Matthew 22:37–40)

This link from the Jewish tradition between love of God and love of one's neighbor became a hallmark of the early Christian church, which cut across class and ethnic boundaries and maintained a strict pacifism. Many in the early community sold their worldly possessions, fed the poor, and lived a communal life focused on loving one another as children of God. This radical ethical universalism, as translated into inter-ethnic relationships, must have been shocking to many first-century Jews who had been taught that God required strict observance of boundaries between their community and others.

Different interpretations of these ideas appeared over time according to their affinities with different social groups. In more conservative versions of Christianity, sin is a central and important aspect of human nature. The concept of "original sin," popular in some circles of Christianity especially since the Calvinist movement in seventeenth century Europe, suggests that humans are born sinful because of the long lineage of disobedience that can be traced back to the original sinful act of Adam and Eve. We are all, according to the famous American Puritan preacher Jonathan Edwards, "sinners in the hands of an angry God." The idea is not popular among most progressive Christians in the twentieth century because of its emphasis on inevitable guilt, which, some then argue, implies a need for tightly bound systems of social control to keep people from sinning. The concept does have some sociological basis, however: individuals face the consequences of their parents' "sin" from the moment they are born because their own values and life situations are shaped by their social context. This phenomenon can be seen in the cycles of violence in human society—children who suffer abuse from their parents, for example, often abuse their own children, and interethnic feuds can be transmitted across the generations.

The classic consequence of sin in Christian theology is to be damned and sent to hell for punishment in the afterlife. Debates about hell have raged through the centuries in Christian theology. There is little hint in the Gospels about Jesus' own understanding of the concept, and our most famous picture of hell was not provided until thirteen centuries later by the Italian poet Dante in his famous *Divine Comedy*. In the Christian tradition evil is personified in the figure of the devil, or Satan, an angel created by God whose pride led to his downfall. By the mid-twentieth century the devil had become a mere metaphor to most people in Western countries, yet popular interest in this figure has been increasing as the end of the second millennium approaches and movies like *The Omen* and *The Exorcist* draw large audiences. In the 1980s, Christian fundamentalists in the United States saw the workings of Satan behind dangerous cultural trends and international events. The charismatic movement revived the practice of exorcism to drive out demons. As a sign of the times, Fuller Theological Seminary—the nation's largest Protestant seminary—introduced a course on how to oppose the devil (see Woodward and Gates 1982).

Widely discredited in secular intellectual culture, then, Satan remains a ubiquitous figure in popular culture and even performs a certain sociological function: the representation of this figure reminds us that evil is a force that exists, like many social forces, above and beyond those individuals who seem to be their instruments. Because demons represent an objectified element of the social construction of reality—that is, something that exists outside of individuals—sociologists must at least remain agnostic about these figures as well as about their positive counterparts, angels. Certainly the concepts of demons and angels correspond to many peoples' experience whether or not they exist objectively. As Peter Berger puts it, people who reject the idea that Detroit is infested with demons miss a certain element of the reality of Detroit!

Christianity and economic ethics. The classic studies of the impact of Christian ethics on the economic functioning of Western society are Max Weber's works in the comparative sociology of religion, beginning with *The Protestant Ethic and the Spirit of Capitalism* ([1904] 1958). Weber's research on his lifelong interest in Western rationality and religious phenomena was inaugurated with this study, which examined the impact of a particular religious system's approach to ordering everyday life conduct. According to Weber, the Protestant Reformation produced a religious crisis when people were no longer able to depend upon the formal ecclesiastical institution of Catholicism and its priestly representatives to assure them that they were saved. In Calvinism and Puritanism, a belief in the omniscience (all-knowing characteristic) of God led logically to a belief in predestination. If God knows everything, then God must know whether we are part of the elect—who will be rewarded in heaven for eternity—or part of the damned—who will suffer in hell. Accordingly, people began looking for new kinds of signs that they were part of the elect.

The anxiety that this dilemma created became linked with the idea of a calling in Puritanism and Calvinism: God calls people to a particular vocation; when one follows God's calling and works diligently at it, one will be rewarded. Worldly economic success consequently becomes a secure sign that a person is saved, thus laying the groundwork, Weber argues, for the systematic life control and inner discipline in the workaday world that promoted the rise of capitalism. Religious ideas, Weber concludes, do play a formative role in history, but the consequences of their impact are not always anticipated. We may also note that although the Protestant ethic has its distinctive elements, the value placed on an individual's working for the good of the collective is a major theme in religious life that runs across traditions.

Religion is often closely tied to economics in a utilitarian way. People, for example, will often appeal to a god for assistance or even intervention in economic activities. From the rain dance and mating rites to facilitate agricultural production to prayer in corporate board rooms, candles to help people win the lottery, and offerings made at the altar of Kuan Kung, humans have invoked the gods to assist the process of economic acquisition. Sometimes the appeal is direct and unambiguous, as in the Reverend Gene Ewing's Church by Mail. Rev. Ewing, a master of the mass-mail market, uses it to entice people to ask God to help them as well as to send money to his organization. His mailings are filled with testimonies of people who have followed his advice and been blessed with "spiritual, physical, and financial blessings." Someone got a check in the mail for $5,000; another person got a new job; someone else was healed of cancer. Modern technologies of television and mass mailings provide a great temptation for people willing to manipulate other people's religious beliefs for personal gain. Rev. Ewing may be sincere himself, but his methods are open to exploitation.

Membership tests and social control. Jesus contended that only God, not other humans, should judge another person's actions (see Matthew 5), but a religion's ethos creates guidelines for daily life. Elites thus use the religious ethos to legitimate a system of social control that does make judgments, so that those who violate normative and legal boundaries can be punished and the existing social order upheld.

The history of the Christian church is replete with the construction of criteria for such judgments. When church and state are closely linked, religious ethical infractions are often punishable by law. Often, however, informal controls are just as important to the ordering of daily life. Within a religious community, and especially in Christianity—in which the boundaries of the community are doctrinal more than social—qualification for membership becomes socially significant, and tests are developed for judging an individual's eligibility. In the early Christian church, all a person had to do was give a profession of faith ("Jesus is Lord") and be baptized in order to join the community. The community quickly established stricter standards, however, engaging in considerable debate over what did and did not constitute appropriate signs of membership. Meeting these additional membership tests was supposed to follow naturally as a voluntary response to the ethical standards of the religious community, including such things as giving away worldly goods to the poor, living communally, and not committing any acts of violence. Soldiers who converted could remain in the military but could not kill anyone.

Such Christian tests of membership, salvation, merit, and the like sometimes led to great disparities between theory and practice. In contemporary Protestant Christianity, for example, a central tenet of the belief system is that each individual has a personal relationship to God with no mediation by church officials (as contrasted with the Catholic practice). Rhetorical and behavioral formulas with little if any biblical basis have emerged, however, that constitute very rigid tests of whether or not one is "truly Christian." In circles where personal faith is most highly valued, conformity to rhetorical standards is strictly enforced: to prove that one has an intense personal relationship with the deity, one must express it in the approved manner that reproduces other believers' equally intense, radically personal encounter with the sacred. In some communities, a Christian is someone who abstains from smoking, drinking, or fornicating (although killing others may be a religious duty, if the act is approved by the right government). In other Christian communities, however, people who approve of killing and disapprove of fornicating are judged as not truly Christian.

Because the ethos of a culture reflects its worldview and a pluralistic culture inevitably engages in struggles over the single acceptable way to define the world and the norms of everyday life, the definition of the family has taken on particular religious importance in the United States.

In the patriarchal Judeo-Christian tradition, the structures of the cosmos and the family typically reflect each other: the father who presides over the family mirrors God the Father in control of the universe. The implications of this perspective for the nature of authority in family and society are instructive. In direct (although somewhat obscured) opposition to the democratic norms of modern political culture, this model of authority requires respect for superordinates at both familial and cosmic levels and harsh sanctions against those who do not follow the norms.

The conservative Protestant movement in the United States is attempting to sustain this metaphor against the protests of the gender equality movement. At issue is what Kenneth Wald and his colleagues (1989) call "authority-mindedness," that is, a model of social life in the family and the congregation that advocates an unequal division of authority. As Ammerman puts it, "They come to expect groups to be divided between sheep and shepherds. The shepherds are entitled to deference and rewards, while the sheep are entitled to love and care" (1987: 128). Within this belief framework, corporal punishment becomes an important part of maintaining the family's structure, just as God punishes wrongdoers.[20] Ellison and Bartkowski (forthcoming) contend that

> Conservative Protestants are convinced that physical discipline communicates a positive spiritual lesson to their children. In brief, they argue that many children develop and express their understandings of God in parental images, and therefore that children will infer God's view of them based on the treatment they receive from their parents. . . . In this view, parents should teach their children by example that God is loving, merciful, and forgiving. At the same time, however, because God's punishment of sin is understood as both inevitable and consistent, it is vitally important for parental discipline to embody these characteristics as well.

Other Christians contend that this authority-minded model is antithetical to their faith, which posits the brotherhood and sisterhood of all humanity.

Such debates take on heightened importance in the contemporary world, in which religious communities are forced to coexist alongside other groups with differing values and standards. Many of these issues can be seen in sharp relief in the strained relationships between the sibling traditions of Christianity and Islam. The way in which these problems are debated and resolved are central to the process of constructing an ethos for the global village.

Islamic Ethics

The ethical and legal code of Islam is centered in the Shari'a, Islamic law, intended to encompass all of human life from the most private areas to the public organization of society. Because early Islam made no distinction between the law and religion, the Shari'a is traditionally the law for Islamic society as well as a set of religious ethical guidelines. Its roots lie in Allah's revelations to Muhammad and the Prophet's efforts to create a disciplined, ordered society in the chaotic, warring tribal culture in which he lived. The concept of the Shari'a as all pervasive is an ancient one in Islamic practice, and is given more emphasis than most doctrines of the faith. As John Williams has said, "for Muslims, consonant with their emphasis on the Law, have been more concerned with what men do than with what they believe, and very slow to reject any group of Muslims for wrong doctrine, unless that doctrine led the group to actively exclude itself, by its deeds, from the Community" (1962: 94). As we will see, however, interpretation of the law is often a matter of dispute.

Islamic economics. In traditional Islam, following the example of Muhammad, a theocratic system was imposed in which polity and economy were essentially under the direction of the *ummah*. The Islamic movement spread rapidly during its formative period, and its military expansion led to Muslim control of the Mediterranean and as far as Southern France, North Africa, the Middle East, and well into Asia, in part because of the practice of Muslim traders, known for their skills and ethical business practices. During the period of Western colonial expansion, the authority of the Shari'a was challenged by the conquering European powers, who tried to impose their secularized legal system on Islamic countries. Whereas economic law (of more concern to the colonizers) was placed under secular jurisdiction, the one area of successful resistance in most Islamic colonies was family law, which became a symbol of the struggle with the colonialists, and is still largely controlled by the religious courts.

In postcolonial Islamic societies, many religious leaders have tried to reinstate their authority over economic matters and in some ways have succeeded in the case of smaller-scale entrepreneurs, but now find that many of the standards of business for larger companies are set by international capitalism. Some of that influence has been bounded by such practices as traditional Islamic hospitality and concern for the poor, including the annual Zakat, which creates some redistribution of wealth within economic society. As other religious communities have discovered, however, it is difficult to resist the powerful forces of international capital, which often emphasizes profit making to the exclusion of other ethical standards.

Religion and Politics

A final dimension of the religious ethos and its impact on collective life is the crucial sphere of politics. Let us now look briefly at the role each religious tradition has played in various political orders and movements, especially in the late twentieth century.

Hinduism and Politics

The relationship between Hinduism and the political sphere is extremely complex in modern India. Religious pluralism apparently thrived on the subcontinent without major disruption until the invasion of the Muslims in the eighth century. The exclusivist claims of Islam, however, were never reconciled with the theologically tolerant Hindu beliefs. Muslim rulers found the worship of the various gods idolatrous and made their condemnation part of the process of conquering the region. Consequently, a virulent form of anti-Muslim Hindu fanaticism also developed over time and has become a major factor in contemporary political conflict, both inside and outside the country. Ongoing territorial disputes with Pakistan and lingering memories of atrocities on all sides following the religiously based partition of British India at the time of independence have kept the flames fanned.

Despite efforts to establish a secular independent state after a century of British colonial rule, India continues to be racked by ethnic and religious strife, and the relationship between Hindu and Muslim sectors of the population is often the source of political rifts. Until fairly recently, the Indian state was virtually a one-party democracy, ruled by the diverse Congress Party that led the freedom movement and drew on the heroic status of its former leaders (notably Gandhi and Jawaharlal Nehru) to maintain its control. A breakdown of that rule occurred following the assassination of Prime Minister Indira Gandhi and again after the assassination of her son, Rajiv Gandhi.

In recent Indian politics, the Muslim-Hindu cleavage has become a central theme recalling ancient divisions and resentments. In the city of Ayodhya is a site cherished as the birthplace of the Hindu god Ram. When the Muslims invaded in the eighth century C.E., they tore down the temple there and constructed a mosque. In 1990, a prominent Hindu nationalist leader (L. K. Advani) mounted a campaign to raise the mosque and construct a temple in honor of Ram. The controversy brought down the Indian government in 1990, and a group of Hindus attacked the mosque in 1992, touching off a series of Hindu-Muslim riots throughout the country.

Buddhism and Politics

Buddhist tolerance of other religions and its custom of private worship tended to promote a general lack of specific alliance with political elites in this religion. An exception was Tibet, where a theocracy was established around the figure of the Dalai Lama. Even when Buddhism was aligned with the state, however, its lack of exclusivism often had a broadening, rather than constricting, effect on the political culture; that is, it encouraged a tolerant and inclusive ethos that cultivated the lowering of boundaries between groups rather than erecting them.

One of the most interesting early developments in Buddhism was the conversion of the Indian Emperor Ashoka in the third century B.C.E. After the bloody conquest of most of South Asia, he became a Buddhist. Horrified at the consequences of the wars he had conducted, Ashoka became legendary for his support of Buddhist institutions, his efforts to lead a nonviolent life, and most of all for his "Golden Age" rule, which promoted religious tolerance and high ethical standards. Although not a strict pacifist, Ashoka was opposed to warfare and animal sacrifice and became a vegetarian. Of particular importance is his famous Twelfth Rock Edict, which declares:

> One should not honour only one's own religion and condemn the religions of others, but one should honour others' religions for this or that reason. So doing, one helps one's own religion to grow and renders service to the religions of others too. In acting otherwise one digs the grave of one's own religion and also does harm to other religions. Whosoever honours his own religion and condemns other religions, does so indeed through devotion to his own religion, thinking "I will glorify my own religion." But on the contrary, in so doing he injures his own religion more gravely. So concord is good: Let all listen, and be willing to listen to the doctrines professed by others. (in Gard 1962: 18–19)

This edict, now almost 2,300 years old, provides a remarkable testimony to the possibility of religious tolerance in a pluralistic cultural context.

Contemporary Buddhists often struggle with modern governments just as early Buddhism often met resistance from the emperors of ancient Asia. In the last three centuries, European colonial conquerors, then the

Japanese, and finally indigenous political movements in China—the Nationalist and Communist parties—have confiscated monasteries or otherwise undermined Buddhist institutions (see Welch 1972: 167ff). Neither four decades of communist rule in the People's Republic of China nor hostile governments in other parts of the region, however, have eliminated the pervasive influence of Buddhism either in the broader cultural milieu or in popular practice. In recent years the repression has lessened, and some temples were refurbished beginning in the 1970s, partly because of efforts to cultivate contacts with foreign governments, especially those like Japan with strong Buddhist traditions. Reforms or a change of governments in East Asia (especially in China) may result in a religious revival comparable to that now going on in the former Soviet states.

Judaism and Politics

Any discussion of modern Judaism cannot fail to mention the two interlinked watershed events of contemporary Jewish history: the Holocaust and the founding of the state of Israel. The Holocaust was an historical event of unspeakable horror: during World War II the Nazis exterminated 6 million Jews, reducing the total Jewish population of the entire world by approximately one-third. The impact of this brutal violence against a people who had sustained their identity for thousands of years will doubtless affect generation after generation of Jews, who have already incorporated the Holocaust into religious rituals such as Passover.

Few, if any, Jewish families and communities were untouched by this tragedy, which precipitated the creation of a national homeland for Jews in the ancient Holy Land so closely associated with the religious tradition. When the British ended their colonial domination of the region after the war, the United Nations voted to divide Palestine into Jewish and Arab sectors, and the state of Israel was established in 1948.

The remarkable sociological significance of these events lies in the fact that the ethnic-religious identity of the Jewish community in many countries was used by the Nazis to torture and kill a major population in an attempted genocide, and then was used by members of the group itself to win international sympathy for their treatment under Hitler and establish a modern state on the basis of a religious vision. Unfortunately, one people's homeland was purchased at the price of another's. The Palestinians, who were living in the area before Israel was created, have become refugees in their own land, pushed out by well-meaning efforts by the international community to provide a homeland for the beleaguered Jewish community. Competing multiple claims by various religio-political groups on the same territory—especially the famous Holy City of Jerusa-lem—threaten to sustain the conflict over many more decades.

Christianity and Politics

The relationship between Christianity and political life is simple in its outline and complicated in detail. Christianity's universalistic doctrines and links with empire expansion facilitated a worldwide diffusion be-yond its Jewish origins, but also made it a convenient ideology for various world-conquering powers, from the Holy Roman Empire to the medieval crusaders and the European colonialists of the early modern period.

After Emperor Constantine's conversion to Christianity in 312 C.E., the church became closely linked with Western power elites well into the early modern period. Although the alliance began to unravel with the Enlightenment of the eighteenth and nineteenth centuries, the Christian missionary movement helped Europeans to solidify their colonial control first over Latin America, and then over large sections of Africa and Asia.

Two events of the last two hundred years have particular relevance to current efforts to construct a multicultural ethos: (1) the disestablishment of Christianity in western Europe (i.e., individual declarations by nations that Christianity was no longer the official state-sanctioned religion), and (2) the separation between church and state and efforts to protect reli-gious freedom in the United States. The second case is significant because it demonstrates how the problem of multiculturalism is forcibly ad-dressed in political discourse when previously separate culture groups begin to share the same space.

At the end of the eighteenth century, the nascent American republic was religiously pluralistic, but not everyone wanted it that way. The colo-nies contained many religious refugees seeking religious freedom who were not about to grant that same freedom to people of other faiths living in their part of the new world.[21] Two mutually exclusive traditions from the Protestant Reformation, Puritanism and Pietism, coexisted uneasily. Puritans (especially in Massachusetts) wanted a theocratic state—liter-ally, a state run by God (as represented, of course, by the political elite). For the Pietists, and others who believed religion to be a private matter, the goal of religious practice was not an external social organization, but internal religious experience.

Boston was essentially a theocracy at the time of its founding, in which only church members could vote; Quakers were executed for reli-gious dissent in 1650. In nearby Salem, witches were tried, found guilty, and hung on the basis of such criteria as not being able to recite the Lord's

Prayer in the courtroom without making a mistake (see Erikson 1966). (In neighboring Rhode Island, however, Roger Williams insisted on no political involvement for religious leaders because he believed that the state corrupts the church.) In most of the southern colonies, the Church of England was the official church.

In the middle colonies the idea of combining the religious and secular—the norm for most, if not all, of human history—was questioned. In Pennsylvania William Penn, a religious Quaker who understood the necessity of religious tolerance, argued against the idea of an established church. This was a radical idea at the time because it raised the fundamental question of basing the state's political legitimacy on a religious basis, a practice common to most societies. Because of competing belief systems the idea of disestablishing religion had an affinity with the interests of many of the colonial elites. The Great Awakening, a strong period of religious revivalism in the New World in the 1730s and 1740s, challenged established religion by emphasizing individual piety. Massachusetts still collected taxes to pay the clergy, but by 1750 people could designate which clergy would receive their taxes.

During the American Revolution, the theme of liberty became an organizing principle of political culture in the colonies. It originally meant freedom from the English Crown, but minority faiths like the Baptists and Catholics also applied it to their freedom from colonial government. Since their enemy's faith—the Church of England, with the king as its titular head—was dominant in the southern colonies, independence forced a reconsideration of the question of an official state religion. In 1784, a group of evangelical ministers in Virginia gained widespread support to obtain state funds for religious instruction, but they were opposed by James Madison, Thomas Jefferson, and others who feared that this would lead to a reestablishment of the Anglican church. In that struggle Jefferson articulated the principle of religious freedom in a way that framed later debates about religion in U.S. political culture by attempting to create a separation between church and state.

At the constitutional convention in Philadelphia in 1787, representatives artfully avoided discussion of religion because they knew it could jeopardize efforts to create a union. It was not that religion was unimportant, but that the Christian denominational pluralism of the colonies prevented any consensus over which single sacred canopy could be erected. Constitutional protection for religion seemed like the most pragmatic solution to a seemingly intractable conflict. Accordingly, religion was not mentioned in the U.S. Constitution, except in Article Six: "no religious test shall ever be required as a Qualification to any Office on public Trust under the United States" (Constitution of the United States [1787] 1938: 192). The First Amendment, however, tackled the issue head on, insisting that "Congress shall make no law respecting an establishment of religion, or prohibiting the free exercise thereof." At the time, three states still had an established religion. Religion did not disappear from public political life in the United States after this clear rejection of established religion, however; it persisted as a civil religion stripped of its most sectarian elements, as we will see in Chapter 6.

The close-knit alliance between the Christian church and secular elites began to unravel in the nineteenth century, and in many places the tradition became a carrier of resistance movements from Third World liberation theology to East European pro-democracy movements and North American fundamentalist revolts against modernity. Christianity has also served from time to time as a focal point of conflict between Western and Middle Eastern powers. As the United States emerged as a world power in the twentieth century, its economic, political, and military invasions of the world were often accompanied by the church, although perhaps more subtly than in the colonial period.

The process by which religious freedom is protected by law is a significant, though not always entirely successful, experiment. Clearly citizens of the global village have to choose some form of religious pluralism in which freedom of worship is vigorously protected by the legal structure or risk subjection to authoritarian efforts to impose a single worldview and ethos on the world's 5 billion inhabitants.

Islam and Politics

Like most new religious movements, Islam was born out of conflict. It began as a reform movement by Muhammad, who, concerned about the materialism and lax moral standards of his society, set out to do nothing less than reform the world on the basis of new revelations from God. Not surprisingly, he encountered much resistance. The idea of the *jihad*, or struggle, remains a central element of Islam—struggle within each individual and between righteous and evil forces in the larger world. Strict boundaries between the Muslim and non-Muslim world perpetuate the struggle today, as do the stereotypes propagated by the non-Muslim media, especially in the West (see Said 1978).

The way in which people within a religious tradition relate to nonbelievers in its formative years prefigures later patterns; a distinctive style emerges that persists over long periods of time. Today's patterns of Muslim–non-Muslim conflict—and to some extent, intensive struggles within Islam itself—must be seen within the context of early Islam, the medieval crusades, and the colonial experience of the early modern period.

The Crusades, beginning in the eleventh century C.E., involved an effort by the religious and secular rulers of Christian Western Europe to expel the Muslims who ruled the Middle East. It may now seem part of the distant past, but this historical episode may be even more important to Muslims now than it was at the time the Crusades took place.[22] Those invasions of Muslim territory by the Roman Catholic Church and its Western European patrons represent a formative event in the centuries-long conflict between "Christendom" and Islam.

Although intense conflict between Muslims and Christians threatened much of the Islamic hegemony of the Mediterranean regions during the period of the Crusades, Muslims managed to retain (or in some places regain, after losses in the initial Crusades) control over much of the region until the fifteenth century. Not only was this sociopolitical hegemony significant to Islam, but also to the European world that later reverted to Christian control. Indeed, much of the great heritage of the West was preserved by the Muslims, including works of Aristotle and classic Greek philosophy and literature that helped to stimulate the Renaissance in Western Europe in the wake of the Crusades. The cosmopolitan centers of learning in Muslim Spain attracted Jewish and Christian scholars, influencing the thinking of Moses Maimonides and Thomas Aquinas; and both the Islamic networks and the ongoing conflict in Christendom led to expanded economic trade and diffusion that prefaced the early modern period.

While Muslim rule ended in Europe by the seventeenth and eighteenth centuries, much of Africa and Asia remained Islamic, and the Muslim influence persists there today. The greatest impact was made during the Ottoman empire based in Turkey, which ruled Central Asia, most of the Middle East, and parts of the Mediterranean and Europe during the sixteenth and seventeenth centuries.

Another Islamic empire was established in the Asian subcontinent, where the Moghuls conquered the indigenous Hindus; other small Muslim states were established in Indonesia, Malaysia, western China, and Africa. This strong political rule of broad territories showed substantial religious tolerance in many instances, although it sometimes destroyed indigenous religious institutions and came into a number of intense conflicts. The Moghul empire finally succumbed to the colonial powers of the early modern period after the voyages of Columbus to the Americas and Vasco da Gama around southern Africa to India at the end of the fifteenth century led to the colonization of large portions of the world by the Christian Europeans. Ironically, when some of the colonial entrepreneurs raided West Africa for slaves, they captured many Muslims and took them to the New World, where Islam was silent under the yoke of slavery until the emergence of the Black Muslim movement in the mid-twentieth century.

European colonial expansion renewed resentments lingering in the collective memory from the Middle Ages and resulted in the defeat of Islamic nations by foreigners. Of forty-two Muslim countries, only four did not experience direct military control by outsiders during the colonial period (from the nineteenth century), a humiliating experience for many Muslims in which Islam was derided and Islamic political and social structures were attacked by Western conquerors.

When colonial domination began to unravel after World War II, superpower interventions in Muslim countries followed. The United States took on Israel as a client state in the Middle East and supported that country in its defeat of the Arab armies in 1967, in the devastation of Lebanon in 1982, and in the occupation of the West Bank. The Soviet Union, although less adventurous in the Middle East, was nonetheless a partisan in several conflicts there and actively suppressed Islam in the Central Asian republics. Since the eighth century, Islamic peoples have been subjected to what the Ayatollah* Khomeini (in prerevolutionary Iran) called "West-toxification" or "Westomania," which many believed poisoned Iranian culture under the shah, Khomeini's predecessor who modernized the country's economy and society. "The goal of the Islamic Revolution in Iran," Mark Juergensmeyer claims, "was not only to free Iranians politically from the shah but also to liberate them conceptually from Western ways of thinking" (1993: 19).

Finally, even the sanctity of the Islamic home was invaded by the West in the form of youth culture and the women's movement. This may prove the ultimate insult, especially for some Islamic men, who have seen their way of life degraded and stereotyped, their political system conquered and controlled by Western colonialists, and their religion mocked by "infidels." It is one thing to have outside powers attack one's state, but quite another to have them invade one's home. This new invasion may be the source of much of the anger expressed by so many Muslims today toward the West. The mainstream of most Muslim societies has reinterpreted many of the strict regulations of traditional Islam, relaxed its segregation of women, and adapted to some of the vicissitudes of the modern world,

---

*An ayatollah, meaning "sign of God," is a Shi'ite leader.

but these developments have simply fueled the flames of those dissatisfied with the direction in which the modern world has pushed them. Many Muslims believe that the authority structure of the family is under siege and the modesty of women and children is eroding, creating an existential crisis.

Although it is not one of the Five Pillars, the Islamic notion of the *jihad* is clearly a core belief that emphasizes the sharp boundaries between the sacred and the profane. Faithfulness to God does not come easily because of the sinful nature of the world, and one's own sinful nature, so one must always engage in struggle. Two types of *jihad* are outlined in traditional Islam: first, the **Greater Jihad,** denoting the internal struggle against one's sinful nature. The Greater Jihad is facilitated by the Five Pillars and the rituals of the faith to remind oneself repeatedly of what is righteous, and to protect oneself from the temptations of the world. The **Lesser Jihad** is the external struggle for which the term is now so famous.

The classic Islamic view—taking its cue from ancient Judaism—divides the world into two parts: (1) the "House of Islam," where Muslim law and faith prevail; and (2) the "House of Unbelief," or "House of War." Because it is blasphemous for unbelievers to rule over the House of Islam, it is therefore a religious duty to overthrow non-Muslim powers if they try to control and persecute Muslims. As the Qur'an puts it:

> Fight against those who fight against you along God's way, yet do not initiate hostilities; God does not love aggressors. Kill them wherever you may catch them, and expel them from anywhere they may have expelled you. Sedition is more serious than killing! Yet do not fight them at the Hallowed Mosque unless they fight you there. If they should fight you, then fight them back; such is the reward for disbelievers. However if they stop, God will be Forgiving, Merciful. Fight them until there is no more subversion and [all] religion belongs to God. If they stop, let there be no [more] hostility except towards wrongdoers. (2:190–193)

The intensity of Islamic thought reflects the harsh environment in which it was formed and the single-minded intensity with which Muhammad and the early Muslims struggled to establish their religious community in the midst of strong opposing forces. Still, there is room within most interpretations of Islamic doctrine for religious pluralism as long as the *ummah* can thrive without persecution. In Chapter 6, we will look in more detail at the Islamic revival of recent years as a protest against the control and invasion of the West. This movement is sometimes called Islamic fundamentalism, although many Muslims object to the use of that term; we will refer to it instead as **Islamic traditionalism.** It is a cry of resentment against the negative stereotypes of Muslims perpetrated by Western media and the development of secular nationalism as a mode of political organization in the West that many Muslims feel is being imposed on Islamic nations in much the same way as colonial rule was in the eighteenth and nineteenth centuries. The Islamic revival is an effort to reassert a positive individual and collective identity, to declare the beauty of the Islamic faith in the face of non-Muslim invasions.

The Ethos of the Global Village

People sharing the same geographical area must develop some agreement on rules of engagement that permit coexistence, unless one group is going to commit genocide against the others, even if the norm is to let various cultures exist in relative isolation and autonomy. The more they are drawn together, either through conflict or cooperation, the more comprehensive must be the norms regulating cross-cultural interactions.

At the close of the twentieth century, the pull of economic benefits from participation in a global economy (at least for elites in various cultures and subcultures) is combined with the availability of technological means for increased interaction, thus dramatically altering the extent to which everyone's fate is shared throughout the world. As we have seen, the global village is governed not by a unifying ethos or a single sacred canopy, but by a marketplace of competing worldviews and corresponding ethical systems that are colliding in many spheres of life in various regions of the world.

We have much to learn about how the process of cross-cultural ethos construction unfolds; we scarcely understand the nature of the religious marketplace in the much-studied American scene, despite important work in that area by a number of scholars (see Sherkat and Wilson forthcoming; Warner 1993; Finke and Stark 1988, 1992; Iannaccone 1991 among others). As Sherkat and Wilson (forthcoming: 26) have noted, religious preferences, like other consumption choices, are developed "not only on the basis of what we want, but how others will be affected by our choices, and how others may react to them." Individuals making a decision to switch Christian denominations, for example, will take into account the potential response not only of members of new groups that they might join, but also of people within their current religious communities, their parents, friends, and so forth.

If there is any truth to Marx's contention that the dominant ideas of any age are those of the ruling class, then we can expect the ethos of the postmodern world order to be disproportionately influenced by the tone of international capital, the owners and managers of multinational corporations. Certainly the value of material gain promoted by capitalist modes of production has already pervaded much of the world's cultures, not so much because it is imposed from the top (although mass advertising certainly influences popular tastes), but because the appeal of consumer goods has its own internal logic.

The role of religious traditions in forming an ethos for the human community is an empirical question not easily tested. At this point, we may be able to do little more than identify the questions that must be asked. All of the world's major traditions have a basic norm of compassion for others that sets moral boundaries around behavior that is harmful to others, especially within one's own society. The way in which those ethical teachings have been interpreted and enforced have varied so widely, however, that they provide no secure basis for our common security. Indeed, religious communities in many places around the world are now, just as they have throughout human history, using their ethical standards to justify widespread slaughter and exploitation, and half of the world's population remains malnourished.

Because religion is so closely linked to social life, it is important to assess the implications for ethical systems of ongoing social transformations. Durkheim's observation that the world system is becoming simultaneously more unified and diverse is instructive. As the world changes, so will the various ethical systems taught by the religious traditions; the ethical transformations may be as riddled with contradiction as the social: we are coming together, but resistance to the globalization of human life is as fierce as are the forces of unification.

The related human rights and democratic movements since World War II, coupled with the dismantling of the European colonial empires, offer some measure of hope in a world that is torn with strife. As democratic revolutions swept the globe and the Cold War came to an end in the last two decades of the twentieth century, these developments seem almost inevitable. Just as important, however, are the movements of resistance to globalization whose participants sometimes see the values of human rights and democratic politics as another attempt by the West to impose a secular nationalism on non-Western cultures still chafing from the colonial bonds.

Juergensmeyer claims that a new Cold War is emerging between the "secular nationalism" of Christendom, which promotes Western models of democracy and human rights, and non-Western religious communities. Significant sectors of the world, he argues, see in these latest trends an effort to thrust Islamic, Buddhist, and other global civilizations under the aegis of Christendom. "From this vantage point," he observes, "it is a serious error to suggest that Egypt or Iran should be thrust into a Western frame of reference. In this view of the world they are intrinsically par to Islamic, not Western, civilization, and it is an act of imperialism to think of them in any other way" (1993: 19).

The current ethical crisis of the global village is not a product simply of the late twentieth century, however. It began in the ancient mists of prehistory, when the ethos of today's religious traditions were born in story form and continued as various localized traditions diffused, collided, and were transformed over the centuries. Although we are always in danger of overemphasizing the importance of our own historical epoch, as the result of the dramatic transformations of society and culture precipitated by the industrial and postindustrial revolutions of the past two centuries, human history seems to be at a critical juncture in our time. To those events we now turn our attention.

5

Modernism: Crisis and Response

The deep and radical changes associated with the globalization of social life are occurring with increasing rapidity as we approach the end of the twentieth century. When social organization changes, so does religious organization; new ideas and new societies are created through mutual, dialectical interaction, and when culture groups interact, each one will be transformed. The impact of the Agricultural Revolution on human life unfolded over many centuries, but the Industrial Revolution was followed almost immediately by subsequent transformations that seem almost as profound. Although considerable continuity exists between the cultures created by the industrial, scientific, and democratic revolutions on one hand and those of the late twentieth century on the other, many now argue that we are living in a postmodern era that is undergoing another transformation as profound as any in human history.

In this chapter, we examine the first of the two great cultural upheavals of the last two centuries, the modernist crisis, and the diverse responses it has provoked among the world's cultures and religions.

From Local to Cosmopolitan

We have seen that each of the world's major religions had its roots in a locally oriented primal religion, usually connected with a particular tribe or clan, and became more cosmopolitan as it diffused, encountering and incorporating other cultural forms along the way. These roots did not disappear as the tradition changed over time but established the form that profoundly influenced each religion's later shape. In a similar transformation process, each tradition has increased in (1) its internal diversity and (2) its structural differentiation. Finally, (3) each religion has had to struggle with the two-horned dilemma of modernism: the challenges of cultural pluralism and scientific criticism. All these aspects of the local-cosmopolitan shift have had profound cultural and organizational consequences for each tradition. Let's look now more closely at some of the specific transformations in religion that the phenomenon we call "modernism" has brought about.

Increased Internal Diversity and Structural Differentiation

The farther a tradition travels from its roots, the more diverse it becomes. Each major religious tradition incorporates a wide range of beliefs under a broad, abstract sacred canopy and thus becomes diverse in terms of beliefs, practices, and institutions. The reason for this development is no mystery. The primal faith of each religion's origins was constructed along relatively homogeneous lines by a group of fairly like-minded people who lived close to nature, in specific ecological conditions. As culture groups migrated, carrying their religious traditions with them, or as they were conquered by invading tribes or conquered their neighbors, their worldview and corresponding ethos were reevaluated and reconstructed to incorporate different perspectives and adapt to new data. These groups borrowed features of other traditions, then reformulated and strengthened the tradition in direct opposition to new challenges. Sometimes the culture changed dramatically as the result of a new technology or environmental condition, as with the Siksika in North America, whose collective, egalitarian buffalo-hunting practices were disrupted by the introduction of the horse, which allowed individuals to obtain their own buffalo independent of the group.

The major religious traditions often adapted to new settings through syncretism or cooptation: Chinese folk gods became Buddhas and local African deities became Christian saints. Even Judaism, which remained an ethnic religion with strictly guarded boundaries, adapted to local conditions, so that a Palestinian and a Babylonian Talmud were produced early in the Common Era, and contemporary Ashkenazi Jews differ from their Hasidic brothers and sisters. After centuries of adaptation, each religious tradition has become remarkably diverse; patterns of rituals and beliefs vary widely around the globe and sometimes even between congregations in the same neighborhood.

The process of **structural differentiation** is a relatively recent phenomenon that involves the creation of specific institutions to fulfill different functions; it can occur both within the religion and between religious and other spheres of life. As societies have become larger and more complex, the division of labor increases (see Durkheim [1893] 1933), so that specialized institutions carry out specific functions. Functions once performed by religious organizations are now carried out elsewhere (e.g., in public school systems) and religious institutions have taken on a specialized role, concentrating more on private than on public life.

The structural differentiation of the social order itself is a striking characteristic of modern societies and has been the subject of much scholarly and political debate. Early sociologists made much of the difference between premodern and modern society, the "Great Transformation" from pre-industrial to industrial society in Western Europe during the nineteenth century, when countless peasants were uprooted from their family and village and flocked to the cities to work in factories. Tönnies's ([1887] 1957) distinction between *Gemeinschaft*, or "community," of pre-industrial life and the *Gesellschaft*, or "society," characteristic of modern social organization implies a loss of communal feeling and family ties. Durkheim ([1893] 1933) distinguished between mechanical and organic solidarity, expounding a more optimistic view of this transformation process than did Tönnies. Elements of that vision were revived again after World War II as modernization theory, which identified parallels between cultural changes precipitated by industrialization in the West and those occurring elsewhere, including the **secularization** of society, that is, the removal of responsibility and authority in certain spheres from religious institutions.

Recent debates on modernization theory have criticized the idea that non-Western societies engaged in industrialization are required to follow the same path of modernization as the West (Wallerstein 1984). Moreover, it turns out that the characterization of a vast gap between primitive and modern culture has not been quite accurate (see Macfarlane 1979). A number of scholars have noted that too much has been made of "pervasive and invidious contrasts" between the old social order and the new (see Bendix 1978; Shils 1981; Wallerstein 1984). Secularization has been a major issue in the sociology of religion, of course, but reflects more of a European experience than a general phenomenon.

What is clear, however, is that religious life has been profoundly affected in the modern era. All the world's religions have had to do battle with the collective social and intellectual giant called modernism. Let us now look more closely at this phenomenon.

The Challenge of Modernism

Modernism can be defined as the emergence of a global, scientific-technological culture since the Industrial Revolution, and especially during the latter half of the twentieth century. The perception among many

European intellectuals in the nineteenth century that religion was dying was the result of two interrelated social movements: the scientific and democratic revolutions. Western science itself was parented by the Judeo-Christian tradition, which put a high premium on cognitive development and scholarship. The scientific movement took on a life of its own, however, and scientists soon came into direct conflict with church authorities because of their questions about particular claims made especially by the Vatican.

This conflict began in the seventeenth century, when church authorities charged the famous scientist Galileo with heresy because he contended that the earth revolved around the sun, and not vice versa. The Jesuit inquisitors forced Galileo to recant his "heretical" ideas (quoted in White 1896–97, I:139). It was not just a specific doctrine that was at stake, of course, but the reputation of the Roman Catholic church and the entire social order legitimated by Christianity. If the church could be wrong about the immovability of the earth, perhaps it made other, more significant mistakes as well. "If the peasants cease to believe that the sun revolves around the earth, they will revolt!" bemoans Father Inchofer in Bertolt Brecht's (1966) dramatized version of the encounter. As the conflict between scientists and church authorities escalated, their positions polarized (as is usually the case in significant social conflict). It became increasingly difficult to be both a champion of scientific inquiry and a Christian; neither side would allow it.

The second challenge to the church occurred through a similar social process: as the democratic revolution emerged in the late eighteenth century (especially in France), its major opponent included not just the monarchy, but also the church. When the monarchy of France was challenged by the French Revolution, the crown and the church stood side by side to defend the *ancien régime*. Positions tended to solidify in nineteenth-century Europe: either one was pro-democratic, in favor of the development of science, and anti-Christian, or one was in favor of retaining the monarch and traditional Christianity, and restricting the development of science.

Because a sacred canopy is woven out of a vast complex of interdependent parts, when one aspect of it is challenged, the validity of the entire system is called into question. Thus, when scientists began to doubt some dogmas of the Christian church, such as the process of creation and the authorship of the Bible, they cast doubt on the validity of the entire Christian tradition. A bitter conflict ensued between scientists and church authorities that persisted for centuries in Western culture. Christianity, and especially the Roman Catholic Church, bore the brunt of the modernist crisis because of its monopolistic truth claims and political alliances with the *ancien régime* and also because modernism came first to the West as it pioneered the Industrial Revolution. Science was used as a weapon in the battle to wrest control of the social order from the church, so the battle lines were drawn sharply, distorting the nature of the conflicts.

The Revolt Against Religion: The Crisis Begins

The philosophical turmoil beginning in seventeenth-century Europe and culminating in the eighteenth-century Enlightenment set the stage for the "warfare between science and religion" (White 1896–97). Besides the new scientific empiricism that Galileo and others initiated, many Europeans exploring the world in the sixteenth and seventeenth centuries had observed common threads in all of the world's religions. Lord Herbert of Cherbury claimed, in his 1624 *De Veritate,* that all humans had a "natural religion," a position that came to be known as **deism**. Although it may not be inherently anti-Christian, deism was an early challenger of some of the church's doctrines and encouraged tolerance of non-Christian religious perspectives.

Advocates of science also came into direct conflict with church officials over the growing development of textual criticism, that is, the scientific study of texts, including scriptures. Scholars examined such questions as the authorship, historical development, and composition of biblical writings and concluded that many of the church's claims about these texts were untrue.[23] Thomas Hobbes questioned the traditional belief that Moses authored the Pentateuch (the first five books of the Bible) and Baruch Spinoza ([1670] 1883) contended that theologians simply used the Bible for their own purposes, pointing out inconsistencies and historical problems in the biblical texts. Some scholars using critical methods were devout Christians, but the methods were appropriated by others who opposed the church and its hold over believers. One of these dissenters was Pierre Bayle, whose *Dictionnaire historique et critique* (Historical and Critical Dictionary, 1697) was widely read and was supported by such influential intellectuals of the eighteenth century as Rousseau, Voltaire, Montesquieu, David Hume, Benjamin Franklin, and Thomas Jefferson.

In the political realm advocates of the 1789 French Revolution attempted to destroy the Catholic church, not so much as a religion, but as a power in society (Tocqueville [1862] 1945). As the battle lines were drawn, people were forced to choose between the church and the monarchy on one hand or science and the Republic on the other. It was almost impossible to hold to any middle ground; people often demonstrated their loyalty to either the King or the new democratic government by choosing to send their children to the traditional church schools or the newly established secular schools run by the state.

The problem of historical contingency. By the nineteenth century, new rifts emerged between theorists of the burgeoning social sciences and ortho-dox Christian belief. Auguste Comte (1853) contended that human thought develops through three historical stages: first, the theological or superstitious; second, the metaphysical; and finally, the positive, or scien-tific. His developmental positivism provided a scientific basis for colonial expansionism and a general euphoria about progress and the future of humanity. The controversy that Comte's framework generated exploded with the theories of evolution that spread throughout Europe, especially in Charles Darwin's *The Origin of Species* ([1859] 1952) and *Descent of Man* ([1871] 1952). Darwin himself claimed that there was "no good reason why the views given . . . should shock the religious feelings of everyone" ([1859] 1952: 239; cf. [1871] 1952: 593), but many church leaders claimed that his theories contradicted the Genesis creation account. In 1865, *The American Church Review* contended that if Darwin's hypothesis is true, "then is the Bible an unbearable fiction . . . then have Christians for nearly two thousand years been duped by a monstrous lie. . . . Darwin requires us to disbelieve the authoritative word of the Creator."

The principle of evolution raised another issue even more profound than specific disputes over the authenticity of the Genesis cosmogeny: did religious doctrine also evolve historically? The major problem raised by the "scientific study of the Bible," or historical criticism, is the issue of **historical contingency**. When religious truth is considered an infallible revelation from the deity, the idea of the historical nature of the tradition can precipitate a crisis because the conclusion of most historiographic science is that each religious tradition has its own history, and the immu-table, taken-for-granted truths of the faith have in fact mutated consider-ably over time. One example is the disputed authorship of the Penta-teuch, traditionally attributed to Moses himself. Study of the texts created problems in Jewish, Islamic, and especially Christian circles when schol-ars discovered that the sacred scriptures changed over time and were written by different scribes; later versions of the Hebrew scriptures were written with vowel marks whereas early versions did not have them.

Evolution and biblical criticism were used by the "anticlerical" (anti-church) movement to undermine the church's authority, and the church (notably the Vatican) responded with a scathing attack on both science and democracy. When Pope Pius X condemned modernism in 1907 as the "synthesis of all heresies," however, in a way he was right. Conflicts about orthodoxy and heresy, in the Christian tradition, have historically concerned the truth or falsity of particular dogmas. In the nineteenth and twentieth centuries, the notion of dogma itself came under attack and the word took on a negative connotation (Kurtz 1986). Not specific doctrines or religious ideas, but the idea of absolute religious truth itself was attacked by modern scholarship and by social reformers who saw the church as an enemy because it supported the monarchy and opposed democracy, supported theology, and opposed science.

The problem of relativism. Although some religions are more exclusivist in their formulations than others, virtually all of them either assert or imply that their own version of the world is true, thereby rendering competing worldviews inferior. Although this position may obtain some legitimacy in isolated cultures, it obviously becomes problematic in a multicultural context. This brings us to the second major problem of modernism, and a central theological issue of the contemporary religions—the issue of **relativism**.

Religious conservatives criticize such modern perspectives as humanism and liberalism on the grounds they erode absolutes, working to destroy the moral basis of a society. Certain ethical standards, the critics of relativism argue, are universally and unequivocally true, and therefore absolute, because they come from God, who is Absolute. This debate is particularly difficult to analyze with any intellectual reliability because first and foremost it involves a framing issue. That is, if one believes that certain truths, values, or beliefs are Absolutes, then any suggestion of relativism will be simply dismissed out of hand. If one refuses to take an absolutist stand, however, a paradox emerges, for the relativist by definition cannot know with certainty that absolutes do not exist.

Georg Simmel (1978) provides a useful perspective on the problem that helps to bridge the gulf between these two seemingly irreconcilable positions. A relativist position, he notes, does not inherently deny the possibility of the existence of an Absolute or Absolutes, but merely insists that one cannot know the Absolute absolutely, but only from a specific point of view, unless one is actually God. Simmel's restatement of the problem suggests that any exclusivist truth claims (such as papal infallibility) might in fact be blasphemous, according to traditional definition, because only God knows the full truth about anything. Without addressing the issue of divine versus human perspective, a sociological analysis of religion can establish that absolutist or exclusivist truth claims are not entirely rare in human history. Moreover, because a wide range of human perspectives tends to represent the world in widely different ways, it is difficult to accept the premise that any single one has a complete corner on the truth.

The Revolt Against Modernism (The Counterrevolution)

When absolutism is threatened, people often respond with fanaticism. If one facet of a tradition seems at risk, people often believe that the entire system is. The conflict between establishment religion in the West and broad cultural movements of modernism in the nineteenth century provides an exemplary case of the scandal modernism created in many religious traditions. During the late nineteenth and early twentieth centuries, the Vatican came down harshly on modernism, unintentionally fanning the flames of discontent, but eventually putting them out by driving some of the dissidents out of the church and silencing many more (Lyng and Kurtz 1985).

Roman Catholicism vs. modernism. As its own authority in European society was attacked by waves of democratic and scientific revolutions, Rome launched a systematic campaign against modernism over a period of several decades. At the First Vatican Council, convened in 1870, the pope was declared infallible in matters of faith and morals for the first time in the history of the church. In 1899, Pope Leo XIII denounced "Americanism" as a heresy in an effort to criticize both modern science and certain forms of democracy as examples of the pernicious practice of adapting religious doctrine and practice to new social circumstances (Leo XIII 1899; Klein 1951).

The church's external enemies, attacking its hold on European society and politics, used scientific criticism as a weapon to undermine the legitimacy of the sacred canopy woven from Christian doctrine. Little could be done by the waning papacy against such formidable enemies, but inner enemies—heretics—were identified and soundly condemned. When Pope Pius X (1908a, 1908b) issued decrees condemning modernism, he set up a system of secret vigilance committees in every diocese to identify and report suspected heretics to Rome.

The modernist scholars denounced by the Vatican faced remarkable ambivalence in their dual roles as Christians (in some cases, clergy) and as scholars, because the culture wars tried to force them to choose sides. The findings of their research contradicted the pronouncements of the Vatican, and Rome exploited their vulnerable positions in order to mask its own vulnerability. The process of identifying and denouncing heretics, of institutionalizing a campaign to root them out of the church, served as a purification ritual for the beleaguered church hierarchy and set the tone for other "counterrevolutions" to follow.

The counterrevolution continues. Conservative Protestant and Catholic Christians in the United States today continue to struggle with many of the same issues the Vatican confronted in the nineteenth century. The evangelical and traditionalist movements of late twentieth-century American culture reflect efforts by a large sector of the Christian community to resist reliance upon scientific and secular thought to establish the moral boundaries of contemporary life.

The modernist crisis has also spread to other religious traditions, especially in what some claim is a "postmodern period," in which all tradition allegedly ceases to function (see Robertson 1991, 1992a, 1992b). It was not long after Christianity's encounter with scientific empiricism that questions were raised about other religious doctrines. Did God dictate the entire Qur'an word by word to Muhammad? Did Krishna really serve as Arjuna's charioteer on some historical battlefield? Have the Vedas really always existed and were never authored by humans? Does Matsu really live in the statues at the temple, or are they just symbolic representations of her? Or, more fundamentally, does a Goddess of Mercy Matsu really exist, or is she just a projection of some social or psychological reality?

As with secularization, the extent to which modernism becomes a problem depends on the nature of the belief system and religious institutions as well as the conflict strategies chosen, especially by religious elites. Each religious tradition faces modernism at its most vulnerable spot. For Judaism and Islam, modernism raises questions about social boundaries and creates a cultural climate in which it is difficult to sustain the rituals that reinforce them. In the Christian churches, modernism attacks the integrity of the belief structure by challenging the tradition's claims about its scriptures and by presenting alternative perspectives that answer the same questions in different ways. Modernism may not offer as much of a challenge to the Eastern religions, which have traditionally coopted, rather than opposed, new ideas. Nonetheless, the more mystical elements of Eastern thought are sometimes problematic in the modern scientific ethos. Both the internal spiritual claims of such disciplines as yoga and the cosmic worldviews that posit cycles of the universe lasting hundreds of thousands of years appear too fantastic and unverifiable to many modern Hindus and Buddhists, despite the effort by some to articulate their claims with scientific rhetoric.

Moreover, the **instrumental rationality**—that is, the utilitarian calculation of means to an end—of the technocratic ethos that now pervades the global village frequently undermines the value rational and nonrational bases of action promoted by Hinduism and Buddhism as well as other religious traditions. The technocratic ethos also values efficiency and practicality above all other values, including justice and personal loyalty. Religious and technocratic values do not always collide, but they often do.

It is clear that a countertrend has also emerged, often not merely a retrogressive or temporary movement but a solid reaction against the dominant worldview that modernism represents. We will return to this issue in later chapters, but a few points must be made here. The rising traditionalist theologies in Islamic societies, North American Christianity, and Hindu nationalism are powerful movements that will not go away and represent a basic revolt against modernism that has persisted long after the first major battles between religion and modernity two hundred years ago. The most hopeful prognosis is that these movements will help to mitigate some of the more damaging effects of modernism without destroying the possibility of rapprochement among the religious communities or between religious and secular forces.

Second, mainstream cultures have begun to learn the limitations of both science and tolerance. Science and technology have been humbled in recent decades, particularly by the ecological crises brought on by unbridled technological development in some sectors of the world and the destructive consequences of scientific and technological research in the development of weapons of mass destruction. Some of the old battles have died down and new areas of agreement have developed between scientific and religious spheres.

Finally, antimodernist movements are now facilitated by modern technologies of mass communications and transportation. Now millions of like-minded people who might have felt isolated in the opposition to the intrusion of modernism into their culture can join together across geographical boundaries, support and encourage one another in their critiques of modernism, and build networks and strategies for collective action.

Historical Outcomes of the Modernist Crisis

Modern culture contains two simultaneous, contradictory trends: increasing unity and increasing diversity (Durkheim [1893] 1933). The emerging global culture has some common denominators and centripetal forces that draw people together as well as profound countertrends that challenge the mainstream—notably, the revival of traditional cultures in many parts of the world, in part as a protest against the flood of foreign influences.

What have been the direct outcomes of the modernist challenge to traditional religion? Some of the consequences were:

1. The substitution of religious traditions with rationalism, scientism, and individualism.

2. The secularization of public life and the privatization of the religious, so that people from different faiths can share a common social life.

3. The revitalization of traditional forms.

4. The construction of quasireligious forms that fulfill many of the social and psychological functions of traditional religions, such as civil religion and nationalism.

5. The creation of new forms of religious belief and practice created through processes of syncretism.

The first two of these consequences were a logical outgrowth of the Enlightenment worldview that precipitated the modernist crisis in the first place. The latter three represent attempts to reshape, rather than replace, the world's religious traditions. We will explore the first two briefly here and the last three when we explore the crisis of multiculturalism in Chapter 6.

Rationalism, Scientism, and Individualism

The first Western solution to the problems raised by modern science was advanced during the Enlightenment: replace the illusions and arbitrary authority of traditional Christianity with a rational system of norms and values based on science. Most of the Enlightenment philosophers and their heirs thus emphasized a **rationalism** that insisted on reason as a source of knowledge superior to religious tradition. As we have seen, the social sciences took the lead in this effort; many were optimistic that a new scientific morality could be founded on either a scientific psychology and economics—Adam Smith and the British utilitarians—or a scientific sociology—Auguste Comte and the French positivists. The German idealists exposed the "illusions" of religious thought in the West, which would be replaced with the rationality of Kant, the socialist revolutions of Marx, and the psychotherapeutic treatment of Freud. In its most extreme forms, this approach resulted in the development of **scientism**, a quasi-religious belief in the scientific method.

The warfare between science and theology that characterized the nineteenth and early twentieth centuries has subsided somewhat, because both sides have pulled back their troops, and because bridges have been built between the two sides. As Ian Barbour (1960) has observed, the relationship between science and religion is now one not of content differences but of methods. Barbour notes a number of similarities and differences between the two methods that are most instructive. Both science and religion involve (1) the interaction of experience and interpretation; (2) the role of community and analogy (neither perspective makes sense to the outsider who is not familiar with the symbolic language of the community); (3) the primacy of relationships rather than objects (relationships among people and with their deities in religion, and among elements of matter—such as probability waves in atomic structures—in science); and (4) the use of reason to test interpretations of the way in which reality is experienced.

Some differences between the two methods remain significant, however: (1) science focuses on means rather than ends; (2) science aims at knowledge of reproducible relations expressible in general laws, whereas religion emphasizes configurational understanding and the significance of a unique part in relation to the whole; (3) science promotes objective detachment as opposed to the personal involvement valued by religion. But finally, Barbour concludes, science and religion are complementary forms of investigating reality. "Either science or religion alone affords a partial view," he claims (1960: 214). "We need to use various categories and frames of reference. The man who says, 'Love is not real because I cannot weigh it' is confusing two frames of reference." The same could be said of the multiple perspectives within and between scientific and religious traditions. Every scientific field, every religious tradition, has its own fields and schools, its own perspectives, which point to reality as it is experienced by people from a given point in the social and natural world.

Various religious traditions have responded differently, of course, to the challenge of modern science, as have schools of thought within each tradition. The historical context and nature of ecclesiastical institutions, as well as flexibility of doctrinal orientations, also influences the extent to which traditions resist or accommodate modern science. Most religions, like Buddhism, have both those who wish to accommodate and those who resist, although the inclusiveness of the tradition favors an incorporation of scientific paradigms into the Buddhist worldview. A few Buddhists have found science inadequate; others have emphasized the similarities between the Buddha's search for truth and the methods of modern science. Buddhist advocates of science point to a passage in which the Buddha encourages testing of his teachings through one's own powers of reason (Kitagawa and Reynolds 1976: 46). Dr. Luang Suriyabongse asserted that "the Buddha was the greatest discoverer and scientist of all time" (quoted in Kitagawa and Reynolds 1976: 47). Other Buddhists were less sanguine about science. G. P. Malalasekera, the first president of the World Fellowship of Buddhists, asserted that the Buddha utilized science when appropriate but that the ultimate mysteries of his teachings went far beyond the knowledge that any purely scientific approach could offer (Kitagawa and Reynolds 1976: 47).

A major feature of the Enlightenment was an individualism that maintains the independence of the human individual as the source of all values, rights, and duties. This claim was a response to the legitimation crisis of the modern West, and the democratic legacy to which individualism gave birth is a hallmark of the Enlightenment. Granting the individual the freedom to make doctrinal and ethical claims independent of religious communities or institutions solves the crisis of faith by making religion a matter of personal choice, but it also creates new social problems. People are not required to rely on suspect institutions, but the dilemma of how to maintain collective life is unsolved if each individual is responsible only to him or herself.

Secularization and Privatization

The second major consequence of the crisis of modernism are the dual processes of secularization and privatization in which religious institutions are differentiated from other spheres of life. The process of secularization was the hallmark of political and religious reform following the French Revolution, when the church, in alliance with the monarchy, had such a monopoly on the organization of public life that those who wished to discard the *ancien régime* felt that they had to eliminate the church's control as well. It is, at first glance, a logical solution to the problem because, like Jefferson's proposed "wall of separation between church and state," it allows a diverse people to build a collective life despite their religious differences. When people enter the marketplace, the statehouse, or the classroom, they can leave their religion at home.

In Europe, the passing of the old regime resulted in the secularization of many spheres of European society, notably in politics and education. As the officially recognized religion in most of Europe, the Christian church had constructed the authorized ethos, socialized and educated the youth, and pronounced judgment on moral boundaries. During the French Revolution, advocates of democracy recognized the power of the Catholic schools in promoting monarchical ideas among young people so made the creation of state schools a major priority (see Durkheim 1961). The schools had been used to promote Christianity; in the secular sphere, they would promote the principles of "liberty, equality, and fraternity" and the civic virtues required by a democratic society (Kurtz 1986: 30ff.; Dansette 1961). In country after country in Europe and the New World, the official relationship between the state and the church was terminated.

As a response to modernism, secularization is closely linked to the scientific ethos, which insists that it is possible to adopt an objective viewpoint that stands above cultural biases; it lies at the heart of the Enlightenment project that would substitute religion with scientific rationality. The problem with this effort, as we have noted, is that the all-encompassing nature of religious perspectives makes it difficult, if not impossible, to "check them at the door" when entering the public arena. A religious perspective by definition involves itself in the ethical standards that apply to all other spheres of life. For most people, historically, and in most cultures, religion is diffused throughout everyday life.

Most sociologists, and many other people living in "modern" society, have trouble understanding this fact because they compartmentalize religion, assigning it to a specific sphere and only attending to it on an occasional basis. Although attention to the sacred has always had a cyclical nature, commonly oriented around festivals and seasonal rites, daily and weekly times of prayer and worship, such differentiation is a fairly recent development in the world's history. The compartmentalization of religion, however, represents one solution to the problem of a multicultural social reality. Here each of many religious perspectives takes its place in a cultural marketplace alongside secular worldviews and ethical standards. If everyone in our interaction space shared the same basic worldview and ethos, we could go about our daily lives taking religious elements for granted. When we encounter a plurality of worldviews on a regular basis in the public sphere, however, we often accommodate that fact by assigning the explicitly religious to certain times and sectors of our lives in the process known as **privatization**.

This process is enforced by social norms of modern Western urban life: when people constantly talk of God or their religious convictions, they are either religious professionals, for whom it is acceptable (although they are alienated somewhat from mainstream society) or religious "fanatics," some of whom are shunned; others are revered, but still set apart (like Mother Teresa). If we think that the copy machine will not work because it is infested with demons or the operator has bad *karma*, we will probably keep our opinions to ourselves. People in heterogeneous urban societies usually approach the sacred with some ambivalence in everyday life. Those who are religious acknowledge that their faith should inform one's entire life, but they are often hesitant to engage in religious talk in a multicultural setting because they get negative feedback. Religious convictions are thus considered *private* concerns that should be kept to oneself, like one's sexual fantasies.

Sociologists of religion have made much of the secularization phenomenon, in large part because it was a major event in Europe and many of the prominent figures in the field were European and tended to generalize from their own experience. In less secularized societies, however, the religious traditions people bring with them continue to shape the ways in which they define the world, the meaning of life, and the nature of ethical behavior in everyday life. A majority of people on the planet live in a much more sacralized environment than do the people who write and read books on the sociology of religion. For billions of people, religious traditions are a natural part of everyday life.

Moreover, because of the highly visible disestablishment of religion in the United States along with the establishment of state schools as well as other spheres of secularization in society, many people assumed that U.S. culture had become secularized in an analogous fashion. As Warner (1993) notes, the secularization paradigm for American religion proposed by Berger (1969) and Parsons (1960, 1967, 1969) was increasingly challenged by an antisecularization thesis growing primarily out of empirical research on American religion, which found it flourishing (see, e.g., Neitz 1987, 1990; Ammerman 1987; and Christiano 1987). Indeed, the counterevidence was so strong that it appears that "the antisecularization thesis . . . has become the accepted wisdom" (Sharot 1991: 271).

This **antisecularization thesis** contends that U.S. culture, far from secularizing, has become more religious than ever; religious participation not only persisted throughout U.S. history, Warner (1993) points out, but actually increased dramatically well into the twentieth century. At the time of the American Revolution in 1776, about 10 percent of the population were church members, compared to about 60 percent in the 1990s, with rapid growth taking place during the half-century preceding the Civil War and the Great Depression (Warner 1993: 1049; Herberg 1960: 47–50; Caplow, Bahr, and Chadwick 1983: 28–29; Finke and Stark 1986). A major reason for the lack of secularization in American society may well be that the battles there have not been as vociferous as in Europe, where they were politicized in an ethos that preferred democracy over monarchy while church officials promoted the retention of the monarchy and fought democratization in every sphere. Although the modernist crisis certainly affected U.S. culture profoundly and the battles have not completely subsided, the working compromise establishing some boundaries between religious and political spheres instituted at the founding of the republic, as well as the forced multiculturalism of American culture over time, have mitigated the polarization between religious and scientific perspectives and among various religious traditions.

The Modernist Crisis and the Twenty-First Century

Not only is religion alive and well in the world's most advanced industrial society, it is thriving in many other areas of the world. Along with the creation of new religious forms, we are now witnessing some dramatic revitalizations of traditional forms of religious life. The growing interdependence of the various human cultures, along with the economic and social webs woven across thousands of former boundaries, is creating an unprecedented series of changes in the nature of human theology. On the one hand, the very notion of religious belief has been called into question by the secular nature of thought in industrial society. On the other hand, the idea of a tightly woven, nearly seamless sacred canopy has clearly become obsolete (if it ever truly existed) as people from various strands of religious thought encounter ideas from other traditions. It is virtually impossible for any believer in the world today to live in isolation.

Each religious tradition faces a similar dilemma, although it is more acute in those that are more exclusivist in their theology: how can they encounter the ideas of another faith expression, and indeed interact with people from that community on a regular basis, without losing the integrity of their own faith? The idea of religious traditions encountering one another is, of course, nothing new. The process has occurred again and again over the centuries, as we saw in our tour of the world's religions.

The scale and significance of those encounters are new. Every major religious tradition now, in a sense, meets all the others on the street, and their members must decide whether to kill each other, pass by indifferently, or somehow engage one another.

One important consequence of these encounters, however, is the rediscovery of the rich diversity each tradition embraces. From within one's own small corner of a faith community, the canopy might appear relatively uniform and seamless. When we look closely at any sacred canopy, however, we discover that it is not uniform at all but a patchwork of contradictory ideas stitched together over the centuries. The great prophets and seers of the planet emerge from the profane order of human existence at times of crisis, when the canopy is ripped apart by wars and invasions, social or economic ferment, and natural disaster. The power of the prophets and the gods comes from being able to restore the canopy so that it can once again be taken for granted. Recognizing the affinities between their interests and the ideas of a particular religious perspective—or even an antireligious belief system—various social strata and classes struggling for a position in a new social order also attempt to seize that power.

The Western Enlightenment worldview, which in essence called for the substitution of religion with modern science, became in effect another competing sacred canopy with its own arbitrariness, contradictions, and truth claims that legitimated a new system of social exploitation. Against those secularizing worldviews and the global military-bureaucratic structures they legitimated arose a series of protest theologies, sometimes from the left and occasionally from the right, but almost always from the bottom up, reaffirming sacred frames for explaining and ordering the world.

Not all responses to the modernist crisis involved either efforts to substitute religion with science or simply to have religion retreat into private spheres as public life became secularized. Other efforts to cope with modern and postmodern life involved the revitalization of traditional forms, the creation of new religious movements, and the formation of quasireligious systems such as civil religion and nationalism. Let's look now at these permutations of religion in the wake of the challenge that followed on the heels of the crisis of modernism: the crisis of multiculturalism.

6

Multiculturalism: Crisis and Response

As modern cultures emerged in the West around the time of the eighteenth century Enlightenment, profound changes occurred in the religious sphere of life as in all other spheres. Religious impulses push toward an all-embracing sacred canopy that pervades everyday life and links it with the broadest theories of the cosmos. The pluralism of the modern world, however, has created a contradictory impulse that limits religious spheres of influence as multiple traditions conflict with one another. New forms of religious life have taken shape out of competing tendencies of the world's religions to provide a sacred canopy for all elements of life on one hand and resistance from alternative traditions to the monopoly of any such system on the other hand. The tension between opposing forces precipitated the privatization of religion and a differentiation of spheres of life in the modern world. Even as private ethics continue to be guided by a person's religious tradition, a wall of separation has emerged between religion and politics, religion and economics, faith and education.

In a structurally differentiated society, every institution is given a specialized task; the task of religious institutions is to tend to spiritual and ethical issues. Religion intrudes on all other spheres, however, because its ethics generally apply to all areas of life. A modern society compartmentalizes institutions, but we cannot compartmentalize people.[24] The cultural life of the global village is a product of an interaction of religious traditions among themselves as well as between each tradition and the multitude of others within which they came into contact as the global society emerged. In itself this is not a new phenomenon; each major cultural tradition is, after all, a product of multicultural encounters. In both form and content, moreover, our late twentieth-century multicultural crisis is similar to the modernist crisis a century ago. What *is* new is the scale and scope of the process.

When cultures collide, the sacred canopy of each tradition is forced to compete in a cultural marketplace and is thus open to the scrutiny of potential consumers. When new gods arrive on the scene, we often react in much the same way as King Kadmeus did when Dionysius appeared in Thebes in ancient Greece—pull out our swords for battle. Multiculturalism creates a crisis, but also an opportunity. We can learn from the successes and failures of the past and, with a sociological imagination, construct new religious traditions in the next centuries. It is not a question of *whether* we will do it, but *how,* and what kind of new traditions will emerge. The construction of new social and cultural forms is never a simple process, however, and the crisis of multiculturalism, following in the wake of modernism, has precipitated culture wars around the globe.

Besides the responses to modernism discussed in Chapter 5—the substitution of religion with alternative ideologies and the secularization of public life—efforts to deal with these crises helped to forge a transformation of religion in the following outcomes:

1. *Antimodernist movements* such as the protest theologies of Christian and Islamic traditionalism
2. *Liberation theologies* from Latin American and the women's movement
3. *New religious and quasireligious forms,* such as individualism and consumerism, civil religion and nationalism
4. *Religious syncretism,* the development of religious movements that bring together elements of various religious traditions in a new (and often controversial) manner

We will examine each of these developments briefly in order to understand contemporary trends and future possibilities for religious life in the global village.

Culture Wars and Protest Theologies

Multiculturalism—the product of sustained encounters among the various religious traditions of the world with each other—along with modernism—the critical force of modern secular thought—fuels ongoing **culture wars** in virtually every corner of the globe.[25] These wars are, in part, a result of what Jürgen Habermas (1975) calls a "legitimation crisis."[26] Many religious movements struggle against the hegemony of modern cultural centers and the invasion of materialistic, relativistic, and hedonistic culture from these centers. These movements, based upon traditional indigenous cultures, have a variety of political agendas, often with diametrically opposed implications for reorganizing society in the global village.

From the liberation theologians of Latin America and Africa to the Islamic and Christian traditionalists of the Middle East and North America, however, all share a common characteristic: religious frames are used as vehicles to empower the participants in their struggles against the oppressive structures of what Weber ([1904] 1958) called the "iron cage" of the modern socioeconomic order and what Simmel (1971) called the growth of "objective culture." In the contemporary world the family and religion are viewed as enclaves of "communicatively structured interaction"—that is, interaction is based on who people "are" rather than what they are "worth," in some market sense. When even that terrain is invaded, people resist (see Habermas 1987: 393). Fields contends that this social context helps to explain the current rise of traditionalism in the United States; it can no doubt apply to other traditionalisms as well. "After years of withdrawal," Fields argues, traditionalist groups are now resisting:

> Thus, the major thrusts of the ideology of activist fundamentalism . . .
> involve a reduction of state intrusion into the economy and the family
> coupled with state promotion of religious doctrine as the basis of law. While
> seemingly contradictory, institutionalization of this ideology would produce
> a shift in the relationship between subsystems and the lifeworld, while politi-
> cal discourse would become more "substantive" than "formal" or "techni-
> cal." (1991: 185)

This two-pronged effort to eject the modern world from private life and at the same time to transform public life so that the gap between private values and the cultural ethos is less striking lies at the core of traditionalism in its various subforms around the world, and in the emergence of liberation theology among the poor, especially in Latin America.

Cultural cleavages in the global village sometimes fall along the lines of the religious traditions. In recent decades, for example, movements in the Islamic world used centuries-old themes of Muslim–non-Muslim divisions as a vehicle for expressing their discontent about the invasions of their lives by "Christians" from the West, "Marxists" from the Soviet Union, Hindus from Delhi, and the like. Protestant-Catholic cleavages in Northern Ireland reflect economic and political divisions that parallel deep religious differences. In many instances, however, new lines of conflict cut across old ones, reflecting competing impulses toward what James Davison Hunter (1991) calls orthodoxy, on one hand, and progressivism, on the other hand, and which I will refer to by the more conventional religious terms of **orthodoxy** and **modernism**. These conflicts involve the question of how to set standards in all social spheres—the family, law, art, education, and politics. They concern, as Hunter puts it, "allegiances to different formulations and sources of moral authority" and "how we are to order our lives together" (1991: 118, 51).

These culture wars are sparked by the interaction of diverse worldviews in the global village and are fueled by widespread dissatisfaction with the way the world is ordered and the ways in which it is changing. Moreover, interpersonal, intertribal, interethnic, interclass, interregional, and international conflicts are often framed in religious terms, intensifying them and giving them a significance to participants that transcends the mundane struggle for survival, wealth, and power. These battles, framed as religious conflicts, take on larger-than-life proportions as the struggle of good against evil.

First, the cultural dimension of the crisis involves the assault on religious traditions by the interaction of various religious orientations and scientific critiques, undermining each system's legitimation. Second, advanced capitalism is in a state of crisis, precipitated, Habermas and others argue, by the inability of political and economic systems to meet expectations about delivering material comforts and economic stability. Finally, these broader crises result in what Habermas (1987) calls the "colonization of the lifeworld," that is, the welfare state and the public realm in general, have invaded the private sphere of lived experience, including the family, which is now subjected to the imperatives of advanced capitalism, "consumerism and possessive individualism, motives of performance and competition" that shape behavior. Everyday life is thus squeezed into a "purposive-rational action orientation [that] calls for the reaction of hedonism freed from the pressures of rationality" (1987: 325). Habermas is writing primarily of the world of advanced capitalism, but elements of his analysis are also applicable to other parts of the world as well. The lifeworld of the poor in the Third World, for example, has been colonized by the advanced capitalism emanating from the West in such a radical manner that many have organized with the only cultural tools they had available, i.e., those from their Christian tradition.

The culture wars of the modern world are often perceived as strictly moral conflicts, but they also have a basis in social organization. Orthodoxy thrives in sociologically simple (small, homogeneous) communities and modernism in complex ones (large, heterogeneous societies). In a small rural village, where everyone comes from the same ethnic group and class differences are minimal, it is feasible to have rigid moral boundaries and a sacred canopy that unifies the ethos of the entire society. In the global village, however, competing claims of diverse groups with radically different ethnic, historical, and class backgrounds render consensus on moral codes virtually impossible.

Sociological insights into religion center on the proposition that religious and social systems are intimately connected. Consequently, they change in a dialectical fashion, influencing and shaping one another. The dramatic transformation of the social world in the twentieth century is both shaped by and in turn produces remarkable changes in the nature of religious life on the planet.

As the world system emerges, many indigenous traditions are either incorporated into broader religious traditions, or eliminated altogether. So many local expressions of religious life were destroyed by colonialism and modernization that it appeared for a while as though few religious traditions would remain. Religious life has proven to be remarkably resilient, however, and we would be mistaken to assume that the shape of religion on the planet will be determined only by the central traditions.

The formation of new religious movements has become widespread, some in the form of movements that syncretize a range of older forms, just as the major religions themselves were created out of intense intercultural conflict in earlier times. Other movements, such as the communist and socialist systems of the twentieth century, claim to be nonreligious but take on many of the characteristics of religions. They attempt to provide a worldview and an ethos, as well as a general sacred canopy that is to guide both the ideology and the structure of life, from the personal to the public. In the Soviet Union the state created a relatively rich, though often cynically practiced, ritual life that was often meant to replace traditional religious practices.

Throughout the modern world, with its nation-state system, various forms of nationalism offer a surrogate religion in which identity is forged not on a religious anvil, but is linked to citizenship in a nation. This development has given us the democratic political institutions so widely cherished in modern life but also nationalistic wars and new forms of ethnocentrism. A similar ambivalence pervades the individualism of contemporary Western culture. It has taken on a quasireligious form as well, leading to both a highly ethical humanism that stresses justice, community service, and civic responsibility and at the same time, a narcissistic hedonism in which the lofty values of individual freedom and self-actualization are translated into patterns of consumption of mass-produced goods.

Revitalizing the Ancient Traditions

The root of the contemporary culture wars is a deep-seated discontent with both traditional and modern culture, which invades virtually every corner of the global village and undermines traditional worldviews and the ethos of indigenous cultures. Instead of showing respect for elders and attending religious ceremonies, many young people from East Asia to Latin America now play brash American rock music, watch Western movies, and drive motorcycles. Instead of following the strict moral codes of their traditions, some young women of the Arabic countries are discarding the veil and demanding to work with men outside the home. These cultural movements lead to conflicts at every level of society, from the intergenerational struggles about conflicting norms and values within families to regional and international conflicts about religious, cultural, and economic issues.

Most individuals experience an ambivalence toward modern culture that pervades the global village, resulting in contradictory behaviors as people express first one, and then another, aspect of their love-hate relationship with the new world. Young people often love their parents and their village, but are drawn toward the lifestyles seen in Western movies. This ambivalence helps explain the penchant for many influences, from rock music to postmodernist theory, through which one can simultaneously emulate and attack the cultural center of the global village. As a representative battlefield, we will briefly examine the culture wars in the United States, in which traditionalist Christians see themselves as struggling with modernists and progressivists to preserve moral values.

Christian Traditionalist Protests

The culture wars occurring in the United States provide a convenient microcosm of the global conflict. American culture is organized in much the same way as culture in the global village: one broadly hewn worldview and its corresponding ethos are hegemonic, but the dominant paradigm is never fully accepted. The vast diversity of religious and ethnic perspectives brought to America by immigrants from around the world, constituting strong religious and ethnic subcultures in the country, present a strong and vocal challenge to efforts to create a hegemonic culture.

Polarized camps in the wars advocate two different styles of social authority, identified by Richard Merleman (1984) and elaborated by James Davison Hunter (1991) as "tight bounded" and "loose bounded." In tight-bounded communities, moral obligations are viewed as rigid and given, whereas loose-bounded groups view moral commitment as more voluntary, contingent, and fluid. We will refer to them as the *orthodox* and *modernist* camps. Reality in American public culture, Hunter argues, is increasingly shaped by the "knowledge workers" of the modernist camp, such as "public policy specialists ... special interest lobbyists, public interest lawyers, independent writers and ideologues, journalists and editors, community organizers and movement activists" (1991: 60). These shapers of rhetoric and definers of moral standards challenge the fundamental religious tenets of many subcultures in the nation, partly because of efforts to create the proverbial "melting pot," and partly as a function of the common-denominator effect of capitalism.

At stake in each area of dispute in the culture wars is the question of authority: Who is responsible for the care of the family and how much shall the state and other institutions intervene? Who can define the role of women in society, and how much authority should men retain in the family? Who defines the ethical boundaries of business, public culture, education, and other issues of public policy? Who can determine when life begins and when it should end?

Specific battles of the culture wars often reveal their fundamental structure, as in the debates over gender-specific language and the Equal Rights Amendment (ERA). The orthodox party, represented by the Christian Right, claims that the ERA would destroy the traditional family and motherhood. Modernists see it as an essential step in the creation of a just society that insures equality for all. The same issues underlie such seemingly unrelated public battles as homosexuality, prayer in the schools, and abortion. Some religious leaders claim that gay rights movements represent a vicious attack on traditional family values, whereas others defend it as an essential struggle for dignity. Modernists see collective prayer in public schools as an intrusion on the religious freedom of those not of the dominant religious perspective. The founder of the Campus Crusade for Christ, however, insists that the 1963 Supreme Court ruling against prayer in the public schools constitutes the primary cause of the social problems faced in the United States today: since the decision, "premarital sexual activity has increased over 200%, pregnancies to unwed mothers are up almost 400%; gonorrhea is up over 200% ... [and] adultery has increased from 100% to 250% [sic]" (Hunter 1991: 204).

The battle between the orthodox and the modernists is not just an American phenomenon but can be found in conflicts within religious traditions around the world that have some common characteristics whether they are between African National Congress and pro-apartheid forces in South Africa churches, secular-oriented and nationalist Hindus in India, or proponents and opponents of women's rights among the world's Muslims.

Despite shared national, linguistic, and geographical bonds, the combatants of the culture wars live in different worlds and talk past one another. The orthodox and modernist camps tend to "operate from different philosophical assumptions and by very different rules of logic and moral judgment" (Hunter 1991: 250). A negotiated settlement is not likely in the near future, Hunter argues, because vocal advocates "at either end of the cultural axis are not inclined toward working for a genuinely pluralistic resolution" (1991: 298).

The New Christian Right. One of the most visible developments in American culture in the late 1970s and 1980s was the rise of the so-called New Christian Right, which soared into prominence with the presidential administration of Ronald Reagan.

Christian traditionalism in the United States during the 1980s contained a number of interesting hybrids that used high technology to promote their decidedly antimodern beliefs.

Television brought the Christian Right into America's homes, however, and made it possible for the movement to become a major force in American culture. In 1970, according to Arbitron, 38 religious programs had a combined audience size of 9,803,000; by 1980, 66 programs had 20,538,000 viewers, significantly transforming the religious landscape of the country (Hadden and Swann 1981: 55).

Television was the most important, but not the only, medium used by traditionalists in mobilizing their movement: computerized direct mail, Lear jets, and even a computer billboard created by John Marler's "Computers for Christ." Marler encouraged the development of a computer network to exchange information about everything from how to attack disturbing social problems to theological debates. Marler himself claims to have "proof" that God dictated "each and every character and word in the Bible" (quoted in "Evangelist Uses Computer Exchange" 1984).

Many Christian conservatives overcame a natural antipathy to partisan politics, beginning in the late 1970s, because they were fed up with the drift of American culture. On the West Coast, where the two sides of the culture wars meet on the battlefield daily; in the South, where many still view the national culture with considerable ambivalence; and across the airwaves into every conservative corner of resistance, they began to talk with a new confidence about changing the country. And this time, they were not just talking about individual conversion; they were talking politics.[27]

In January 1979, a number of anti-gay, anti-pornography, and pro-family groups on the West Coast were brought together by California ministers Robert Grant and Richard Zone to found Christian Voice. Pat Robertson featured Voice on his "700 Club" and it quickly amassed a mailing list of 150,000 laity and 37,000 clergy, including Catholics and Mormons as well as Protestants. A few months later, in July 1979, Jerry Falwell founded the Moral Majority, with a strong southern contingent and a serious computer-based fundraising effort that gathered $1,000,000 in the first month, largely with support from the "Old Time Gospel Hour" audience. Falwell traveled to all fifty states holding "I Love America" rallies; by 1981, he claimed to have 4 million members in his organization—hardly a majority, but certainly a substantial bloc.

Another significant Christian Right organization, Roundtable, sponsored workshops to teach clergy how to mobilize their congregations to support conservative political candidates. At a Dallas extravaganza in August 1980, Ronald Reagan and other right-wing stars spoke, endorsing the organization's goals. These organizations and others joined with the televangelists to oppose the Strategic Arms Limitation Treaty between the U.S.S.R. and the U.S. in late 1979, to protest state interference with Christian schools, to oppose abortion and endorse school prayer, and to elect a new set of political leaders. Although not very successful at recruiting people to run for Congress, the New Right did play an important role in defeating Senators Packwood, Church, Bayh, McGovern, and Culver, as well as several House members from conservative districts.

The Christian Right's greatest coup, though, was the election of Ronald Reagan as president. Not only did the conservatives mobilize people in the church to vote, but they raised large sums of money for political action committees (PACs). Whereas liberal PACs only raised about $1.2 million in 1977–1978, conservative PACs raised about $6.4 million. In 1979–1980 the disparity was even greater: liberal PACs raised about $2.1 million and conservative PACs $11.3 million (Latus 1983).

Some students of the Christian Right predict that the movement may have the resources to dominate U.S. politics by the end of the twentieth century, for the following reasons:

1. A loss of confidence in the liberal philosophy because of persistent military defeats, failed leadership, poverty, crime, drug use, and the like

2. The legitimization of a conservative cultural revolution during the Reagan era and the linkage between Christianity and free enterprise capitalism, prayer in schools, and the protest against secular humanism

3. The New Christian Right's monopoly of religious broadcasting, with 1,370 religious radio stations and 221 religious television stations (in 1987), far surpassing that of any other single interest group

4. Their mastery of fundraising skills so essential to sustaining a social movement organization, in terms of grass-roots fundraising (especially through television and direct mail) and contacts with wealthy individuals

5. The New Christian Right's appeal to the growing number of Americans over the age of sixty-five (3.1 million in 1900 and 29 million in the late 1980s), who are more likely to be religious than a demographically younger population

To this impressive list, Hunter (1991: 299) adds another: the extensive network of parallel institutions: the schools, colleges, universities, and publishing firms of the New Christian Right. Moreover, despite a number of scandals and difficult times for televangelists during the 1980s, many persist in having widespread influence. A more secularized version of the Christian Right's agenda has a widely heard supporter in the strident voice of syndicated radio and television talk show host Rush Limbaugh.

A number of countertrends call the above predictions into question, however:[28]

1. When Ronald Reagan left the presidency, the initial fervor of the New Christian Right evaporated quickly; Reagan's charismatic authority held together a rather disparate movement with serious internal cleavages.

2. Those people most likely to support the movement—a disproportionate number of working class and minorities—are traditionally drawn to the more liberal Democratic Party, so that few issues unite the movement beyond school prayer and abortion.

3. The institutional resources and power behind the modernist camp—notably the knowledge industry itself, so central to the process of constructing public opinion, and with a relatively secular ethos—are probably stronger than those supporting the orthodox camp.

4. Because of its general orientation and modes of operation, the ethos of the modern state does not support an orthodox stance.

5. The ethos of the country's major cultural centers—Washington, New York, Boston, Chicago, Los Angeles, and San Francisco—tends to be progressive or modernist.

6. Finally, the style of contemporary policy debates assumes the autonomy of rationality, thereby excluding the appeal to traditional authority of the orthodox message. The orthodox camp tends to lose simply by accepting this ground rule for participation in debate. (see Hunter 1991: 306)

The culture wars are far from over in the United States, and bickering occurs even within each camp as well. One of the most difficult problems in political culture is the lack of tolerance on both left and right. For example, even some of the traditional conservatives were displeased with the New Christian Right's efforts to label those who disagreed with them as immoral people. Senator Barry Goldwater, a longtime spokesperson for the conservative community, declared in 1981 that he was "frankly sick and tired of the political preachers across this country telling me as a citizen that if I want to be a moral person, I must believe in A, B, C, and D. Just who do they think they are?" (Nelson 1981)

Because of the pluralistic character of the U.S. population, pressures to have a broad, flexible collective moral code have permeated American culture from the country's beginning. Those forces favoring less rigid common morals have always collided with others attempting to install a hegemonic culture and to enforce a particular brand of Christianity on everyone. They have never been fully successful, however, and part of the reason for the New Christian Right's emergence in the 1970s and 1980s was their perception that they were losing the battle for the country's hearts and minds, especially as various minority groups began to assert their own subcultures in the wake of the cultural ferment of the 1960s.

Christian fundamentalist and evangelical movements in the United States provide an important anchor for identity in a sea of change and a means of expression for people dissatisfied with the direction in which the world is moving and grieving over the loss of their world as they knew it. They also present a serious challenge to American multiculturalism and religious pluralism because of their strong opposition to religious tolerance and their certainty of the truth on certain moral issues against which other groups hold competing beliefs just as strongly.

Islamic Traditionalism: Antimodern and Anticolonial

Many believers in the Islamic world have picked up their own banner of orthodoxy in a manner similar to that employed by the New Christian Right in the United States. In some ways, these two groups fight the same enemy—the Western establishment, the modernists who attempt to establish cultural hegemony in the contemporary world based on secular scientific thought that undermines the ethos and worldview of the religious community. The Islamic traditionalists emerged from a very different historical context, however.

In the last century, issues of modernism and colonialism became deeply intertwined in the Islamic community. On one hand, life in the

twentieth century raised the question of how to respond to the globalization of culture, the interaction among the world's religious traditions, and
the challenges to all religious dogmas presented by science. On the other
hand, the humiliation of colonial subjugation that so many Muslims endured in the hands of Westerners fed fuel to the fire of conflict. In the
polarized climate of charges and countercharges, it became virtually impossible, in many parts of the Muslim world, to be faithful to Islam and
also tolerant of other religious faiths and scientific inquiry—much like
the Catholic church aligned itself against science and democracy in the
West during the eighteenth and nineteenth centuries.

By the end of the nineteenth century, nearly all of the Muslim world
had been conquered by European colonialism: Britain controlled the Gulf
area, Egypt, portions of Africa, India and Malaysia; France took over
North Africa and much of West Africa and the Middle East; the Soviet
Union incorporated major Muslim areas of Central Asia after the 1917
revolution.[29] During this colonial period Jamal al din Afghani (1830–1897)
and Muhammad Abduh (1849–1905) attempted to elevate the dignity of
Islamic thought and encouraged self-determination among Muslims in
the Middle East. Afghani argued that Islam was not inherently opposed
to modern science, but that European domination should not be tolerated; he encouraged the formation of a pan-Islamic federation of states.
A number of independent Muslim nation-states were created, although
at the beginning they tended to follow, rather than reject out of hand,
trends initiated by the European colonials. Ataturk (Mustafa Kemal)
founded Turkey, a secular state replacing the disintegrating Ottoman empire, in 1923. Ataturk essentially disestablished Islam in Turkey, limiting
the scope of the Shari'a to personal matters, and adopted many European
practices in government and culture.

Iran underwent a similar process, beginning in 1921 with Reza Khan,
who proclaimed himself Shah (Persian for Emperor) and set his country
on a process of modernization, despite resistance from the religious scholars, the mullahs, who had always played a significant role in governing
the country. Hasan al-Banna founded the Muslim Brotherhood in Egypt,
and the movement spread to Syria, Palestine, the Sudan, and elsewhere
in the Arab world. In South Asia, scholars such as Sayyid Ahmad Khan,
Sayyid Amir Ali, and Muhammad Iqbal participated in an Islamic intellectual revival at the turn of the century, including the founding of the
Aligarh Muslim University in India. Muhammad Ali Jinnah pressed vigorously for the formation of a separate Muslim state when India was
pushing for its independence from the British Empire, and succeeded in
getting it, despite the strenuous objections of Gandhi and others.

Sayyid Abdul Ala Maududi, a Muslim intellectual and religious leader in India and Pakistan in the early 1940s, spoke for many Muslims when he decried the moral decadence and corruption of the West. "Islam and Western civilizations are poles apart in their objects as well as in their principles of social organization," he insisted (Maududi 1979: 23). Moreover, he claimed that Islam is self-sufficient and provides a viable alternative to both Western and socialist ways of life. The Muslim Brotherhood (Jama'at-i Islami), founded in 1941, was vital under Maududi's leadership and laid the basis for an educational campaign, influencing many Muslims outside of Pakistan, including those in Europe and North America (see Cragg 1965).

Two years later, in 1949, Indonesia gained independence from the Dutch after a struggle led by Sukarno that was motivated by nationalism and Islam. Although the independent republic succumbed to military rule, Indonesia's Muslims remain a vital part of the country, which has the largest population of Muslims in the world. North and west African Muslims also gained independence during the mid-twentieth century, producing a number of Islamic states. Considerable conflict ensued, however, between the orthodox and modernist Muslims within these new nation-states, as well as struggles with external powers. Dreams of establishing a unified Islamic Brotherhood of nations has not materialized, and the difficulties of doing so are exemplified in the eight-year bloody war between Iraq and Iran, in which each side claimed to have God on its side.

The traditional alliance between Islam and the state, an alliance also enjoyed by other Western religions until very recently, has exacerbated the tensions between those wishing to make a transition to modernity and forces wanting to revive a more traditional Islamic society. The emergence of Islamic traditionalism—which some call Islamic fundamentalism—represents the orthodox camp's effort to reassert itself in the wake of Western colonialism and in the face of rapid changes in many Islamic states. Those internal conflicts have been exacerbated by continued struggles with the non-Muslim world as well, especially since the founding of the state of Israel and the intrusion of the United States after the disintegration of European control over the region. Many of the orthodox thus perceive a dual enemy attacking the sanctity of their traditions: the Western outsiders, especially the United States and Israel, and the modernizing insiders, who reduce the power of religious leaders and the Shari'a, the rule of Islamic law, in regulating society's affairs as they press for a modern, secular state.

These developments in the Muslim world have led to tremendous misunderstandings in the West along with considerable fear fueled both by misleading stereotypes in the media (see Said 1978) and popular culture, and by the visibility of life-threatening terrorist groups, sometimes operating in the name of Allah. Now for the first time these groups have launched significant attacks on targets within the United States, heretofore relatively unscathed by the Islamic struggle. The bombing of the World Trade Center in New York in the spring of 1993, and the subsequent arrests of suspected terrorists planning to bomb other key U.S. targets, has left many in that country suspicious and fearful. On the other side, the United States government, usually in league with the other major Western powers, has inflicted much violence on Islamic populations as well, having destroyed the infrastructure of Iraq during the 1991 Persian Gulf War and attacked other targets in the Arab states over the years.

When the battles escalate, religious traditions are often called into play to justify the political stance of the conflict. This practice is particularly obvious in the Islamic world, in which religious rhetoric is a more central part of the political culture than in other societies. Thus, the orthodox attack their enemies—both internal and external—with an intensity that only religious framing can justify.

Islamic reformers enrage the traditionalists. It is one thing to have infidel ideas imposed by foreigners. It may be even more outrageous to have such ideas championed by insiders, who are, in the long run—like all heretics—more dangerous than outsiders because they undermine the faith.

The case of King Amanullah of Afghanistan (1919–1929) is instructive.[30] He declared Islam to be the official religion of Afghanistan in 1923, provided the country with a written constitution, and endeared himself to many with his *jihad* against the British. In 1927, he toured India, the Middle East, and Europe, and his wife Soraya appeared unveiled at receptions in Europe, causing a scandal when her photographs circulated in Kabul. Despite resistance, Amanullah pressed forward with his efforts to reshape his Islamic society. He championed women's rights, outlawing polygamy among civil servants and permitting women to discard their veils. In October 1928, the queen led a hundred women in appearing unveiled at an official function in Kabul, outraging the religious establishment. The act was not simply a matter of women's rights, according to some; it rent the entire fabric of the sacred canopy: as one cleric declared, "When reforms come in, Islam goes out" (Hiro 1989: 234). Instead of retreating, the king escalated the conflict. In 1929, he required all Afghans in Kabul to wear Western dress, including European hats. When clerics pronounced this practice blasphemous, the king forbade students to enroll in the famous Deoband seminary. When the Hazrat of Shor Bazaar collected signatures of protest, he was arrested. At this point rioting broke out in Kabul and an insurrection ousted King Amanullah from power, despite his last-minute concessions.

The significance of this scenario lies in the role of religion and religious leaders in the debate over the ethos of Afghan society and the extent to which people were willing to allow Western influence to affect the norms and values of their culture. It was not the monarchy itself, but the king's alliance with the West and his subversion of Islamic tradition that precipitated both the popular revolt and the organized resistance of the *ulama*. Afghan traditionalism waxed and waned throughout the rest of the century, but it was almost always used as a tool to resist both modern culture and Western intervention in that society.

As the case of Amanullah suggests, one test for ethos-related conflicts between orthodox and modernist camps in the contemporary world is the role and status of women. Some highly visible and influential Islamic women insist on their equality, and many equally visible and influential Islamic men resist their efforts ferociously. The Pakistani Muslim leader Sayyid Maududi, for example, was innovative in trying to develop Islam as an alternative to Western and socialist systems, but on the issue of women he maintained a strict orthodox position. Maududi advocated strict sexual segregation and the necessity of the veil to close the "main gate," that is, the face: "nothing can be more unreasonable than to close all the minor ways to indecency but to fling the main gate wide open" (Maududi 1979: 197–198).

One reason for the intensity of these conflicts now is that the social organization of the family often represents for Muslims the last bastion of traditional Islam. During the colonial period, Muslims were forced by the colonial powers to secularize their legal system, taking power away from the Shari'a, the rule of Islamic law. The family was exempted from many of these developments, probably because it was so important to traditionalists and did not substantially affect the economic interests of the colonizers. By leaving the family under the aegis of the Shari'a, Islamic elites and the general population could be more easily persuaded to cooperate with the colonial government.

Revivalism Around the World

The Islamic world is not the only place where colonialism and modernism are challenged by efforts to revive indigenous religious practices. The prototype is Mohandas K. Gandhi's revival of Hinduism in India as part of his campaign for independence from Britain. In his famous *Hind Swaraj* (Home Rule; [1908] 1939), Gandhi denounced the corrupt influence of Western, especially British, influence on Indian culture, calling for a return to Hinduism. Gandhi successfully used the stories and rituals of several religions, but especially those of Hinduism, as a vehicle for his development of the Indian Freedom Movement.

The first major element of the Indian movement's campaign of noncooperation with British rule to protest the colonization of their country was initiated with a Day of Prayer and Fasting. "Do you mean a strike?" he was asked. "No, a Day of Prayer and Fasting," Gandhi replied. The entire country came to a standstill as people prayed and fasted. The British might try to punish people for engaging in a general strike, but how could they suppress a religious celebration? Subsequently, Gandhi used daily prayer meetings and his status as a religious holy man to press his message of Indian home rule and to mobilize the social movement that opposed British rule. Despite the fact that it was presented in an orthodox fashion, Gandhi's interpretation of Hinduism was novel. His charismatic authority was so great as leader of the Freedom Movement, however, that no one was able to challenge him directly on religious grounds.

Other colonial countries followed suit, especially after World War II, often emulating Gandhi's tactics and adapting them to their own situation. A 1947 Nigerian editorial, for example, bemoaned the invasion of Christianity and advocated a revival of traditional religion as a means of resistance.

> The native dweller in Nigeria had a religion before the advent of Christianity. His religion was perfect, and taught him the brotherhood of man and the fatherhood of God. He lived for the other man. His one sole aim was to carry sunshine and happiness into the home of his fellow man. . . . The African has a religion which, unfortunately, is fast giving place to the imported form of worship. His religion takes him closer to the Divine Presence, and enjoins him in true love for his fellow man. Hence the African has always been found a child of nature, docile and unsuspecting. This copyist attitude in all phases of his life has robbed the African of his innate godliness, and it was time our people turned to find God, to worship Him, and to serve Him in the true African way.[31]

In Latin America, Roman Catholicism was used from the beginning of the colonial period to legitimate the imposition of European rule over the indigenous people of that continent. Over the centuries, Catholicism became the core of Latin American popular culture, and people in power there used the faith's symbols and the authority of the church to maintain their hold over the masses. With the emergence of indigeneous Christian leaders in the twentieth century, however, Christianity began to legitimate movements of resistance against the power structure and was used to mobilize reform movements and even revolutionary activities.

Christian Liberation Theology

A social protest movement challenging the social status quo of the modern world—the theology of liberation—represents one of the major religious movements of the twentieth century. As with Islamic and Christian traditionalism as well as the Indian Freedom Movement, **liberation theology** frames the desire for freedom from political subjugation in a traditional religious perspective. The birth of this movement among the poor of Latin America signaled a reshaping of traditional Christian symbols in a way that some argue is truer to the spirit and teachings of Jesus and the early Christian church than is the establishment church, which legitimates an oppressive social order. A traditional reliance upon God as a personal savior—or liberator—is taken for granted by people in this movement, but the classical theological questions of modernism—Does God exist? Are the scriptures infallible? Is the pope infallible? Can a Buddhist be saved without becoming a Christian?—mean little to them. They ask instead: How can we participate in God's liberating activity in the world?

Christianity from the bottom up. Liberation theology grows, first of all, out of Latin American attempts to break out of the historical oppression of colonialism and then hierarchical systems in which a small wealthy elite is sustained in power by the United States. As Penny Lernoux (1982: 10) puts it,

> From the moment Columbus set foot in the New World cross and sword had been indistinguishable. Priests and conquistadors divided the plunder in people and land—it was a toss-up which was the greedier. And long before Latin America's military regimes installed their torture chambers the Inquisition was at work with whip and rock. By the time of the wars of independence at the beginning of the nineteenth century, the Church was the largest landowner in Latin America. It was also the most conservative political force on the continent.[32]

Other forms of liberation theology have emerged elsewhere in the Third World, especially in Africa, and among feminists, black Christians in the United States, and German philosophical theologians criticizing the middle class gospel of consumerism. Liberation theology constitutes a new paradigm in Christian theology (Chopp 1986), as well as a practical liberating activity in the *comunidades de base* ("base communities") of Latin America.

Two events in the 1960s laid the groundwork for the emergence of the liberation theology movement: the Second Vatican Council in Rome, beginning in 1962, and the Medellín Conference (CELAM II) in 1968. Vatican II, and Pope John XXIII's attempts to "open the windows" of the church, established a precedent in taking note (in *"Gaudium et Spes"* [1965] 1976) that Christians have a special responsibility for "those who are poor or in any way afflicted." This emphasis on the church's responsibility to the poor struck a chord in Latin America, where the church was deeply enmeshed in the lives of the poor. At the General Conference of the Latin American episcopacy in Medellín, Colombia, in 1968, the Roman leaders of the church contended that "the Lord's distinct commandment to 'evangelize the poor' ought to bring us to a distribution of resources and apostolic personnel that effectively gives preference to the poorest and most needy sectors" (Latin American Bishops 1979: 175).

The Medellín conference gave a green light (Berryman 1976) to the development of Christian base communities in which small groups of people—often meeting without clergy, because of a shortage of priests and Rome's relaxation of regulations after Vatican II—met throughout Latin America for prayer and Bible study, rediscovering the radical liberating message of the New Testament often lost in contemporary Christianity. This message—and the process by which it emerges from the pages of the Bible in the hands of the peasants—comes through clearly in the four volumes of *The Gospel in Solentiname*, transcripts of Bible studies led by the poet-priest Ernesto Cardenal in Nicaragua. In the discussion following their reading of Luke 4:16–30, in which Jesus announces that he has come "to give the good news to the poor," Cardenal (1976) explains, "The good news is for the poor, and the only ones who can understand it and comment on it are the poor people, not the great theologians. And it's the poor who are called to announce the news, as Jesus announced it." Similar communities emerged in other parts of the world, including Africa and Asia, although with their own local agendas and languages. In Zimbabwe before independence, people from all across the country would meet early in the morning to pray and sing and ask God for their liberation.

The preeminent figure in articulating the ideas of liberation theology was Gustavo Gutiérrez, whose *Teología de la liberación* (A Theology of Liberation, 1973) served as a manifesto for the movement. Bridging the gap between the church hierarchy and the base communities that flourished in the slums,[33] Gutiérrez's theological reflections were amplified by such figures as Camilo Torres from Colombia (who studied sociology at Louvain, where he was a classmate of Gutiérrez's), and Dom Hélder Camara in Brazil.

Ironically, the initial ecclesiastical actions that led to the liberation theology movement grew out of conservative efforts to defend the institutional interests of the Roman Catholic Church in the face of Marxist and other left-wing critics (Adriance 1992). Moreover, the practical measure of forming base communities in the wake of Vatican II reforms and a shortage of priests cultivated the growth of base communities among the poor, which unexpectedly resulted in a movement that gradually sought some independence from the church hierarchy. Adriance's examination of developments in Brazil and Chile "provide illustrations of the paradox of institutionalization. They show how measures taken by some bishops to restore the church's influence in the context of a secularized, pluralistic society unleashed a potential for social and ecclesial change that may prove to be more radical than the bishops had ever intended" (1992: 60).

The Vatican found the liberation theology movement a highly disturbing phenomenon, in part because of its independence, not only from the political establishment, but also from the ecclesiastical one. The Polish Pope John Paul II was also concerned about its links with Marxism, because in his experience Marxism was more the oppressor than the liberator. When the pope visited Nicaragua in 1983, he shook his finger at Father Cardenal, who was Minister of Culture in the new communist Sandinista government, and scolded him for his political involvement.

Liberation theology had many critics in the church because it was too politicized, too Marxist, and sometimes advocated violence. It also had many supporters at high levels and represented one of the fastest growing-sectors of the church, and so the movement was difficult to suppress. As with Islamic and Christian traditionalism, liberation theology provided a vehicle for discontented people to express their protest and try to change the world around them. A similar, and in some ways more successful, movement for change with a religious base occurred in recent nonviolent movements in Asia and Europe, where the church played a key role in organizing resistance against various dictatorships.

A theology of "nonpersons." Although not always articulated by the poor,[34] liberation theology is a perspective of and from the poor, or as Gutiérrez puts it, "nonpersons"—that is, the people who are ignored to the extent that they do not even exist for people in power. Erving Goffman (1959) explains the dynamics of this role in social life in the example of the servant, who is a convenient "nonperson" to have around but does not exist for social interaction and is treated as less than human. In the most extreme instances, a "nonperson" in the role of a servant sleeps in the master's bedroom as part of the furniture in case anything is needed during the night. Most of us find ourselves in this role, to a lesser extent, when people of power and privilege simply ignore our presence.

Entire classes of people are nearly invisible to the mainstream, and especially to the elites, of most modern cultures. The invisibility phenomenon enables the rich to cope psychologically with the existence of mass poverty and starvation in their environment. In India, the millions of people living in abject poverty on the street are simply screened out of existence by the middle and upper classes, who go about their daily routines pretending that they do not exist. The number of people who live in such dire poverty that they scarcely live at all is so enormous that we ignore their existence in order to enjoy our own lives. Even the news media, which usually focus on problematic aspects of human life, manage to ignore what is certainly one of the most significant stories about our world every day: that is, that roughly 40,000 children die each day of malnutrition and related causes, and a similar number are permanently damaged each day by the same state.

Since the 1960s, the world has witnessed what Gutiérrez calls an "eruption of the poor."[35] Religious thinking grows out of the social context in which the thinker lives; liberation theology constitutes a form of reflection on the nature of the sacred from the point of view of those who suffer, from those who constitute the majority of the world's population at the end of this century (see Chopp 1986). Sociologically, we expect "nonpersons" to view the world differently, of course, from people in other social roles, and to have affinities with different religious expressions from those of the rich. Gandhi said that God should appear to the poor in the form of bread. Liberation theology recovers the perspective of the poor from the Judeo-Christian tradition, a rich and deep element that has been conveniently subordinated by the alliance between the church and the Western establishment.

Civil Religion and Nationalism

Every airplane of the aggressors in the Iraqi skies should be a target for you, and you fight in the name of God, and you shall down these aircraft. God is great, God is great, God is great. And the aggressors will be thwarted and defeated. God give us victory, and peace and the blessings of God may be upon you. —President Saddam Hussein, January 1991

If the Lord is our light, our strength and our salvation, whom shall we fear, of whom shall we be afraid? No matter where we live, we have a promise that can make all the difference—a promise from Jesus to soothe our sorrows, heal our hearts, and drive away our fears. He promised there will never be a dark night that does not end. . . . And by dying for us, Jesus showed how far our love should be ready to go: all the way. —President Ronald Reagan, February 1984

Along with the revitalization of ancient traditions in the form of traditionalism and various religious revivals and reformulations of religious traditions, a number of new religious forms have emerged as a response to modernism. These forms include civil religions and syncretic religious movements that draw upon elective affinities between the interests of particular groups of people and the interaction among various religious traditions and secular forces.

One of the most significant forms of quasireligion in the twentieth century has grown out of the social organization of the nation-state, which often replaces traditional religious institutions as a focus of identity and basis of the cultural ethos. This significant element of political culture, especially in modern nation-states, is usually called **civil religion**, a concept developed by Jean Jacques Rousseau ([1762] 1901) and Alexis de Tocqueville ([1862] 1945) that is congruent with Emile Durkheim's understanding of the role of religion in collective life. The growth of civil religion has been widespread primarily for two reasons: (1) to provide cultural unity among a set of pluralistic belief systems created by population migration or artificially constructed states (usually established by colonial powers); and (2) as a functional substitute for a religious tradition that was deliberately attacked because of its alliance with the old order (especially in the socialist states).

American society provides a particularly instructive model of civil religion because of the parallels between the multicultural U.S. society and the emerging pluralistic world system. Many of the struggles faced first by Western Europe, and then the United States, as they moved into the heterogeneity of the modern world are now encountered in other countries, even when the paths and contents of cultural transformation have been substantially different.

Civil Religion: The American Case

Civil religion in the United States, though still highly Christian in its tone and basic beliefs, is a general religious orientation that emphasizes belief in a generic God and a specific role for the United States of America in world history. Robert Bellah is the sociologist who has applied the notion of civil religion most thoroughly to the U.S. context:

> Behind the civil religion at every point lie biblical archetypes: Exodus, Chosen People, Promised Land, New Jerusalem, and Sacrificial Death and Rebirth. But it is also genuinely American and genuinely new. It has its own prophets and its own martyrs, its own sacred events and sacred places, its own solemn rituals and symbols. (1970: 186)

Gehrig concludes that civil religion in the United States is "the religious symbol system which relates the citizen's role and the American society's place in space, time, and history to the conditions of ultimate existence and meaning"; it is differentiated structurally from the political and religious communities of the U.S., and performs "specialized religious functions performed by neither church nor state" (1981: 108).

Generic religious images and rituals are frequently evoked to underscore the sacredness of U.S. tradition and culture, practices that reflect the ambivalent and tenuous framing of religion in American political culture: "In God We Trust" is inscribed on the currency, but the referent is deliberately ambiguous. Every presidential inaugural address, except George Washington's second one, includes references to God. In the 1950s, the phrase "one nation under God" was added to the pledge of allegiance, which is recited in most public schools around the country. In the 1980s, Ronald Reagan's unprecedented Christian rhetoric broke traditional rules about the relationship between politics and religion because of his specific references to Jesus.

Civic rituals in the United States have a strong religious flavor. The major holidays in the American liturgical calendar unite religion and political culture, if not church and state:

> Thanksgiving is at the core of the practice, with its explicit link between the "status legend" (as Weber might call it) of the country's founding and the deity of American civil religion.

> The period around "Christmas," now sometimes generically referred to as "the holidays," embracing Christmas and New Year, and in recent years an adopted holiday of Chanukah.

> Martin Luther King, Jr.'s birthday, a recent addition for the purpose of inclusivity, celebrates a Christian pastor's contribution to national political life.

> Memorial Day links the nation's wars with the deity.

> July 4th is explicitly a secular holiday, but God's name is often invoked in official ceremonies.

Hammond summarizes the ideology behind the peculiar alliance between the state and religion in the United States as follows: "(1) There is a God (2) whose will can be known through democratic procedures; therefore (3) democratic America has been God's primary agent in history, and (4) for Americans the nation has been their chief source of identity" (1980: 41–42). This ideology is multifaceted: on one hand, it has been a useful cultural tool for uniting people from diverse backgrounds into a single body politic; aspects of the civil theology facilitated a critique of slavery in the eighteenth century and legitimated the civil rights movement in the nineteenth (see Bellah 1975). On the other hand, civil religion in the United States has cultivated hegemonic ambitions and a sense of religious superiority that has legitimated some of America's worst episodes of adventurism, from the earlier doctrine of "Manifest Destiny" which justified in retrospect the genocide of the people living in the New World before the Europeans arrived to more recent efforts to police the world with the American military.

Debates about Bellah's characterization of American civil religion all reflect the problem of collective religious ideas in a pluralistic society so characteristic of both U.S. culture and the global village. Richard K. Fenn (1972, 1974, 1976) developed a series of critiques, the core of which resurfaced on a broader scale with Stephen Warner's (1993) important proposal for a new paradigm for the study of religion in American society in which the metaphor of the marketplace replaces that of the sacred canopy. Fenn contended that because cultural integration is impossible in modern societies, civil religion is a useless concept. It is probably more accurate to say that cultural integration is a necessary but extremely difficult process in diverse societies and that the idea of a broad civil religion that lacks any sectarian character but still aids the construction of a collective identity is one important response to the dilemmas of multiculturalism.

Civil Religion in the Global Village

Political elites attempting to achieve national consensus will, of course, find some form of civil religion, or its functional equivalent, desirable to give legitimacy and (at least the appearance of) higher purpose to the political order. The more diverse the citizenry, the more difficult it is to suspend a sacred canopy across the state. Independent India, for example, has had great difficulty developing a secular state that embraces Hindus, Muslims, Sikhs, and Jains because questions of religion and politics are always intertwined. Efforts to use Mahatma Gandhi, the universally acknowledged "father of the country," as a figurehead have sometimes backfired because Gandhi, despite his own universalistic approach to religious belief, alienated large portions of the Muslim and Sikh communities because he employed Hindu rhetoric and symbols in his public presentations (although he also included symbols from many faiths, including Muslim, Sikh, and Christian as well as Hindu).

Like Western Europe following the French Revolution, twentieth-century communist countries attempted to replace traditional religious forms with new versions, not always successfully. Civic rituals in the Soviet Union looked remarkably like Russian Orthodox ones, with some new content. The public processions of Party and military looked much like ancient religious processions, and the celebrated saints of Christianity were replaced with Saints Marx and Lenin. Every winter people put up elaborately decorated "New Year's trees," exchanged gifts, and even received visits from a gift-bearing white-bearded man in a red suit named "Father Frost." Meanwhile opposition movements throughout the Soviet bloc were supported in significant ways by both the ideologies and the institutions of the Christian church. Religious organizations provided a space for organizing alternative institutions and resistance movements, training workshops in nonviolent workshops, and a general legitimacy within the larger population.

In China, efforts to replace Confucianism, Taoism, and Buddhism with Maoism were only partially successful. Because diverse religious beliefs have lived together in relatively peaceful coexistence in Chinese culture over the centuries, many people simply add Mao to the pantheon, or at least worship him in public and their traditional gods at home. Buddhist religious officials, with a long history of negotiating with Chinese political elites, discussed affinities between Buddhism and Marxism.

The Republic of China (Taiwan) presents an interesting case, because the nationalist leader Chiang Kai Shek was a Christian, as were many of his followers (converted and educated by missionaries). When the government fled to Taiwan from the mainland in 1949, it tried to suppress "superstitious" Chinese folk religions but allowed free worship of Confucianism and Buddhism, which place relatively little emphasis on transcendental theology and have traditionally promoted public order in Chinese culture. Because K'ung Fu tzu is regarded more as a philosopher and founder of Chinese social and political thought than as a god, the conflicts do not seem so sharp. Confucian temples are maintained by the state and are the site of major celebrations every year at K'ung Fu tzu's birthday, when he is honored—not so much as a god, but as the "Great Teacher"—by government officials and the general public.

Efforts to create civil religions within and among national societies are now complicated by intercultural conflicts almost everywhere, even in places where new states have been carved out more or less on the basis of ethnic identities—such as Pakistan and Israel—because of persisting internal diversity and, more importantly, because no nation lives in isolation and the dilemmas of multiculturalism cannot be avoided.

Religious Syncretism and Alternative Religious Movements

In the new context of multiculturalism we witness the revival of a venerable phenomenon in the history of the world's religions: religious **syncretism**, that is, the combination of elements from more than one religious tradition to weave a new sacred canopy that competes in the cultural marketplace. All the world's religions were created over the centuries through processes of intercultural conflict, amalgamation, and creative synthesis. The current religious scene presents a dynamic interplay between traditional practices on one hand and widespread transplanting of traditions and experiments with syncretism on the other.

Vast movements of migration and the creation of modern means of communication and transportation have increased the tempo of syncretism in the late twentieth century, now occurring on an unprecedented scale. New versions of old traditions emerge as alternatives to mainstream culture in contexts where the tradition has been dominant, as well as in new settings where a religious movement is transplanted. The potential for conflict between established and alternative religious communities is thereby greatly increased, posing a significant social problem for the global village.

The Sociology of Alternative Religious Movements

Conflict between religious movements and the religious and social establishment is not a new theme, nor is it a marginal one. It is an age-old story about the relationship between religious expression and the social order, between heresy and orthodoxy. Most religious movements—including those which now constitute the mainstream—begin as small, intense rebel groups at odds with the religious and political establishments of their own origins. Early Christians, for example, were in constant conflict with authorities: Jesus was executed by Rome after complaints by the local religious establishment, and many of his disciples were also put to death. New religious movements tend to attract primarily people who perceive themselves as marginal or opposed to the dominant society and its value system (Glock and Bellah 1976). Consequently, some form of tension between these movements and the larger society they inhabit is inevitable.

This section will examine briefly some alternative religious movements and traditions. By alternative movements, I mean those religious groups outside the mainstream popularly called "cults," although sociologists sometimes refer to them as **new religious movements** (NRMs) to avoid the negative connotations of the popular term. We will adopt the term NRM in this discussion, though reluctantly, because it is something of a misnomer; "there is nothing new under the sun," to quote Ecclesiastes. Some NRMs are imported versions of ancient religious perspectives from the other side of the global village; others are new interpretations of ancient indigenous religions. In this sense, North American religious life offers a microcosm of the broader processes taking place on the planet; and the experiments have had mixed results.

New Religions in the United States

The history of religious life in the United States is a story of ongoing struggles among various religious communities to coexist within the same polity and geographic area. What is so interesting sociologically about the U.S. case is that it foreshadows many aspects of the process the entire global village is now experiencing. Because of the diversity of religious groups in the New World from the very beginning of American colonial history, a variety of faith communities—some of them with highly incompatible worldviews—have been required to forge a working relationship with each other.

Religious diversity has been normative in U.S. history from the beginning, but the cultural ferment of the 1960s and the waves of new immigrants from various parts of the world in recent decades have precipitated an explosion of new religious movements in the United States. The degree of multiculturalism has never been so high in American culture, especially with the introduction of large numbers of Asian immigrants in the late twentieth century as a consequence of the relaxation of immigration laws against them. Although the American religious landscape has always been diverse, this large influx of people from the Far East made a dramatic difference in the number of non-Christian believers living in the United States.

We can make three related sociological observations about the alternative religious movements of late-twentieth-century American life:

1. Not all religious movements are alike, and they cannot accurately be classed together under the single label "cults" to distinguish them from "legitimate religions."

2. The appearance of large numbers of new religious movements around the world in recent decades reflects ongoing globalization processes: the "anticult" movement is often a protest against those changes, sometimes from an ethnocentric point of view.

3. Those characteristics of NRMs that people most detest are as much a consequence of social hostility toward them as properties inherent in the movements themselves.

Let's examine each of these observations more closely.

Not All "Cults" Are Alike

Alternative religious movements are remarkably diverse in their beliefs and rituals, organization, membership, relationship to the broader society, and virtually any other dimension, with one exception: most are forged in deliberate contrast to existing mainstream religious groups in the culture or as a subgroup within these groups.

The original meaning of the term *cult* comes from the Latin *cultus*, "care" or "adoration." It also refers to formal religious veneration, worship, or a system of religious beliefs, or its rituals. More recently, the term has taken on a third meaning; as Webster's puts it, "a religion regarded as unorthodox or spurious" (1979: 274). In its latest sense, the idea of a cult, at least in American popular culture, has absorbed a range of negative images that include brainwashing, fanaticism, mind control, and so on. (See Table 6.1.)

Asian and countercultural movements. The most significant group of NRMs in the United States are imported from Asia and derive especially from Buddhist and Hindu traditions. Like other NRMs, the Asian movements were transported through two different routes: (1) immigrants from the region bringing their own native religious beliefs and practices with them, and (2) indigenous countercultural movements that emerged, especially in the 1960s. These two distinct groups of practitioners are sometimes in conflict with one another: while the immigrants are busy attempting to assimilate to their new environment, counterculture participants are attempting to jettison the American cultural milieu they are rejecting. Thus, any embarrassment that immigrant groups have

TABLE 6.1

Major Religious Movements in the U.S.

	Movement Name	Roots	Major Figure	Doctrines, practices
Mormon	Latter Day Saints	Christian	Joseph Smith	Restoration of Christianity
Communal/ Counter- cultural	The Farm			
Asian	Zen Buddhism	Buddhist	Gautama Buddha	Meditation school; parables
	Yoga	Hindu/ Buddhist		
	Transcendental Meditation	Hindu/ Buddhist	Maharishi Mahesh Yoga	Meditation to improve clarity
	Krishna Consciousness	Hindu	A. C. Bhaktivedanta	Bhagavad Gita
	Divine Light Mission	Hindu	Maharaj Ji	New incarnation of God
	Unification Church	Syncretic	Sun Myung Moon	New incarnation of God; anti-communist, ascetic

Feminist	WICCA (Witchcraft)	Syncretic		Feminism, Goddess worship
Neo-Christian	Christian World Liberation Front ("Jesus Freaks")	Christian		Radical counterculture Christian
	Children of God	Christian		Counterculture Christian
	Campus Crusade	Christian		Evangelical Christian
	Jews for Jesus	Judeo-Christian		Converted Christian
New Thought	Christian Scientist	Christian	Mary Baker Eddy	Healing through positive attitudes
Psychic/ New Age/ Personal Growth	EST	Asian/syncretic	Werner Erhard	Sensitivity training
	Scientology	Syncretic	L. Ron Hubbard	Auditing of past lives
	Synanon		Charles Dederich	Substance abuse therapy
Neopagan	Satanism	Pagan	Anton Szandor LaVey	Magic, hedonism

Sources: Glock and Bellah (1976); Wuthnow (1976); Bromley and Shupe (1981).

about their religion is exacerbated by having it embraced by people who criticize the new culture to which the immigrants are trying to adapt.

Buddhist groups in the United States, especially the Zen and Pure Land schools, most commonly have Japanese origins. Zen Buddhism was a particular favorite of the 1960s counterculture movements because of its spontaneity and its thoroughgoing challenge of Western utilitarian rationality and materialism. The Beat generation of the 1950s set the stage for its introduction, with such writers as Jack Kerouac (with his novels such as *On the Road* and *The Dharma Bums*) and Gary Snyder making the precepts of Buddhism familiar to a large American audience. The counterculture of the next decade provided a fertile soil for both Buddhism and Hinduism, demonstrating

> a clear affinity between the pure self-determinist notion of the hippie movement and the law of karma as stated in Buddhism. Despite a present shaped by past actions, freedom of action in each new moment persists, enabling the practitioner to claim complete responsibility for, and control over, the future, religiously and otherwise. Further, the practitioner is enjoined not to look outside of himself to any agency of control such as God. (Prebish 1978: 162)

The association between Asian religions and the American counterculture had mixed consequences for the Buddhist tradition: on the one hand, Asian traditions flourished as an outlet for disgruntled Americans, especially young people, and they received a great deal of attention. On the other hand, versions of Hinduism and Buddhism arrived on the U.S. scene in a variety of popular forms, often substantially modified from their Asian roots, and focused on a critique of American culture rather than on developing a true religious vision (see Johnson 1976: 48). Yoga classes were given on television and techniques of yoga were sold as a form of self-therapy as well as consciousness expansion and relaxation.

Many Indians who were gurus in the Yogic tradition—such as Yogi Bhajan of the Happy Holy Organization; and Swami Satchidananda, who performed at Woodstock; Swami Vishnudevananda of the International Sivananda Yoga and Vedanta Society; and the Maharishi Mahesh Yoga, with whom the rock group the Beatles associated—came to America with their message. Transcendental Meditation, a particular technique of Yoga promoted by Maharishi Mahesh Yoga, became very popular; by 1975, half a million people had taken his courses.

The International Society for Krishna Consciousness (ISKCON) was founded in 1966 by A. C. Bhaktivedanta, who had been an active Krishna devotee in India before going to New York in 1965. The movement flourished in San Francisco in the 1970s, claiming 10,000 members (half of them in the U.S.) and 200 centers and communities worldwide (Rochford 1985). Bhaktivedanta believed that the world was near the end of the materialistic age of Kali-Yuga, the last cycle of a four-cycle millennium. If the populace could be aroused, a new age of peace, love, and unity would be discovered. With an interesting twist of irony, Western counter-culture and modern mass culture technology together created a wide-spread dissemination of ancient Hindu and Buddhist ideas. When the Beatle George Harrison praised Hare Krishna in his songs, millions of American teenagers had their first positive encounter with Hinduism.

Satguru Maharaj Ji, a young Indian with some 5 million followers (including at least 80,000 Americans), was believed to be an incarnation of God (see Messer 1976). He established the Divine Light Mission, which maintains households (*ashrams*) throughout the world for devotees who work full time for the movement. When she studied the group, Jeanne Messer (1976: 58) found that the guru was often identified within the movement as Christ, despite the Hindu form of his religious rhetoric and rituals: initiates are often told that "Guru Maharaj Ji is Christ, that Christ has been on the earth many times as Jesus, as Buddha, as Mohammed, as Krishna, or that Christ has always been on the earth."

One of the most popular—and widely studied—movements with Asian roots is the Unification Church (see Bromley, Shupe, and Ventimiglia 1979), whose members are nicknamed the "Moonies" because their leader is a Korean minister named the Reverend Sun Myung Moon. Reverend Moon's followers consider him a manifestation of God and incorporate a number of Korean traditions, from a virulent anticommunism to arranged marriages. Followers of the church's ascetic practices are active in many parts of the world. A number of profitable businesses supporting their activities have become the subject of continued investigation by the U.S. Internal Revenue Service, which may be a form of official harassment.

Another successful group drawing widely on Asian religions is Scientology, which claims 5 to 6 million members. This movement, founded by L. Ron Hubbard, combines Buddhist, Hindu, Taoist, and Christian ideas along with principles of psychoanalysis and business administration, and has been the subject of much controversy and the object of numerous attacks by U.S. officials and mainstream cultural elites. Scientology features a brand of psychotherapeutic technique called "auditing" that adherents claim helps one to free oneself not only of the burden of painful memories of early childhood, as in psychoanalysis, but also those stored away from past lives.

Goddess worship. Whereas Asian religions have been used as a framework for much countercultural resistance in American culture, a number of feminist movements have turned to so-called pagan religions and witch-craft as a way of embodying their discontent with the patriarchal struc-ture and content of the dominant religions.

What Mary Jo Neitz calls the **Goddess movement** encompasses a vari-ety of countercultural groups that, although they have "no unifying or-ganization, written scriptures, or dogma, no defining ritual practice," be-long to two intersecting currents: neopaganism and feminism. The neopagan movement revived witchcraft in the countercultural ferment of the 1960s, drawing upon pre-Christian Celtic folk religions from ancient Europe. The term *witch* is used deliberately, in spite of (or because of) its negative connotations, because participants in the Goddess movement are protesting the sexism of their culture.

Witches organize in *covens,* small grassroots women's circles that focus on bonding and empowering one another as women (although some neo-pagan circles include men as well). When witches gather, they draw syn-cretically upon ancient rituals of religions from what Eisler (1988) calls the "partnership" societies of ancient Europe, and new rituals that in-clude one reported by Neitz in which women sit in a circle and give their names and the names of their matrilineal ancestors as far back as they can go. The participants quickly realize that the patrilineal naming prac-tices have caused them to lose even the names of their foremothers. God-dess movement participants have experimented with the use of dance and music to tap the energy of the religious spirit.

Goddess worship is an interesting phenomenon that many North Americans find threatening because it represents a deliberate rebellion against the Christian cultural mainstream. Long a source of denigration by Western patriarchal culture, witchcraft calls up images of devil wor-ship and black magic in the minds of many. For feminist witches, how-ever, the Goddess is "a symbol for the empowerment of women" (Neitz 1990: 353) and provides a vehicle for creating an alternative social space within the patriarchal culture. Some witches have emphasized the more generally accepted positive characteristics of the Goddess image, how-ever, interpreting her as "an archetypal figure based in the early human experience of nurturance from a mother" (Neitz 1990: 356). In that sense, the witches share much in the tenor of their religious movement with other Goddess movements around the world, including Chinese and In-dian folk religions and, in a less obvious way, with the cult of the Virgin Mary that has permeated a broad spectrum of the Christian church.

Because of its deliberately rebellious spirit and negative image in the mainstream culture, Goddess movement participants have often faced considerable opposition. In a recent series of events in Jonesboro, Arkansas, Terry and Amanda Riley were forced to close their shop, the Magick Moon, which sold books on witchcraft, incense, wands, and cauldrons. Area merchants banded together to prevent the two from finding another location. When asked by a *Newsweek* reporter about protecting their religious freedom, one local resident replied that he naturally supported religious freedom, but the Rileys did not have a religion (Shapiro 1993).

According to Carol Christ, a feminist theologian involved in the movement, the contemporary Goddess movement in North America "is the acknowledgement of the legitimacy of female power as a beneficent and independent power" (Christ 1987: 121).

Neo-Christian and charismatic movements. Some rebels against contemporary American culture turn not to ancient pagan rituals or Eastern religions, but to aspects of the diverse Christian tradition not normally emphasized by the religious mainstream. In the 1960s, a number of such movements, such as the Christian World Liberation Front, an outgrowth of the "Jesus Movement," or "Jesus Freaks," as they were sometimes called, emerged as part of the youth counterculture. Their leftist political orientation appealed to campus radicals in Berkeley, but these movements were opposed to Marxism and were somewhat introverted, so did not attempt aggressively to recruit new members.

A related movement called themselves the "Submarine Church," after the Beatles song and movie *The Yellow Submarine,* because they considered themselves a Christian community that went underwater, not underground; they emphasized the idea of a radical faith community that challenged the establishment and championed the poor much like the early church. When the United Methodist Church held its quadrennial conference in St. Louis in 1972, the Submarine Church was there as well. At the major local church downtown on the day the conference convened, as a number of international dignitaries were gathered for worship, members of the Submarine Church unfurled a banner from the balcony with a bright yellow submarine and a cross on it. One of the members stood up from the floor just as the worship service began to make a "testimony" of concern about the poor people living in the neighborhood of the church. As he was arrested and escorted from the sanctuary, a number of people in the congregation stood up to voice their protest against the arrest; they too were taken off to jail. (Two Methodist bishops later visited the police station and negotiated their release, and all charges were eventually dropped by the church.)

Other new Christian groups had a more conservative message but also represented a counterculture movement within the church. One of these was Campus Crusade, a popular evangelical movement that appealed to a different audience from the other groups mentioned thus far, but differed from mainline Christian campus ministries in aggressive recruiting methods and sectarian organizations. A fast-growing and vital alternative Christian group is the **charismatic movement**, which swept the United States and many other parts of the world. This movement protests the formality and "dryness" of contemporary establishment Christianity and emphasizes so-called "gifts of the Spirit" (see Neitz 1987). Although originating in Protestant churches, the charismatic movement became very popular in the American Catholic church following the Second Vatican Council. In 1966 faculty members at Duquesne University in Pittsburgh began meeting regularly to pray for these "gifts," which included "speaking in tongues," or glosalalia, vocalizations that are linguistically unintelligible despite recognizable phonetic features (Lane 1976) that seem to express intense religious experiences. The Catholic Pentecostal movement, or Catholic Charismatic Renewal as it was later called, spread quickly; at their first annual convention in 1967, ninety persons came; five years later, ten thousand attended, and the following year more than twenty thousand.

The charismatic movement has touched a deep chord in contemporary popular culture, "a concern that the world is falling apart," as Mary Jo Neitz put it in her ethnographic study of a Catholic charismatic group. "Yet the problems on which their actions focus are overwhelmingly personal, with concern for protecting oneself and one's family" (1987: 232). The intense community of the movement and the idea of a powerful personal relationship with Jesus has provided an important source of support for thousands of people living tenuously in the postmodern world.

Who participates? Glock and Bellah's (1976) study of new religious movements in the San Francisco area gives an informative portrait of participants and groups in the major center of cultural ferment at a significant time, the early 1970s. Robert Wuthnow's (1976) contribution to that study identifies three broad categories of movements: (1) *countercultural* movements that provide an alternative to mainstream American culture (e.g., Zen Buddhism, Yoga, Transcendental Meditation, Hare Krishna), (2) *personal growth* movements that combine religious practices with psychology and an emphasis on personal development (EST, Synanon), and (3) *neo-Christian* movements that are sectarian in nature and draw upon the

Christian tradition to create an alternative, usually sectarian, Christian community (such as Campus Crusade, Jews for Jesus, Children of God, and the Christian World Liberation Front).

The countercultural movements tend to overselect young people, with slightly higher than average educational levels. Not surprisingly, they are likely to reinforce values and lifestyles that contrast sharply with convention. Participants in all groups (but especially the countercultural) are more likely to be single and employed part time or looking for work, and more geographically unsettled than the general population. Counterculture movements appear to be stronger than their small numbers would indicate because they attract better-educated people and consequently have greater influence. The movements in general may continue to find a more responsive chord among the young, the educated, and those interested in more general forms of cultural and societal transformation.

"Networks of faith." Sociologists usually emphasize what Rodney Stark and William Bainbridge (1980) call **networks of faith** in explaining why people join religious groups, whether more conventional, mainstream groups, or the unconventional groups under discussion here. Two slightly different emphases emerge in the literature: (1) on the appeal of the ideology of various groups and the needs of those who join them, and (2) on the importance of interpersonal relations. The latter position contends that membership spreads through social networks and that people adjust their religious beliefs to conform to those of people who are important to them.[36] Stark and Bainbridge (1980) provide evidence from studies of three groups (a doomsday group, an Ananda commune, and the Mormon church) for the importance of social networks in recruitment to both types of NRMs. They conclude that a sense of deprivation (e.g., social isolation, people with a grievance of some sort, etc.) and ideological compatibility "limit the pool of persons available for recruitment," but since many people are deprived and ideologically predisposed to cult membership but do not join, a number of situational variables must be explored to explain why some do and others do not.

The number of new religious groups in the United States jumped dramatically between 1950 and 1970: that is the period in which the U.S. became fully integrated into the world economy, large numbers of immigrants came to the country, tourist travel flourished, and television brought the far corners of the globe into the nation's homes. Moreover, many Americans became disenchanted with their own cultural milieu and religious traditions. The same impulse that led to the hippie movement, the New Left, and the civil rights and antiwar movements of the 1960s influenced many to search for alternative religious communities in which to pursue their spiritual quests.

The institutional and technological infrastructure facilitating the spread of NRMs, including cable television and video technologies, developed dramatically in the 1970s and 1980s. The International Society for Krishna Consciousness, ISKCON, for example, developed its own network of print and video newsmagazines, and ISKCON TV began producing instructional videos with lectures from Swami Bhaktivedanta and reports on ISKCON activities around the globe. Distant religious practices no longer appeared so foreign, and as young people rebelled against their own culture and their parents' values and religious traditions, large numbers of Western youth sought spiritual and social support in these alternative communities. In some instances, religious traditions from other parts of the world provided a significant alternative to the conventional (mostly Christian) traditions of their families.

Finally, Stark and Bainbridge (1980: 1393) conclude that potential recruits must receive *direct rewards* from their participation if they are likely to join a movement. Although the affection of the movement network is often an important factor—especially for people who suffer from isolation and low self-esteem—successful groups also include other rewards. The Hare Krishnas and Moonies often provide food, clothing, and shelter as well as a meaningful occupation with potential for advancement within the organization. The Mormons have a thirteen-step recruiting plan that showers potential new members with tangible rewards.

Contemporary empirical research on reasons for joining NRMs does not advance us theoretically much beyond Max Weber's concept of elective affinities between ideas and interests, although it does spell out the nature of the relationship in more detail. People tend to join a new religious movement primarily for social reasons, adopting first the ethos of a group, and gradually accepting its worldview as well. Most people, of course, choose the religious tradition of their families and other immediately relevant social groups. In the global village, however, switching may become more common. The role of elective affinities in the conversion process can be seen quite clearly within some social groups, which, as they undergo dramatic transformation, construct an ethos and worldview they feel a stronger affinity for than those traditionally available to them in their social situation.

In the late twentieth century, the number of new religious movements in the United States has skyrocketed, in part because of unprecedented new immigration of ethnic groups from parts of the world where Christianity did not predominate (such as Asia), but also because of the cultural upheaval of the 1960s, in which—as we have just seen—many, especially young people, turned to alternative forms of religious expression as part of the counterculture movement. In the first decade of the twentieth century, only eleven new religious groups had formed in the United States. In the 1960s, 105 new communities were founded; in the 1970s, 177 (see Hinnells 1984). The only time the trend was reversed during the century was during World War II, which fostered a climate that discouraged cultural experimentation. When the global economy emerged in the postwar world, social networks expanded and cultural patterns were widely disrupted and reformed. The most obvious reason for the birth of new religious movements anywhere in the world is that people live increasingly in a global context. People living in a heterogeneous culture generally have more freedom of choice and more religious options in the religious marketplace.

Cult and Anticult

Many Americans find alternative religious communities repulsive and threatening, and the negative label *cult* is popularly used to refer to all of them. Some of the reasons for this criticism are quite valid: many horrible things are done in the name of these new religious movements, just as much evil has been committed in the name of every one of the more established religious communities. People also object to new religious movements because they are different, intense, authoritarian, and often cause family members and friends to break with kin and friendship networks, much to the dismay of those left behind. Finally, a great deal of misinformation is spread about alternative religious groups by those who are critical of them.

Ironically, the anticult movement that emerged in the wake of the proliferation of religious movements in the 1960s has often exacerbated the very characteristics that trouble many people about the NRMs in the first place. Under attack by the outside, participants in alternative religious communities become more alienated from the external world and consequently more amenable to authoritarian structures and leadership.

Brainwashing and deprogramming. As NRMs attracted widespread attention in the 1970s, the anticult movement became increasingly aggressive in its opposition. A major source of the movement was the hostility and fear from family members of converts who felt abandoned, sometimes under stressful conditions. A network of anticult movement organizations mounted a campaign against the NRMs and clashed with the elites of these groups, creating what Bromley and Shupe (1981) call a "social scare," that is,

> (1) a sociocultural climate characterized by heightened tension as a result of (2) intense conflict between two (or more) social groups in which (3) the more powerful group mobilizes control claims by (4) denigrating the moral status of the less powerful groups through (5) construction of a subversion mythology. (Bromley 1988a: 186)

The key element in the "subversion mythology" constructed about NRMs was the idea of brainwashing—that individual recruits had been robbed of their free will through mind control techniques.[37] The anticult movement focused on Reverend Moon's Unification Church because of its visibility, aggressive recruitment of young adults, direct challenge of the authority of traditional churches, and provision of a single target on which to concentrate its efforts most effectively (Bromley 1988: 188–189).

The most remarkable part of the campaign was the creation of what anticult activist Ted Patrick (1976) called the **deprogramming** process, intended to help "victims" snap out of the hypnotic trance into which cult members were supposedly put by the brainwashing process. In the process, NRM members were kidnapped, taken to a secluded location (such as a hotel room), and subjected to various techniques, including eliciting

> guilt for rejecting family members and educational plans, expressing love and concern about the dubious future the individual had charted, refuting the group's doctrines, revealing esoteric beliefs and practices that were not known to the individual, challenging the motives and sincerity of the group's leaders, providing testimonials by former members that they had been brainwashed but failed to recognize their own psychological captivity, and threatening that the individual would be released only on the condition that membership in the group was renounced. (Patrick 1976: 194)

Although deprogramming incidents involved varying degrees of coerciveness, these anticult tactics raise many questions about the reality of religious freedom in the United States. Bromley contends: "The practice of forcibly separating individuals from religious groups for the purpose of inducing them to renounce their membership is unprecedented in American religious history" (1988a: 203). The extreme measures of deprogramming were given justification by the mythology of brainwashing and supported by much of the general public. The news media in the United States further legitimated deprogramming and other attacks on the movements by disseminating "atrocity tales" about NRMs (Bromley, Shupe, and Ventimiglia 1979). By evoking outrage at the alleged acts of religious groups, newspaper accounts facilitated the "social construction of evil" about these religious movements.

In their study of 190 newspaper articles about former members of the Unification Church between 1974 and 1977, Bromley and colleagues (1979) found that all but two contained at least one atrocity story and were primarily hostile toward the church. The most frequently reported atrocities were:

1. *Psychological violations of personal freedom and autonomy.*
2. *Economic violations*: reports that the church forced members to sell their private property and give it to the church.
3. *Severing of the parent-child bond*: the most sensational of the reports, growing out of the hostility of families who were rejected by members joining NRMs.
4. *Political and legal atrocities*: stemming from the fact that the church was founded and run by a foreigner.

Although there was an element of truth in many of these stories, the point is that these problems are present in many other organizations and the kind of coverage provided was entirely negative.

That people should be *forced* out of the Unification Church in order to regain their freedom was an irony lost to many. The movement in and out of most NRMs is relatively high, however, and the average stay within the communities is rather short. Eileen Barker (1988: 167) found "that the majority of members joining the Unification Church seem to leave voluntarily within two years of joining." Long-term affiliation and involvement seems even more tenuous; only 3 percent of a thousand people attending a workshop in 1979 were full-time members by the end of 1985. People left the movement for a variety of reasons, and many of the deprogramming efforts were successful,[38] but the cost of extricating them was extremely high to those involved, and to the society, as a blow to religious freedom.

What to Do About "Cults"

Alternative, or new religious movements, do present a threat to the established sociocultural order in the United States, not only because of what the movements themselves do, but also because of the anticult movement's campaign against them. Families are disrupted and people are cut off from former social networks, sometimes causing pain and anguish;

those developments are often symptoms of deeper problems in the relationships and in the broader culture, rather than something caused by the NRM itself. The record of the response to these threats has been mixed. Alternative religious movements have not been accorded the kind of protection guaranteed in the U.S. Constitution. They have been harassed not only by the anticult movement, but even by agencies of the state (see Wallis 1976; Bromley and Shupe 1981). Unfortunately, such responses are more consistent with historic practices than is a thorough protection of religious freedom.

A tragedy at the Branch Davidian compound in Waco, Texas, in 1993 is an extreme but not entirely unrepresentative case. Federal agents came to arrest the leader of a Christian sect, David Koresh, whose community had stockpiled a vast arsenal of weapons and were awaiting the Battle of Armegeddon, which, according to Christian scriptures, would signal the end of the world. Several government agents were killed in the raid; after a long standoff between the FBI and Koresh's followers, remaining members of the religious community perished as their building went up in flames. On one hand, confronted by a heavily armed group of "religious fanatics," the federal government responded with violence. The standoff in Waco involved two groups of people who were well armed and willing to fight to the death for higher principles. Although the religious movement involved may have been unjustified in its stockpiling of guns and David Koresh may have misled members of the group by using his charismatic authority to exploit their fears, the question remains as to whether the most appropriate way to respond was in kind, i.e., with the same violence and pressure tactics that Koresh was condemned for using. Criticism of the government's response to the Branch Davidian situation was widespread, and an investigation was initiated by the Attorney General's office. Even though such investigations are often an attempt to justify and cover up the actions taken rather than to expose mistakes made, the norm requiring a clear explanation for such actions was affirmed.

Science fiction writers have often evoked the theme of what we would do if confronted by an "alien force," by a life form from another planet with different customs, beliefs, and rituals. Perhaps we can see the answer to that question in how dissident groups are treated in any given society. Kai Erikson's *Wayward Puritans* (1966; Erikson 1965) concludes that the kind of deviance most likely to be defined and sanctioned in any given society will reflect the important values of that society. The outlier and outlaws provide something of a mirror image of the dominant norms and values, but both criminal and police operate by the same rules and share many of the same values.

Without attempting to prescribe public policy recommendations regarding alternative religious movements, it does seem important for societies to consider the following questions.

1. How should the freedom of all religious movements be protected? This would not be an easy, absolute task, and certainly society will draw boundaries around acceptable and unacceptable behavior. Most modern constitutions make religious freedom an official tenet of each nation's political culture (although as we have seen the norm is not always adhered to, e.g., in the U.S.). Consequently, actions taken by the state against any religious group should be done within the boundaries of strict due process and not because of prejudice or theological disagreements. Religious movement members should be accorded the same legal rights as rapists, murderers, and the KKK.

2. How can religious movements be evaluated on the basis of their "fruits," i.e., in terms of the personal and social consequences of their religious beliefs? Disagreements should take place within the confines of the moral debates about what is acceptable and unacceptable *behavior*, as far as the law is concerned, and questions of theology should be debated theologically. In a heterogeneous society, some people will obviously find some groups more attractive, and others more repulsive; is it possible for people to debate those differences freely, rather than trying to suppress those with whom they disagree?

From a sociological point of view, these questions are ultimately the kind of questions that must be asked about the way in which religious movements will be treated in the global village as we attempt to fashion a global ethos that permits the peaceful coexistence of diverse social groups.

New Forms of Religiosity

One variant of the secularization thesis suggests that the new cultural forms of the modern world are, in fact, a sort of invisible religiosity. Thomas Luckmann (1967: 113) argues that the central cultural themes of "individual 'autonomy,' self-expression, self-realization, the mobility ethos, sexuality and familism," as well as a number of other less important topics, constitute something of an "invisible religion," because they have some claim to a "sacred" status in modern culture, but are not explicitly organized religious traditions.

Durkheim's study of aboriginal Australian religion in his formative book, *Elementary Forms of the Religious Life*, was part of his lifelong search for functional equivalents of the mobilizing power of religion to revitalize the social order and provide a basis for social solidarity. His sociological predecessor Comte capped his career by elaborating a secular "religion of humanity," basically Catholicism without the supernatural, and Durkheim appeared to be taking somewhat the same path, although with a more sophisticated method. He concluded that the phenomena being worshipped in religious ritual were actually social forces themselves that ritual could be harnessed for the common good if science were used to provide a moral basis for the collective life.

Durkheim was not alone in his quest for functional surrogates for religion; many other moderns who were "spiritually musical" (that is, were spiritually inclined and talented) but disillusioned with traditional religious forms have sought to replace them with a new worldview and its corresponding ethos. Others have replaced some of the social and psychological functions in a less deliberate manner, through other social activities as voluntarism, dance, music, sports, or nationalism. Even on a relatively mundane level, collective life is now often expressed through secular rituals that take on a quasireligious character, especially for those most dedicated.

The line between religious and secular rituals is very thin, as both lie along the same continuum of social forms that run from the most sacred to the most profane. In modern and postmodern societies, secular rituals from political campaigns and television ads to rock concerts and Olympic games fulfill many of the functions identified by Durkheim as religious, promoting social solidarity and facilitating the process of collective identity construction.

Cultic practices often emerge around charismatic cultural figures like popular rock singers or political figures. Many of the groups surrounding particular rock groups, such as the Grateful Dead, take on many characteristics of a religious movement. In its most extreme forms, fans become devotees and exhibit behavior that borders on worship. During the height of their popularity, perhaps the most famous group of the late twentieth century, the Beatles, were thought to have such miraculous powers that people were brought to their dressing rooms for healing. The singers themselves tried to downplay these practices, and John Lennon even wrote a song protesting such attitudes and providing a long list of things he did not believe in, including God and the Beatles, concluding that he only believed in himself.

Constructing and Reconstructing Religious Life

As we have observed in this chapter, religious life has not died in the modern world, as many scholars expected. Instead, religious beliefs and practices have been reformulated in a variety of ways. The ancient traditions of the mainstream have been revitalized, for example, as traditionalist protest movements on one hand and as liberation theology on the other. Other forms of religiosity, notably civil religion and nationalism, though they are decried by the traditionalists as examples of the disappearance of the "true religion," nonetheless function much as religious traditions do. Religious syncretism at the margins of society and a new ecumenical spirit among the mainstream religious groups also constitute a crucible in which a new generation of religious traditions may now be forming. The emergence of alternative religious movements, especially in the United States, reflects a religious ferment that stimulates creative theologizing in a way reminiscent of the formative periods of the existing mainstream religions.

In addition to the emergence of some deliberately syncretistic religious traditions, such as the Baha'i faith, a new spirit of dialogue seems to be widespread as the twentieth century comes to a close. In 1893, at the World's Columbian Exposition in Chicago, the first World Parliament of Religions brought representatives from a wide variety of religious traditions together to explore their similarities and differences. A century later, the second Parliament of Religions convened—again in Chicago—to discuss the possibility of constructing a human ethical consensus out of the world's religious traditions, and an institutional basis, a sort of religious United Nations, to encourage ongoing dialogue among religious leaders from a wide variety of traditions.

Religious diversity will no doubt remain the hallmark of the global village well into the next millennium—perhaps as long as human life persists—and the major issue is probably not how to eliminate religious conflict among different traditions and perspectives, but how to facilitate constructive and creative, rather than destructive, conflict. That issue will be explored in the final chapter.

7

Religion and Social Conflict

Few concerns of social life can lead as readily to conflict as the combination of religious differences with other forms of struggle. In the twentieth century, the twin crises of modernism and multiculturalism have added a religious dimension to many ethnic, economic, and political battles, providing cosmic justifications for the most violent struggles. Multiculturalism produces complex patterns of conflict both between and within religious traditions that feed off one another and often intensify over time. Given the destructive capabilities of modern weaponry and the consequent necessity for peaceful coexistence, the potential for religious traditions to promote either chaos or community becomes a crucial factor in the global village.

In this chapter we will examine the nature of conflict and the special character of religious conflict, contending that conflict itself is not inherently a sociological liability, as Simmel puts it; conflicts can be either constructive or destructive. As we have seen in this exploration of the world's religious traditions, conflict is a major source of cultural innovation and the crucible in which our current traditions were forged. We should not fear conflict itself, but battles that rage with escalating violence. Violent conflict has been an integral part of human history for thousands of years and has been intimately associated with religious practice. In the global village, where automatic rifles and weapons of mass destruction have replaced stones, the cost of violent conflict has simply become too high. The problem created by the special confluence of modernism, multiculturalism, and the modern technologies of violence is not conflict itself, but destructive conflict. In this chapter, we will explore the insights that the sociology of the world's religions provides for our understanding of the relationship between religion and social conflict in the global village.

A Theory of Religious Conflict

As Georg Simmel observes, social conflict is a form of **sociation** (social interaction); the social order is itself fashioned out of attractive and repulsive forces:

> Society . . . in order to attain a determinate shape, needs some quantitative ratio of harmony and disharmony, of association and competition, of favorable and unfavorable tendencies. But these discords are by no means mere sociological liabilities or negative instances. (1971: 72)

Religious traditions also take shape from a combination of harmony and disharmony. Religious conflict can be extraordinarily bitter, however, and is often destructive because the parties to the dispute view themselves as "representatives of supraindividual claims, of fighting not for themselves but only for a cause," which, as Simmel argues (1971: 87), "can give the conflict a radicalism and mercilessness. Because they have no consideration for themselves, they have none for others either; they are convinced that they are entitled to make anybody a victim of the idea for which they sacrifice themselves" (1971: 87).

Extremes of thought and behavior are often defined as inappropriate for selfish causes, but not for religious purposes; in most traditions, believers should be ready to die, perhaps even to kill for their deity. Ironically, the most intense extremism may be reserved for conflict with those whose values and beliefs are in reality not so different from one's own. That is why, for example, ancient Jewish law permitted bigamy but prohibited simultaneous marriage with two sisters. The principle here, Simmel notes, is "that antagonism on the basis of a common kinship tie is stronger than among strangers" (1971: 90). Thus, the most intense form of religious conflict may be that between heretics and religious authorities, i.e., conflict *within* a tradition (see Kurtz 1986). A similar volatility may emerge in relations between sibling religions, such as Judaism and Islam, with the same roots, many overlapping beliefs and practices, but significant divergences as well. Such controversy combines the intensity of religious conflict with that of a sort of kinship. Simmel suggests that the strongest examples of hatred are "church relations. Because of dogmatic fixation, the minutest divergence here at once comes to have logical irreconcilability—if there is deviation at all, it is conceptually irrelevant whether it be large or small" (1971: 90). Although religious conflicts threaten our coexistence in the global village, not the struggles between, but those within traditions may be the most dangerous.

The Politics of Heresy

It is no accident that the concept of heresy comes from the Christian tradition, which, in the absence of ethnic or tribal memberships, has placed so much emphasis on right doctrine. Formally, **heresy** in the Roman Catholic tradition refers to "a sin of one who, having been baptized and retaining the name of Christian, pertinaciously denies or doubts any of the truths that one is under obligation of divine and Catholic faith to believe" (Buckley 1967: 1069). Although originally it did not have a negative meaning, the idea of heresy as evil surfaced during bitter battles in the early church councils (see Hughes 1961; Cross 1925). Looking at heresy as a social construction can be useful in understanding the relation between belief systems and social organization.

Elsewhere (Kurtz 1986: 3ff), I have suggested a number of characteristics of heresy:

1. Heresy is simultaneously near and remote. That is, heretics are within the relevant social group and therefore close enough to be a threat, but distant enough to be considered in error. A heretic is thus a "deviant insider" and is considered a danger to the institution and its leadership. Heresies are internal, but they represent a pollution from external sources—an inevitability in the global village, where traditions collide.

2. Heresy is socially constructed in the midst of social conflict. As people fight with one another, their interests become associated either with the heresy or with its refutation. Consequently, the problem of heresy is primarily a problem of *authority*, that of beliefs and structures.

3. Heresy has social consequences as well as social origins. It is a double-edged sword, sometimes disruptive (the conventional view) but often is used for the creation of group solidarity and for purposes of social control. By labelling a group of people as heretics, elites rally support for their own positions but may inadvertently stimulate a rebellion.

4. Campaigns against heresies have doctrinal consequences as well as social ones. In the heat of escalating conflicts, groups often clarify just what they believe about a particular issue.

5. The process of defining and denouncing heresies is a *ritual* that helps to relieve social and psychological tensions and deal with institutional and religious crises. Christian rituals for denouncing here-

sies began in the first centuries of the church's history as the church began to encounter non-Jewish influences and people fought for control of the institution and its belief systems. Antiheretical rituals reached their peak with the formation of the Inquisition and the use of the formula *coge intrare*, "to force them to join" (see Weber 1968: 480), which justified the use of force against heretics, sometimes giving infidels and heretics a choice between either conversion and submission, or death.

The phenomenon of heresy is important to our understanding of religious conflict, which is fueled by differences on issues of great significance to people. The issue of heresy is also critical in the global village for two reasons. First, in the face of external attacks by other religious and nonreligious perspectives, people within a tradition will often turn on insiders who have slightly deviant points of view, especially if they echo aspects of the undesirable outsiders' arguments. Second, there is a sense in which everyone is now an insider—as a citizen of the world—so that insider-outsider distinctions become blurred, a situation ripe for escalating conflict and the social construction of evil, as people attempt to redraw boundaries that once seemed safe. The problem, again, is not conflict per se, but its potential for destructive violence.

Religious conflict is frequently associated with violence, either directly or as a way of legitimating violent means for handling conflict that originally had a nonreligious basis. Because of the centrality of the problem of violence in the twentieth century, it is important to understand the ways in which violence and the sacred are intertwined.

Religion and the Problem of Violence[39]

The norms against the overt use of violence are so strong in the global village that those who would use force must justify it eloquently. Religion is one of the most convenient and effective ways of making such a justification, and the link between violence and the sacred is an ancient one that grows out of the roots of human cultures (see Girard 1977). Religion has also been the source of powerful rationales for nonviolence. Violence has been simultaneously condemned and condoned in the twentieth century (see Turpin and Kurtz forthcoming). Although most people abhor violence, many use it either defensively to respond to violence or offensively for coercive purposes. The same violence committed by "illegitimate" forces is considered acceptable when carried out by the state. Age-old killing practices—usually in the name of one or another God—now produce destruction on an unprecedented scale because the technological means of destruction have become so effective. Not only are individuals or tribes now at risk from acts of violence, so are entire populations. With the advent of nuclear, chemical, biological, and space-based weapons, the ecosphere itself is endangered.

We will now explore the role of religious traditions in the origins of violence, critiques of violence, and the construction of nonviolent alternatives. Then we will examine the cases of two sharply different religious protest movements that put people of faith in intense social conflict.

The Religious Roots of Violence

The use of religious arguments to justify violence waxes and wanes historically, but few justifications of violence are as universally upheld as those supported by the world's religious traditions. In the religious context, violence is usually done in the name of some good, and often in the name of a god. Discerning whether violence is truly religious, or merely a profane act which its perpetrators try to endow with sacred purpose, is a difficult business, perhaps altogether impossible. It is, nonetheless, an important question to raise if we are to judge the nature of any empirical case. Religious deities and their institutions sometimes appear to sponsor violence directly, but the most significant role religion plays in promoting violence is an indirect one in which sacred traditions are called on to justify its use.

Because violence is considered legitimate only when done for the "right reasons," it often takes on the character of a religious sacrifice (Girard [1977: 1]). When a sacrifice is carried out by "divine command," it is defined as more legitimate than if it is done for profane reasons such as fame or profit. Thus, when violence is committed or people engage in warfare, such acts are often framed with religious purpose by invoking God's blessing at the beginning and offering thanks after a victory. A portion of the spoils are given to the deity or its representatives in an effort to sacralize the enterprise, allowing the interests of the victors to be masked by religious ideals.

Every major religious tradition includes its justifications for violence (see Ferguson 1977). Behavior that is prohibited under ordinary circumstances becomes obligatory when it carries a divine sanction (Girard 1977). Although the killing of other human beings is usually prohibited, in times of warfare (especially holy war) it is required. Primal religions typically frame violence as part of the natural process. The creatures of nature die and kill one another on a regular basis as part of their struggle for survival. Killing may not be taken lightly, however, and may not be done often (especially the killing of other human beings), although the frequencies vary widely from culture to culture.

The "religions of the book" contain ample precedents for justified killing. According to the Hebrew scriptures, held authoritative by Judaism, Christianity, and Islam, God kills people, and instructs others to do so, when an injustice has been committed or holy law has been disobeyed. In Asian religions, killing is usually prohibited by the principle of *ahimsa* (nonviolence or nonharmfulness) but is sometimes required by one's *dharma*.

The western god of war. In the Judeo-Christian tradition, Yahweh is praised as a God of war. As the Psalmist writes,

> Thou doest arm me with strength for the battle
> and does subdue my foes before me.
> Thou settest my foot on my enemies' necks,
> and I bring to nothing those that hate me.
> *(Psalms 18:39–40)*

Yahweh not only caused acts of violence while liberating the Hebrew slaves from the Egyptian pharaoh, according to the tradition, but also gave the Hebrews victory in conquering the inhabitants of the "Promised Land" to which they fled. In the Hebrew scriptures, violence by or on behalf of God seems to favor the poor; it is condemned when undertaken for personal gain, and offensive violence is allowed only in the holy wars against the tribes of the "Promised Land." The Holocaust perpetrated by the Nazis on the Jewish community in the twentieth century, in which perhaps a third to a half of the entire Jewish population was killed, imposed such a toll on Jewish identity that all subsequent discussions of Judaism and violence have to be seen in light of that tragedy.

A similar attitude is perpetuated by portions of the Qur'an and the concept of the *jihad*. Although the idea of Islamic *jihad* has been widely misunderstood and distorted, it does offer a clear legitimation for violent acts against those who allegedly disobey Allah. As noted earlier, an accurate translation of the word is "struggle," and the "Greater *Jihad*" takes place internally, within one's own heart, whereas the "Lesser *Jihad*" refers to struggle of all kinds in the external world, including war (see Ferguson 1977). Those who do not "heed God" should "be prepared to face war declared by God and His messenger" (2:280).[40] The Qur'an states, however, that God, not humans, should decide who deserves punishment, and sets strict limits about what kinds of violence can be done under what conditions.

The early Christian church, as we will see, fostered strong pacifist beliefs marking a break with ancient Judaism, but the church's position shifted dramatically after about three hundred years with the conversion of the emperor Constantine to Christianity in 327 C.E. (see Bainton 1960). By the eleventh century C.E., Christianity had shifted from being a pacifist to a warrior religion. It is not difficult to discern why the shift occurred: early Christianity was a small religious sect devoted to a radical new version of Judaism taught by the rabbi Jesus. Although originally popular among marginal social groups in an isolated province of the ancient Roman empire, gradually its influence reached the elites of the time, until the Emperor himself was converted. Gradually an effective affinity emerged between the religious institution and Rome, an alliance that was to transform the church more than the empire in the centuries to come.

Violence in eastern religions. The Asian religions are just as complicated in their attitude toward violence as the Western religions, although support for violence is not quite as well developed doctrinally as in the West, for several reasons. First, both of the major religious forces in the East, Hinduism and Buddhism as well as other traditions such as Jainism and Taoism, contain strong nonviolent doctrines in their core teachings. Second, religious doctrines in the East are not as authoritative as in the West (especially Christianity); they are more diverse and less binding, especially in the political sphere. Because the pantheon has a division of labor, some gods are more likely to support the use of violence than others, so it is unnecessary to develop a definitive stance on the issue of violence. Such a position could not be enforced anyway even if it were proposed. Third, the charismatic authority of first Mahatma Gandhi and then the Tibetan Dalai Lama have transformed much of modern thinking about violence in Hinduism and Buddhism, highlighting some previously subordinate strands valuing the doctrine of *ahimsa,* or nonharmfulness.

Finally, and relatedly, the major religions of the East are somewhat less closely linked with the political establishment than Western religions are, although that generalization must be carefully qualified. Many heads of state have at least formally adhered to Buddhism, and the teachings of K'ung Fu tzu have formed something of a state religion, or quasireligion, in China until the twentieth century. The fortunes of religious institutions are not so closely linked with those of the state, however, as in the West.

Both Hindu and Buddhist leaders have advocated the use of violence and warfare over the centuries, however, tracing their justification to the sacred texts and traditions in which they operate. The Hindu tradition, despite its current nonviolent emphasis, is replete with war stories that are understandably interpreted by many believers as sacred legitimation of the use of force in battle. In the Bhagavad Gita Krishna explains that "there is no greater good for a warrior than to fight in a righteous war" (Bhagavad Gita 1962: 51). In this case, fighting (and consequently, killing) is required by the god himself, not because of the act's inherent moral value, but because it is the warrior Arjuna's duty to fight. The warrior battles as a sacrificial act of duty to the god, but also because that is what the universe expects of warriors. Fulfilling one's duty to fight becomes a religious sacrifice—as selfless action (*anasakti*) for a larger purpose than personal gain. One should fight regardless of the outcome, because the focus is on the effort of battle, not whether one wins or loses. One does not take personal responsibility for a loss or credit for a victory, nor is one to blame for the devastation caused by war. The deaths of warriors are preordained by fate; they will die if their time has come, so the one who "kills" them is only an instrument of a larger cause. Furthermore, one cannot kill the soul, but only the body, so the apparent act of killing is merely an illusion.

The Buddhist tradition is more difficult to cite in defense of war because of the Buddha's emphasis on compassion for all creatures and the admonition against killing at the gate of the Eightfold path. Despite that clear prohibition, some Buddhists (including monks) have made fierce warriors in parts of Asia, especially China (see Ferguson 1977).

It is important to note that religion is often the *content* of a conflict, though not its basis (Kurtz 1991a). The conflict may be political, class, familial, or even psychological, but religious issues become the subject around which the conflict evolves and religious rhetoric is used to carry it out. When fighting breaks out between Protestants and Catholics in Northern Ireland, or Hindus and Muslims in India, the conflict is usually as much economic as religious, though it may be couched in religious rhetoric. In these cases, the conflict's religious significance lies purely in its justification of violence and the sacralization of the cause for which the parties are fighting.

Religious Critiques of Violence

Religious institutions or their adherents have not only justified violence throughout human history, they have frequently criticized it as well. Religious critiques of violence include the contentions that it is

1. Against human nature, or the nature of things in the universe
2. Ineffective in the long run because it simply produces a spiral of violence
3. Sinful or unjust, and the deity does not like it

In most cultures, a sort of *Realpolitik* hypothesis reigns, however, in which common sense "dictates" that realists must be hardheaded and willing to engage in violence in order to accomplish anything and especially to defeat evil forces that engage in violence. Ideas such as nonviolence may be acceptable—even admirable—for saints and holy people, this thinking goes, but they should not be binding rules of morality for ordinary individuals.

Religious arguments may run counter to these conventional cognitive frames, especially concerning issues of power and politics. Religious perspectives are often quite different, especially when they draw upon a theory of the world that allows for a benign universe that will eventually prevail even if evil seems to be temporarily in control. Often this counter-system point of reference can facilitate a nonviolent approach that rejects the more conventional attitude toward violence. In this framework, what appears to be efficacious is only temporarily so, and one needs a larger perspective in order to see the shortcomings of violent methods.

Messianic eschatologies, found especially in the Western religions, of Judaism, Christianity, and Islam, are replete with beliefs about the unanticipated turn of events that will elevate the downtrodden.[41] Similar perspectives are found in Eastern religions in which a *bodhisattva* or a god may intervene, or things will just work themselves out according to the law of *karma*, which helps to explain why things are not the way they superficially appear to be (e.g., one's rewards may come in the next incarnation).

According to the Tibetan Buddhist leader Tenzin Gyatso (the Dalai Lama), people are, contrary to popular belief, naturally more nonviolent than violent; they are naturally filled with compassion, seek affection, and recoil from violence. The universe itself is naturally inclined toward nonviolence; consequently, the Eightfold path that guides the Buddhist's life contains a set of Five Precepts, the first of which is not to kill (see Ferguson 1977: 43). The outcome of taking life is to have an inferior incarnation. Second, even if one does use violence to solve a problem, it is not going to be a successful resolution in the long run. The Dalai Lama (Gyatso 1990) claims: "Even if you achieve something through force, physical force . . . very often it creates a situation [in which] . . . the other party . . .

[is] not happy. . . . Therefore, as soon as another opportunity happens, then they'll take retaliation." According to the Taoist principle of *wu-wei*, violence simply begets violence: "The use of force usually brings requital. Wherever armies are stationed, briars and thorns grow. Great wars are always followed by famines" (Lao tzu 1972: 30; Ferguson 1977: 65).

Finally, some individuals refuse to commit violence simply because they believe that God has told not them to do so. Admittedly, this position is a minority one in most religious traditions, but it is significant nonetheless. Russian novelist Leo Tolstoy, for example, contends from the Christian pacifist tradition that "a Christian, whose doctrine enjoins upon him humility, non-resistance to evil, love to all (even to the most malicious), cannot be a soldier; that is, he cannot join a class of men whose business is to kill their fellow-men. Therefore it is that these Christians have always refused and now refuse military service" (Tolstoy 1987: 11). From this point of view, refraining from violence has nothing to do with whether or not the alternatives will "work" in any conventional sense of the term, but whether or not they are morally superior.

Religious Contributions to Nonviolence

The irony of the relationship between religion and violence is that the most potent violence *and* the most powerful nonviolence both have religious roots. Both Eastern and Western religions have strong pacifist traditions that lay one part of the foundation for the twentieth-century tradition of active nonviolence. Violence often appears to require religious justification because it is negatively valued as undesirable, nonviolence because it is equally negatively valued as ineffective.[42] One religious figure who challenged that argument in both theory and practice was Mohandas K. Gandhi (1869–1948). The remarkable growth of nonviolence as a political strategy in recent decades is Gandhi's legacy to the modern world.

Gandhi's Experiments in Nonviolence

Gandhi's response to the problem of violence centers around his formula that one should separate the doer from the deed, that is, hate evil but respect the person, an idea rooted in his religious understanding of the nature of humanity. This differentiation of the adversary from his or her behavior changes the nature of conflict; it depersonalizes (and demilitarizes) the conflict but personalizes the opponent. The attack is not against individuals who will respond in kind but against evil itself.

Gandhi's advocacy of nonviolence combines all three religious arguments against violence. First, he claims that nonviolence is the law of the universe. Because nonviolence is "in harmony with the nature of existence and reality," it "must in the final analysis therefore be action which 'works' and is 'practical'" (Sharp 1987: 41). If the universe itself is basically good, then all people are good; that is why they should be treated with respect. Whether one is convinced or not that one's adversaries are good people, acting as if they are may well evoke a positive response from them. That was not only Gandhi's theory, but also his practice. It sometimes seemed as if he *forced* people to do good rather than evil, even when they seemed inclined toward the latter, by calling out the best in his opponents rather than humiliating them.

Second, Gandhi demonstrated that nonviolence can work even in the most unlikely situations. Perhaps it was the efficacy of nonviolence, more than the ineffectiveness of violence, that shaped his attitudes. Gandhi contended that "even the most despotic government cannot stand except for the consent of the governed which . . . is often forcibly procured. . . . [When] the subject ceases to fear the despotic force, the power is gone" (Gandhi 1962: 154).

Third, Gandhi believed that nonviolence was morally superior to violence, and must be carried out even if one feels as if one is acting alone: "There are moments in your life when you must act even though you cannot carry your best friends with you. The still small voice within you must always be the final arbiter when there is a conflict of duty" (*Young India*, August 4, 1920 in Gandhi 1962: 152).

Because religious history is replete with persecution, most traditions have many inspiring models of individuals or groups of people who stand up against overwhelming powers and win. This is one central element of nonviolent action that is always in tension with the efficacy argument: some would argue that even if nonviolence does not always work, it is always right.

Transforming the Traditions

Despite the widespread presence of nonviolence in the world's religious traditions, however, the warrior motif remains dominant; the concept of God as pacifist or nonviolent activist is supported only by a minority strand (Kurtz 1991b). For religion to become a vital force against violence, the traditions would need to be transformed in their dominant manifestations and institutions, as Gandhi tried to do with some success in the Hindu tradition. Although the process would be opposed in many circles, it is already unfolding in a number of religious traditions. Three major developments in this area are worth mentioning here: (1) criticizing contemporary warfare by means of traditional criteria, (2) spiritualizing the old war stories to make them parables of nonviolent struggle, and (3) secularizing religious traditions in such a way as to diffuse their moral lessons into the broader culture without the entire religious "package."

New critiques with old criteria. The Christian concept of a just war, with its roots in the writings of fourth century C.E. Augustine and the medieval theologian Thomas Aquinas, contains a fundamental bias against war but allows it as morally justifiable under certain extreme conditions when certain criteria are met. One of the most significant developments in religious responses to violence has been the effort by Christian leaders, beginning with the U.S. Catholic bishops, to reevaluate just war theory in light of contemporary means of mass destruction, which make traditional justifications for war extremely problematic. It is no accident that this radical critique of violence by an established religious institution emerges from a society that threatens to annihilate the species.

In traditional just war theory, the criteria governing the decision to go to war rely primarily on the issue of proportionality: that is, is the good to be gained from the battle proportionate to the cost to be incurred? According to the U.S. Catholic bishops (National Conference of Catholic Bishops 1983), a decision to go to war is possible only when the following conditions are met:

1. Just cause
2. Competent authority
3. Comparative justice
4. Right intention
5. Last resort
6. Probability of success
7. Proportionality

The final two criteria especially have forced many Christian authorities to reevaluate the traditional legitimation of warfare in the latter part of the twentieth century. It is impossible to envision any way in which a total nuclear war could meet either the criteria of probable success or that of proportionality. Even after the decision is made to go to war, the conduct of war itself must be subject to two principles: proportionality and discrimination. The principle of discrimination prohibits action against innocent civilians (see Ramsey 1961, 1968; Johnson 1981: 350). In modern wars it is difficult, if not impossible, to discriminate between retaliation against aggressive parties and actions taken against noncombatants.

The Second Vatican Council (Vatican Council II [1965] 1982) concluded that the nature of modern war requires "a completely fresh reappraisal of war." The implications of that conclusion are profound and have precipitated a rediscovery of the pacifist elements of Christianity lost since the conversion of Emperor Constantine fifteen hundred years ago. Even though many Christians continue to use just war arguments, and even the "Crusade" tradition, to justify modern wars, responsible religious leaders throughout the church are giving the matter serious consideration. Other religious traditions have undergone similar efforts to reevaluate, or even transform, their positions on violence and warfare. Such a transformation of religious ideas is neither as unusual nor as formidable as some might think. It is a normal aspect of socioreligious development and has occurred innumerable times in the history of religious thought.

Spiritualizing the war stories. Religious traditions cannot simply repudiate the stories of violence in their history that are often used to legitimate the use of violence in the name of the deity. To escape the trap of violence, these stories must be reinterpreted. One significant model for the process is Gandhi's recasting of the Bhagavad Gita.[43] In the pivotal scene, as we have seen, the warrior Arjuna is facing his kinsmen on the battlefield of Kurukshetra, anguished over the decision about whether or not to fight. If he undertakes the battle, he will most likely kill members of his family and his teacher. Finally Lord Krishna convinces Arjuna that it is his duty as a warrior to go to war.

This difficult legend would appear to create cognitive dissonance for anyone attempting to live a nonviolent life. Gandhi, who relies heavily on the Gita for his own thinking, turns the story into a metaphor: "The battle-field of Kurukshetra," Gandhi writes, "only provides the occasion for the dialogue between Arjuna and Krishna. The real Kurukshetra is the human heart. . . . Some battle or other is fought on this battle-field from day to day." The meaning of the Gita is thus not that one should engage in physical violence, but that one must engage in the struggle that is associated with one's duty. It is, moreover, a detached action; "it is up to us to do our duty without wasting a single thought on the fruits of our action. . . . Gain or loss, defeat or victory, is not in your power" ([1930] 1987: 8, 11).

Finally, one must be prepared to sacrifice. The gist of the Gita, Gandhi contends, "is that life is given us for service and not for enjoyment. We have therefore to impart a sacrificial character to our lives" ([1930] 1987: 20). That is not to say, however, that the religious life itself is simply a spiritual exercise for Gandhi. On the contrary, he contends that "the spiritual law . . . expresses itself only through the ordinary activities of life. It thus affects the economic, the social and the political fields" (quoted in Sharp 1987: 39; cf. Sharp 1979). The legend of Arjuna and Krishna, which easily could be taken as providing a religious legitimation for violence, becomes instead the direct opposite: it is a story about the obligation to serve others with sacrifice and without self-gain. Instead of legitimating violence, Gandhi's interpretation of the scripture moves toward a radical nonviolence.

This transformation of tradition, like that accomplished by the U.S. Catholic bishops in their study of just war theory, is a characteristic tactic employed by Gandhi, who constantly reinterpreted traditional concepts and "grafted them onto the modern setting" (Kothari 1970: 54).

Secularizing religious nonviolence. The previous example demonstrates that religious ideas never have a widespread impact unless they enter the cultural mainstream and become diffused throughout both elite and popular cultures. In the contemporary world, that process often requires the decoupling of a specific theme from the broader religious message. That is, in fact, precisely what has happened with the theme of nonviolence in recent years. As the idea of active nonviolence (or "nonviolent direct action") has diffused throughout the world, it has become increasingly secularized (see Kurtz and Asher, forthcoming). The religious nonviolence of Gandhi and then Martin Luther King, Jr., was systematically developed in many modern political movements and in some popular developments such as conflict resolution and mediation. King's strategy was to translate Gandhi's philosophy and strategies—relatively universalistic, but with strong Hindu overtones—into Christian rhetoric. Others, such as Gene Sharp (1973–1974; 1979, 1987), removed most of the religious bases for nonviolent action altogether, and much of the moral justification for it, to construct a set of pragmatic strategies for engaging in nonviolent struggle.

In Eastern Europe, similarly, various Christian churches, such as the Roman Catholics in Poland and the Lutherans in Germany, provided important leadership, but the idea also captured the imagination of the intellectuals, who translated many of the core ideas of nonviolence into a more secular language (see especially Havel 1990). Although religious imagery has persisted in the peace movements in Europe, North America, and elsewhere, and Gandhi and King have remained the "saints" of the movement, many participants have toned down the explicitly religious rhetoric and now speak in more secular terms about the moral aspects of nonviolence.

Religion and Nonviolent Social Movements

Nonviolence was first "baptized" by Christians in the U.S. civil rights movement and in the Philippines "People Power" movement, thereby removing the concept from its Hindu moorings. Martin Luther King, Jr., adapted his strategy of nonviolence from Gandhi for the American context. Since it took root in the black church in the United States (see King 1986), the concept remained explicitly religious, with a strong Christian flavor. African-American slaves, historically forced to convert, used the symbols of Christianity for their own liberation, not only to talk about rewards in the world to come to sustain them through the suffering, but also to mobilize resistance movements and anti-slavery activities. Thus, African-Americans used Christian symbols and myths to resist the very culture that imposed Christianity on them. When the slaves sang spirituals like "Come and go with me to that Land," they were not only talking about a heaven in the afterlife, but also about escaping on the underground railroad to the north and their freedom.

King and others in the civil rights movement captured that spirit in the black church to give people the courage to struggle against the racism of the system in the United States. The pulpits of Christian churches, both black and white, and other resources of the institution, played a crucial role in making the movement. In the daily struggle of the civil rights movement, participants were sustained by their faith and assisted by their religious tactics. Resistance movements elsewhere also found essential support in the ideas and institutions of religious traditions. In South Africa, for example, where anti-apartheid forces were often led by religious leaders, protesters encountered advancing police by kneeling in prayer, thus gaining broad sympathy for their cause.

Nonviolent protests in Asia and Europe. A series of nonviolent social movements in Asia and Eastern Europe modeled their campaigns for social change after Gandhi's Freedom Movement and the civil rights movement in the United States, especially Martin Luther King, Jr.'s Christian nonviolence. In the Philippines, where a majority of the population is Catholic, base communities were established throughout the country and an indigenous form of liberation theology emerged. Moreover, in the 1980s, the church became the site of training for nonviolent resistance against Ferdinand Marcos's dictatorship. An astounding "People Power" revolution in 1986 overthrew the Marcos regime, demonstrating the power of committed people who believed they had God on their side in the face of brutal right-wing oppression (see Deats forthcoming). Members of the Christian church took the leadership of the movement and many were trained in nonviolent tactics by the Fellowship of Reconciliation, a nonsectarian religious pacifist organization (see Lee forthcoming).

After Marcos tried to steal the election from popular opposition leader Corazon Aquino and key members of the military defected from the regime, the Cardinal of Manila called on people to join him in the streets. Hundreds of thousands did so. When the troops were sent to stop the rebellion, the demonstrators confronted the tanks and armored personnel carriers, as vividly described by Father José Blanco (forthcoming):

> with our bodies, our prayer, our Filipino piety with images of Mary and the crucifix. Our faith has made us this kind of a people, both we who were resisting, as well as the soldiers who were ordered to attack. We venture to suggest when the soldiers saw praying, unafraid people, cheerful, offering flowers and cigarettes, willing to come under the tank treads; these effectively tied their hands and changed their wills not to carry out their mission of destruction. They might as well have had no tanks and armored cars, because their human concern for the lives of literally thousands was a stronger brake that kept their armored vehicles at a stand still. . . .
>
> This miracle is the mystery of God's grace powerfully working in the hearts of each one of us. The miracle is God bringing about events both big and small, which no one of us thought about, much less planned.

Although the socioeconomic conditions for rebellion were clearly present in the Philippines at the time of the People Power movement, it was the combination of the religiously motivated nonviolence and the institutional resources of the church that made a successful revolt possible.

Similar, and even more dramatic, change took place in the Soviet bloc a few years later, again largely propelled by the church in a context ripe for change. Although some people explain the collapse of the Soviet empire in terms of a bankrupt economic and political system, religious ideas and institutions played an important, and perhaps formative, role. An elective affinity emerged between the interests of dissident forces and the ideas and strategies of a religiously forged nonviolence. Perhaps the turning point in the pro-democracy movements of Eastern Europe was the visit of Pope John Paul II to Poland in 1979. Millions of Poles met him enthusiastically in the streets and were empowered to support movements of change by the introduction of this radically different frame.

As Adam Michnik explains, the Worker's Defense Committee (WDC, a crucial organization in the initial stages of the dissident movement)

> had a model in Polish civic life: the Catholic Church. Not all WDC members were Catholics, although the overwhelming majority of Poles are Catholics. Not all of them would admit at the time that the Catholic Church was actually the first to provide definite proof that it was possible to be an independent institution in a totalitarian political environment, and that the Church itself demonstrated the first type of antitotalitarian action. (1992: 242)

In 1989, the Berlin Wall fell, symbolic of the division between the two superpower camps. Behind the movements for change was the quiet, persistent work of the church and people of faith whose allegiance was to another system. The institutional resources of the church, more than any other single organization, helped to facilitate the dialogue, first quietly and then openly, that led to the resistance movements of Eastern Europe and the Soviet bloc. At first, much of the opposition took the form of worship services and discussion groups in church basements. When the movement came out into the open, it was not suppressed, in large part because it had the powerful backing of the institutional church, and therefore the broad population. Operating in a spirit of reconciliation and nonviolence, the pro-democracy forces fearlessly continued to press for change. It was, in fact, when the military forces tried to suppress the movement that the general population began to voice their opposition and demand change.

Women's Movements

> "I'd like to be a priest when I grow up," she said.
> "You can't," I said, "you're female."
> "So what?" she said, in the tone she defies her grandmother but not her mother in.
> "Girls can't be priests," I said. "Our Lord said so."
> "Where?" she insisted.
> I told her He didn't say it in so many words, but He chose no women to be apostles, and priests are successors to the apostles. That means they would have to be like the apostles.

"But the apostles were Jewish, and you're not Jewish," she said.

"What's that got to do with it?" I asked her.

"So, you're not like them, and you're a priest." She glowed with success-ful argument.

I thought of all the foolish, mediocre men who were permitted ordina-tion because of the accident of their sex. And I thought of this child, obvi-ously superior to all others of her age in beauty, grace, and wisdom. I told her to pray that the Church would change its mind by the time she grew up.

"You pray, too," she said.

I said I would, but it must be a secret between us. And so each morning, at my mass, I pray for the ordination of women. —Mary Gordon, *The Com-pany of Women*

Nowhere do interreligious encounters occur more intimately than in the separate voices of men and women as they encounter the sacred, not in different parts of the globe, but within their own homes. One of the most profound of modern movements—that affects all levels of society as well as all societies—is the demand for equality by women. This movement, in its various forms, challenges the very roots of the major world reli-gions, each of which has its own liberating traditions, but all of which have consistently legitimated patriarchal culture and male domination. The related social problem, of course, lies in the ways in which female identity is shaped from a very early age, so that religious legitimations of inferior status affect the lifelong socialization process and the ways in which women (or any other group of people) will be treated and, conse-quently, think of themselves.

Every major living religious tradition has a patriarchal tendency, and the Western religions, especially Christianity, have been soundly criti-cized for their sexism. As with critiques of that tradition during the French Revolution, the basis of the complaint is the use of religious insti-tutions and ideas to impose inequality. Some of the early women's leaders in the United States found aspects of Christianity downright immoral. Elizabeth Cady Stanton, for example,

> was shocked by the frank misogyny of the original [bible]. Genesis, for ex-ample, read to her like "gross records of primitive races," and the stories of Lot's daughters (who got their father drunk and then seduced him) and of Tamar (who dressed as a whore to seduce her father-in-law) she found un-worthy of comment. As for contemporary Christianity, she wrote: "So long as ministers stand up and tell us that Christ is the head of the church, so is man the head of the woman, how are we to break the chains which have held women down through the ages? (Ehrenreich 1981: 38)

A different strategy of some contemporary critics, like Mary Daly and Rosemary Radford Ruether, has been to forge a feminist theology that reshapes the traditions in a less sexist manner. Ruether (1981: 388) developed a feminist critique of religious studies that begins with the historic exclusion of women from religious leadership roles in the Judeo-Christian tradition. She notes that women were prohibited from studying the scriptures in Judaism, as in the rabbinic dictum "cursed be the man who teaches his daughter Torah." Christianity has had similar practices, noted in the New Testament statement, "I do not permit a woman to teach or to have authority over men. She is to keep silence" (I Timothy 2:12).

Because of this exclusion, women were usually permitted only an inferior role in shaping the major traditions, and a number of derisive characterizations of women have been made by the core figures of Western thought: Thomas Aquinas, for example, defined a woman as a "misbegotten male." In the medieval scholastic tradition, efforts to ordain a woman for the priesthood were considered simply impossible—the ordination "would not 'take,' any more than if one were to ordain a monkey or an ox" (Ruether 1981: 390).

Finally, Ruether argues,

> the male bias of Jewish and Christian theology not only affects the teaching about women's person, nature and role, but also generates a symbolic universe based on the patriarchal hierarchy of male over female. The subordination of woman to man is replicated in the symbolic universe in the imagery of divine-human relations. . . . Thus everywhere the Christian and Jew are surrounded by religious symbols that ratify male domination and female subordination as the normative way of understanding the world and God. This ratification of male domination runs through every period of the tradition, from Old to New Testament, Talmud, Church Fathers and canon Law, Reformation, Enlightenment and modern theology. It is not a marginal, but an integral part of what has been received as mainstream, normative traditions. (1981: 390–391)

Ruether's response to this situation is not to reject the entire tradition, but to reshape it, first by documenting the male bias and tracing its sociological roots (see Daly [1968] 1975 and Ruether 1974). The second step is to discover "an alternative history and tradition that supports the inclusion and personhood of women" (1981: 391), either within the Jewish and Christian traditions or elsewhere. A number of well-documented studies show, Ruether contends, that the exclusion of women from leadership roles is not the whole story. Women were probably not so excluded in first-century Judaism, and the rabbinic dicta against teaching women Torah is only one side of an argument, albeit the side that won (Ruether 1981: 392).

Similarly, the passage in I Timothy just cited is a second-generation reaction, Ruether claims, against the widespread participation of women in leadership positions in the early church. It is unlikely that anyone would bother to oppose female involvement if it were not happening. Ruether argues that the participation of women in early Christianity was a natural part of its theology, in which "baptism overcomes the sinful divisions among people and makes us one in the Christ: Jew and Greek, male and female, slave and free" (Galatians 3:28; Ruether 1981: 393).

Some support for feminist perspectives on the early church have come from unexpected quarters, as in Robin Scroggs's contention that

> we must make a radical reversal in our interpretation of Paul's stance to-
> ward women. Far from being repressive and chauvinistic, Paul is the one
> clear and strong voice in the New Testament speaking for the freedom and
> equality of women. Paul lucidly sets forth the equal rights and responsibili-
> ties of male and female, grounds this freedom in the liberated humanity of
> the new creation, and assumes that women will live in this freedom in the
> eschatological communities he has helped create. (Scroggs 1972: 309)

Some authorities in the early church, Scroggs contends, "found this freedom too radical and quickly rewrote Paul to make his writings conform to the practices of the establishment church" (1972: 309). The charge is a serious one, based on textual criticism concluding that portions of the text were altered, that should be taken in light of different norms of the status of texts in the ancient world, where individual authorship rights were not rigidly defined as they are in modern cultures.

Women and the priesthood. Debates about the role of women in religious institutions often focus on their eligibility for the priesthood. Some branches of Protestant Christianity, especially in the mainline denominations, include women in leadership roles, so that there are even some women bishops. In several areas of Protestantism and in the Roman Catholic and the Eastern Orthodox churches, however, resistance is still very strong and unlikely to change soon, despite shortages of priests.

In the meantime, barriers are falling elsewhere, albeit in isolated instances. In Pune, India, in 1984, for example, a group of Hindu women began chanting hymns and conducting rites previously reserved for male Brahman priests. Shankar Hari Thatte, a seventy-six-year-old Brahman, brought them together for that purpose, contending, "The men priests were cheating people, their lives had degenerated, they were unable to honor the holy books and I felt I should organize the women because there is no specific ban on them performing these rites in the religious texts" (Hazarika 1984: 4). Although some priests and scholars voiced objections, no one attempted to stop them. Ganesh Shastri Shinde, an eighty-six-year-old priest, contended that what they are doing is "against religious traditions," but added, "we will not interfere with their ways. We will let them go on their path and we will continue on ours" (Hazarika 1984: 4).

A year later, Amy Eilberg was ordained as a Conservative Jewish rabbi after graduating from the Jewish Theological Seminary in New York (Goldman 1985). Following a vote of the Rabbinical Assembly allowing the ordination, Eilberg was admitted into the ancient priesthood as the first Conservative woman member (Reform Judaism had been ordaining women for the previous decade). Although Rabbi Eilberg fulfilled a life-long dream and broke another barrier, it remains to be seen how long it will take before women rabbis are accepted as full equals. As one rabbinical student put it, "Men are rabbis and women are women rabbis" ("Women Studying" 1984).

Nonpatriarchal traditions. Finally, some people have used historical and anthropological studies to explore alternative religious traditions that are not patriarchal, including both ancient Mother Goddess traditions and popular contemporary feminist spirituality groups. In a provocative analysis of archaeological research in recent years, Marija Gimbutas (1982: 236) contends that because "the task of sustaining life was the dominating motif in the mythical imagery of Old Europe," that is, in the period before about 4500 B.C.E., "the goddess who was responsible for the transformation from death to life became the central figure in the pantheon of gods." Male and female divinities were presented side by side, however: "Neither is subordinate to the other; by complementing one another, their power is doubled" (1982: 237).

Rianne Eisler's *The Chalice and the Blade* (1988) analyzes these findings by positing a partnership society in which males and females were equal partners that was overrun by male-dominated warrior societies at the end of the Neolithic Age, during the third to fifth millennia B.C.E. For about 20,000 years, Eisler argues, most European and Near Eastern societies were based on simple, supportive technologies, matrilineal descent, and common ownership of the means of production. They had a cooperative social organization and a gynocentric culture, with the deity represented in female form. Their Kurgan conquerors imposed a dominator model of social organization with male deities, "a social system in which male dominance, male violence, and a generally hierarchic and authoritarian social structure was the norm" (Eisler 1988: 45).

Although the jury is still out on the exact nature of the evidence and its implications, a number of discoveries are quite remarkable. First, representations of weapons appear only after the Kurgan invasions, with "the earliest known images of Indo-European warrior gods" (Gimbutas 1982, 1989; Eisler 1988: 49). The weapons apparently represent the power and function of the gods, with the Goddess gradually appearing as the wife or consort of the male deities. Moreover, the nature of burial sites begins to shift at about the same time, from more egalitarian graves to hierarchical "chieftain graves" with marked differences in size and "funerary gifts," that is, the contents found in the tomb along with the deceased. For the first time in European graves, an exceptionally tall or large-boned male skeleton will be accompanied by the "skeletons of sacrificed women—the wives, concubines, or slaves of the men who died" (Eisler 1988: 50).

If the obvious interpretations of these findings are true—and it seems plausible—the implications are profound. They are both horrifying and hopeful. On one hand, a radical cultural revolution occurred in human prehistory thousands of years ago, a revolution in which we are still participating, that values hierarchical, male-dominated culture at the expense of partnership models, and warrior gods over peaceful, nurturing deities. On the other hand, these archaeological discoveries—like some of the existing alternative religions in the twentieth century—also suggest that human social organization can be different from the way it now is, and that our worldviews might once again be transformed before our own warrior gods overtake us.

Female deities and quasideities. A number of contemporary religious traditions contain a strong female presence. One of the most prevalent figures worldwide is the Virgin Mary, a particularly potent symbol for women and the poor around the world, although she remains a somewhat suspect figure for most Protestant churches. Pope John Paul II, apparently recognizing her importance, and echoing the longstanding popular interest, has actually promoted interest in Mary from the Vatican. The Beatles' Paul McCartney's popular song "Let It Be" captures the spirit of the religious adoration of Mary, claiming that she comes in times of trouble.

Chinese religious symbols include three major female deity cults: Kuan Yin, Ma Tsu, and the "Eternal Mother" (see Sengren 1983). Although they do not represent a simple transfer of men's and women's social roles, these deities contrast sharply with the male bureaucratic deities in Chinese folk religion. The female deities provide some alternatives to the hierarchical models of the male deities and reflect the mediation role that mothers often play in Chinese family life. Kuan Yin, Ma Tsu, and the Eternal Mother all intercede in times of danger and are approachable in ways that the bureaucratic deities are not, just as Mary seems closer to humans in need (especially women) than the Christian God, as either a father or a son (see Warner 1976).

Sengren suggests that whereas one can approach "ancestors or territorial-cult deities only as a representative of a patriline or household, one can approach female deities as an individual" (1983: 20). Male deities act as officials, responding to justice and bribes and promises of payment, but female deities are moved more by a worshipper's devotion and dependence. Thus, the female deities provide an alternative model of authority within the religious sphere that reflects differences in authority elsewhere. They facilitate the empowerment of women in religious life in a way that is difficult for the male deities, because they respond to the models with which women are socialized in Chinese society.

In practical matters of worship, the female deities in China may act more as opiate than activists despite their "proven" powers, thus covering over any symptoms of discontent among women that might emerge as a result of inequality within religious institutions. Men tend to run the important temples, even those with female deities, who are often more prominent as domestic gods. Moreover, the attributes the goddesses possess reflect those of women in the traditional patriarchal society, even if in a subtly subversive way. In the sectarian cults of the Eternal Mother, a subversion of the hierarchical structure of celestial bureaucracies reflects the coalitions between children and mothers against their fathers in extended Chinese families (Wolf 1968, 1972; Sengren 1983).

Religious deities or quasideities such as Mary, Ma Tsu, and the Eternal Mother thus reinforce the hierarchical, male-dominated social order under normal circumstances but also contains the seeds of rebellion—sometimes as a subtle form of covert sabotage, but also potentially as a direct confrontation. Most importantly, as Neitz notes, "The symbols of the goddess movement in themselves represent cultural change. For many the rituals are new forms of play. For others the rituals express their deepest hopes for social transformation as well" (1990: 370).

The introduction of goddess worship into the contemporary religious life of advanced industrial cultures is not limited to those who have rejected mainstream religious forms altogether and opted for alternative systems, or even to the more subtle inclusion that surrounds the adoration of Mary in Catholicism. Controversy recently erupted in the mainline

Protestant denominations of the United States over the use of a ritual devoted to Sophia, an ancient feminine image of God in Christianity. At an ecumenical gathering of women in Minnesota, elements of the ritual were included in a worship service, provoking a series of attacks on the Women's Division of the United Methodist Board of Global Ministries, which had financed the participation of several United Methodist representatives to the conference.

All of the major living religions of the world are essentially patriarchal and male dominated. They explain the world in masculine terms and tend to reinforce male-dominated social structures. Underneath the surface of these religions, the feminine face of God persists, kept alive sometimes quietly, and sometimes loudly. As Gimbutas writes, "Now we find the Goddess reemerging from the forests and mountains, bringing us hope for the future, returning us to our most ancient human roots" (1989: 321). As women become increasingly prominent in public life in the global village, they may change the face of religious beliefs as profoundly as the interaction among the major world traditions now dominating the religious landscape.

Environmental Movements

Many of the religious traditions—like the goddess worship of Old Europe—that emphasize a harmonic relationship with the natural environment have been destroyed by industrialization, along with the destruction of the environment that has accompanied so much of modern economic development. The more utilitarian attitude toward nature emphasized in the dominant cosmopolitan religions of the twentieth century has been challenged on a number of fronts in recent years. For some practitioners of ancient religious traditions like those of some Native Americans and other indigenous groups around the world, the idea of harmony with the environment and a critique of modern ecological destruction have forced the basis of a protest theology that has a clear affinity with the interests of these groups, which are often exploited by the "advance of civilization."

The environmental movement, like the pro-democracy and women's movements, was born largely out of a religious sensibility but contains an ambivalence toward religious traditions because of the legitimation for environmental devastation those traditions have provided. A new sensitivity to ecological issues has emerged in many religious traditions in recent years, however, in part because of the emphasis on placing ethical values and broader universal causes above short-term profit motives that often fuel environmental destruction.

Attention to environmental issues has fanned the flames of multicultural conflict and protest theologies. Of particular interest are questions surrounding the role of Christianity in creating and solving environmental problems. A number of Christians have attempted to mobilize attention to the environment as a faith issue, as Ian Bradley in his *God Is Green: Ecology for Christians* (1992) and James Nash's *Loving Nature: Ecological Integrity and Christian Responsibility* (1992). Others claim that the environmental crisis is symptomatic of deep-seated problems in the Judeo-Christian tradition that must be dramatically changed (see Ruether 1992); a third group attempts to replace or supplement Christianity with other religious perspectives, whereas a final argument contends that environmentalism is an anti-Christian movement undermining the authority of the church (see Wilkinson 1992).

At the Earth Summit in Rio de Janeiro in 1992, leaders from many religious traditions gathered to focus their attention on the environment along with official governmental representatives and people from various nongovernmental groups around the world. Loren Wilkinson (1992) reported in *Christianity Today* that

> the Christian presence at the forum was swamped by a plethora of feminist, universalist, and monist groups, who argued that a new religious paradigm must replace the old one, which was shaped by patriarchy, capitalism, theism, and Christianity. Many blamed the "old paradigm" for the environment's destruction.

The charge against Christianity is considered inaccurate by the Jesuit Drew Christiansen (1992: 449), who contends "that there is something disingenuous in maligning those who, only a generation ago, were considered insufficiently modern as perpetrators of modernity's capital crime." The root of the problem, he claims, is not any religious tradition, but "social systems built on material accumulation" (1992: 451).

Christian theologian Rosemary Radford Ruether argues, however, that such groups as the "deep ecology" and feminist movements are correct in identifying Western culture, sanctified by Christianity, as the major cause of destructive conflict. Ruether claims that "ecofeminism brings together . . . two explanations of ecology and feminism in their full, or deep forms, and explores how male domination of women and domination of nature are interconnected, both in cultural ideology and in social structures" (1992: 2). Her approach, though not opposed to looking for insights from non-Christian traditions, is to "sift through the legacy of the Christian and Western cultural heritage to find usable ideas that might nourish a healed relation to each other and to the earth" (1992: 2).

Chaos or Community?

> We must realize that all traditions are ambivalent and that it is therefore necessary to be critical about all of them so as to be able to decide which tradition to maintain and which not. —Jürgen Habermas (1994)

The increasing unity and diversity of the global village has had a profound impact on religious life on the planet. On one hand, each of the world's faiths has been increasingly forced to take account of the multitude of others. On the other hand, specific religions have become internally diversified as they absorb a broad range of indigenous cultures and as they rediscover diverse elements within their own history. The encounters of American young people with Eastern religions, for example, has helped to stimulate a rediscovery of the mystical traditions of Christianity and Judaism, just as Eastern encounters with Christianity may have revitalized some of the ancient ethical teachings in Hinduism. The richness of individual traditions has been highlighted by encounters among the various faiths.

The Sociological Imagination

Solutions to the cultural dilemmas of the global village will require a great deal of what C. Wright Mills (1959) called the "sociological imagination." The use of that creative imagination in examining contemporary religious life leads, I think, to three fundamental conclusions. First, religion is intimately linked to social life. Any analysis of religious life has to attend both to social structures and cleavages and to the ways in which religious systems are engaged in sustaining hegemony or rebellion. Relatedly, any analysis of the current global human situation must take the significance of religious beliefs, practices, and institutions into account. Religious traditions are vehicles of protest for many currents of social change in the late twentieth century, from the anti-Western revolt of the Islamic world to nonviolent and liberation theology struggles of various social movements. Religious institutions—in their pluralistic and contentious variety—comprise the one significant force that possesses some relative autonomy from the dominating centers of international capital and political structures.

Second, the existing religious traditions, having been formed out of a long-term process of diffusion across cultural boundaries, are already multicultural, incorporating a variety of indigenous beliefs and practices in the midst of considerable conflict both within and between traditions. No pure monolithic cultures exist as the twenty-first century approaches. If humanity's future is anything like its past, the challenges of science and diverse religious traditions will not simply go away; rather, they will be essential ingredients in new socially constructed forms.

Third, models do exist for a combination of both unity and diversity in social life that could result in a shared ethos in the global village that does not destroy the rich fabric of human religious life or force anyone to participate in religious practice who does not wish to do so.

Religious traditions are broad cultural abstractions that link worldviews with daily life through rituals and institutions that symbolize and sustain certain values and norms. The link between society and culture is a dynamic one, characterized by elective affinities between ideas of a particular cultural orientation and the interests of particular social groups. Consequently, cultural and social change go hand in hand: when societies change their form of organization, so do cultures; the cultural styles of a previous era will prefigure the way in which societies change, and the kind of change that occurs will shape the worldviews and ethos of the next era.

In recent centuries, a new form of social organization, global in scope, has emerged. Picking up pace in the latter half of the twentieth century, it will profoundly affect the nature of human life for some time to come. One consequence of that change is that religious traditions—which play a key role in both precipitating and resisting the transformations—face a crisis of multiculturalism that calls the taken-for-grantedness of every major religious tradition into question.

Multicultural Religious Themes of Tolerance

Religious traditions, we have argued, grow out of social life, change over time, and have considerable internal diversity when diffused across a variety of indigenous cultures. As they transform from local to cosmopolitan traditions, they incorporate the diversity of a wide range of beliefs and practices, worldviews and norms, yet somehow maintain their integrity. Often when they are in the very process of transformation, the tradition's guardians of orthodoxy claim that it never has and never will change. The most serious challenges to religious toleration and diversity usually come from exclusivist truth claims in general, and especially from monotheistic traditions because of their inherent tendencies toward intolerance. Yet history does demonstrate that monotheistic religions have found ways of building tolerance into their belief systems, and monotheistic political elites have incorporated it into their public policies. That it has historical precedence is important and encouraging.

The struggle to live together will force people of faith to search their traditions for those points of contact or to fight the people whose village they share, perhaps to the death. Each of the major traditions in the global village, however, can make a contribution to a multicultural ethos. Hindus suggest that many paths lead to the same summit and that each person and social group must find their own way, guided by their own traditions. Buddhists subscribe to the same "multiple-paths" premise but suggest that the world is so full of suffering that one should try to escape it; the way out of the world, for the Buddhist, is to treat its creatures with compassion for their shared suffering, thus embracing the world they are rejecting. Judaism begins with a particularism that favors one ethnic group but declares that the group's very purpose is to be a light to others, to lead all of humanity to an ethical lifestyle that sustains a world of justice and peace. Muslims demonstrate an intensity of commitment that could lead to destructive conflict but turns to justice and tolerance whenever they are allowed to practice their worship in peace. Christianity has been spread by world-conquering colonial and neocolonial powers, but in this violent century Christians have rediscovered the nonviolent strength of their founder, who insists that all people are children of God and that the test of one's relationship with God is whether one loves one's enemies and brings good news to the poor.

The fact that these sacred traditions are each formed out of a specific and different social context creates an ambivalence. On one hand, faith communities can facilitate the process of ordering a common life since all traditions change and diversify as they encounter other perspectives and all traditions are now sharing more life experiences in common. On the other hand, however, the process is fraught with danger, precisely because of the close link between religious and social life. First, some people's identity and statuses are threatened by the changes and they will resist, perhaps violently. Second, change may come more slowly, and the resistance may run more deeply, than the overall community can tolerate, especially if some people decide that they would rather die than live with pluralism.

If we are to share the planet successfully without redividing it into a set of isolated fiefdoms, the increased unity and diversity of the world's cultures and religious traditions will probably intensify. That will inevitably lead, it seems, to secularized political orders at the broadest level—

barring some religious miracle by which the current religious traditions are quickly transformed and consensus develops among the world's religious leaders and at the grassroots. Within that secularized polity—or set of polities—the religious freedom of individual traditions must also be protected if we are to share the planet peacefully.

Second, we must demilitarize our conflicts and learn how to conduct them creatively. One of the most hopeful developments for the global village has been the development, in the 1970s and 1980s, of a set of conflict resolution techniques that have been elaborated by conflict experts and diffused widely in a number of settings. Our self-conscious development of nonviolent and nondestructive means of conflict and experimentation with them in various arenas from the school playground to corporations, interethnic, and international affairs, is still rudimentary, but nonetheless promising. Interreligious conflicts, especially when they run across social fault lines, can be particularly deadly, as we have seen, so they must be attended to in a deliberate and creative fashion. Secular forms of conflict resolution might be supplemented with techniques couched in ecumenical religious rhetoric so that it appeals to each faith community within the cognitive frames of its beliefs and draws legitimacy from its respective traditions.

Finally, each of the major religions has ethical standards that would promote a basic sense of justice and compassion that would transform the current situation if they were applied to daily life and the construction of human institutions. A set of minimal cultural norms, a global ethos that protects us from one another, must be codified in secular media. The human rights tradition, for example, emerging on a global level in recent decades, declares that every human is entitled to a set of basic rights and due process; this tradition has been widely accepted in recent decades and is sustained by secular rituals and institutions such as the United Nations. It is unlikely, moreover, that the injustices of the current global economic order, in which half of the world's population lives on the verge of starvation and lacks minimal levels of shelter and clothing, can sustain a peaceful world. Religious traditions must legitimate a global ethos before it can be widely accepted and (more importantly) practiced.

Stories of Conflict and Change

Many stories embedded in religious traditions on the planet recall the traditions of courageous men and women who responded to times of social crisis and intercultural conflict by forging new religious systems. Moses came from a group of people who had become enslaved and were under attack from the establishment. Thanks to the bravery of the Hebrew midwives who defied the Pharaoh and hid the babies whom he had ordered slaughtered, Moses was saved. As a young man, he became enraged when one of his compatriots was beaten; Moses killed the Egyptian overseer and fled for his life, only to encounter his God.

Mary, a young Jewish woman living under the shadow of the Roman empire in a time of social turmoil, proclaimed that God blessed the poor and sent the rich away empty and gave birth to Jesus, who challenged the religious and political establishment of his time. Siddhartha, raised as a prince, turned his back on his heritage of kingship and wealth and sought a different path. The wealthy Arab merchant Muhammad denounced the emptiness and materialism of his day and set his sights on a more meaningful struggle to live an ethical life.

These stories, and many more from ancient times to the present, suggest that people can rise above fear or apathy and meet the challenge of transformative times. Despite the centuries, if not millennia, of religiously based conflict, the various religious traditions share some essential norms. They posit the significance of collective life and of ethical values; they encourage people to treat others at least with respect, better yet, with compassion or love; and they inspire people to reach beyond their profane everyday lives and to strive for something higher.

The religious path is fraught with danger, however; those who encounter the sacred can be consumed by its fire. Most religions warn through ancient legends that the power of the gods can destroy those who do not approach them correctly or call upon them for the right purposes. Most malicious deeds, moreover, are usually done in the name of good; humanity's religious traditions are used to destroy as well as to create, for greed as well as altruism.

Max Weber contended that the groundwork for the modern socioeconomic order of capitalism was laid inadvertently by the Puritans and their specific notion of the "calling." It may well be that the ideas of active nonviolence, growing out of a fertile confrontation between Eastern and Western religious traditions, may be preparing the way for a new order that mitigates the spiral of violence and that a new spirit of interfaith dialogue will prepare the way for a multicultural ethos that will respect everyone's beliefs while cultivating our common life. Given the current sophisticated state of violence and the persistent inequalitites on the planet, such an order would come none too soon. For, as Martin Luther King, Jr., contended, the choice is now between nonviolence and nonexistence: we must learn to live together as brothers and sisters, or we shall die together as fools.

Notes

Chapter 1

1. Throughout this work, I will use the terms Before the Common Era (B.C.E.) and Common Era (C.E.) to refer to the time periods traditionally called Before Christ (B.C.) and Anno Domini, "in the Year of Our Lord" (A.D.). This compromise position acknowledges the widespread adoption of the so-called "Christian calendar" while moving away from its ethnocentrism.

2. I am grateful to Sheldon Ekland-Olson for his insights on this matter.

3. Robert Wuthnow outlines four major approaches in this emerging field in his important work, *Meaning and Moral Order* (1987). At the risk of oversimplifying his rich discussion, I will briefly summarize his arguments in the following discussion.

4. Readers who need more background on the religious traditions are encouraged to supplement Chapter 2 with readings cited in the bibliography.

Chapter 2

5. Weber typically surrounds this typology with a series of caveats, admitting that it "may be sketchy" and seeming to imply that its main purpose is to show "how complicated the structures and how many-sided the conditions of a concrete economic ethic usually are" ([1922–1923] 1946: 267).

6. This idea is a standard interpretation, but is the subject of some controversy.

7. From the *Vammika-sutta* of the Pali text *Majjhima-Nikaya*, quoted in Gard (1962: 120); and in Buddha (1954: 180).

8. All quotations from the Christian and Jewish scriptures are from the Oxford Annotated Bible.

9. Quotations from the Qur'an are from the American version translated by T. B. Irving (Al-Hajj Ta'Lim 'Ali).

Chapter 3

10. Taken from Leach (1956: 145–146; cf. Eliade 1967: 91–92).

11. Most people have only one death, at least per lifetime, out of the countless events of the life course, and will seldom if ever have religious visions. The

frequency of sexual intercourse varies significantly, but people have sex much less often than they engage in other activities they consider less significant.

12. For the discussion that follows, I found Weightman's (1984: 215ff) summary very helpful; cf. Bhardwaj (1973); Diehl (1956); and Stevenson ([1920] 1971).

13. The following discussion draws heavily from Jagannathan (1984: 70ff), as well as my own observations and conversations with Hindus while living in India. It should be noted that this source, though written in a popular style, is carefully done by a woman from a scholarly tradition. More important, it contains a blessing from Shankaracharya Jagadguru Shri Jayendra Saraswathi, a significant authority in contemporary Hinduism.

14. Quoted in Gard (1962: 53–54). Because a threefold confession of faith is a central ritual in Buddhism, the formula is then repeated twice.

15. Quoted in Ch'en ([1964] 1972: 474), who excerpts these quotations from Tokiwa, *Bukkyo to jukyo dokyo*, 529–531.

Chapter 4

16. I am grateful to Poorno Pragna for his insights into the Vedic traditions.

17. Apparently the fifth precept, the rule against drinking intoxicants, is not considered serious enough for expulsion. Additional rules require either a formal meeting of the order to consider the violation or a confession of guilt. A wide range of practices evolved, however, as the *sangha* was organized throughout Asia.

18. I have taken them from the King James version, in order to use the traditional "Thou shalt" formulation lost in the new, but more accurate, translations.

19. Aaron, who is left in charge, has a wonderful account for Moses, which seems to be an effort to avoid responsibility for the events: they handed him the gold, and "I threw it into the fire, and there came out this calf" (Exodus 32:24).

20. I am indebted to Christopher Ellison's insights on this topic and rely heavily on Ellison and Bartowski (forthcoming) for the discussion that follows.

21. In this section I am indebted not only to the authors cited, but also to Howard Miller and Douglas Laycock, colleagues at the University of Texas.

22. Suggested by Yvonne Haddad, in "Islam and the Transformation of Society," paper delivered at the University of Texas at Austin, March 2, 1988.

Chapter 5

23. The discussion that follows draws heavily from my discussion of these issues in *The Politics of Heresy: The Modernist Crisis in Roman Catholicism* (Kurtz 1986).

Chapter 6

24. I am grateful to Teresa Sullivan for this way of articulating the problem.

25. The term *culture wars* comes from the *Kulturkampf* of the Enlightenment period of eighteenth- and nineteenth-century Europe and is used effectively by Hunter (1991) in his analysis of conflicts in contemporary political culture in the United States; cf. Kurtz (1994).

26. See Echo Fields's (1991) discussion of Christian fundamentalism along these lines, as well as more theological explanations, but with a similar tone, in Harvey Cox (1984).

27. See Guth's (1983) review of the movement's history and strategies.

28. The first two observations are my own and from Crippen (1988). The others are from Hunter (1991: 299ff).

29. For a brief summary of these developments, see Nanji (1988a); for a more detailed discussion of the intellectual issues, see Marty and Appleby's (1993) three-volume edited collection of evaluating fundamentalism.

30. The following account is taken from Hiro (1989: 232–235).

31. From "Revive Native Religion" (1947), quoted in Assimeng (1978).

32. This view is not universal, although there is considerable truth in it. Renato Poblete (1970), for example, claims that there was little struggle in the transition from the indigenous religions to Christianity.

33. It is telling that when Gutiérrez was delivering a lecture series in Austin, Texas, as a world-famous visiting theologian, he quipped while struggling with the microphone, "I am not exactly a modern man."

34. The conventional wisdom is that liberation theology emerged from the grass-roots poor of Latin America, an assumption challenged by Madeleine Adriance (1986). Certainly its key spokespersons, like Gutiérrez, are college-educated elites, but many come from poor families and others live and work with the poor, listening to and articulating their perspectives on the Christian tradition.

35. The following discussion relies heavily upon Gutiérrez's important *A Theology of Liberation* (1973), as well as a lecture series he delivered at Austin Presbyterian Theological Seminary October 24, 25, and 26, 1983. See also Chopp (1986); Ferm (1986); Berryman (1984); Boff and Boff (1986); Lernoux (1982); Novak (1986); Gutiérrez (1977; 1983); Segundo (1976, 1985).

36. On the importance of religious belief in decisions to join, see Clark (1937); Wilson (1959); Smelser (1963); Glock and Stark (1965). The emphasis on interpersonal bonds and networks can be found in Lofland and Stark (1965); Lofland (1977); Bainbridge (1978); and Snow, Zurcher, and Ekland-Olson (1980).

37. The concept comes from the purported "mind control" techniques used on American prisoners held in Korea and China during the Korean War who became sympathetic with their captors' belief systems (see Anthony 1990: 299–300, who considers the brainwashing argument a hoax, used first as an

anti-communist propaganda tool during the Korean War, and again in the 1970s and 1980s against new religious movements).

38. Bromley (1988a: 204) and Barker (1988: 175) both estimate that about two-thirds of the coercive deprogrammings of Unification Church members were successful.

Chapter 7

40. Parts of the first section of this chapter appeared in an earlier version in S. Jeyapragasam (1993), *Communism: The Crisis in India and The Way Out*, and is used by permission.

41. All quotes from the Qur'an are taken from The First American Version, translation and commentary by T. B. Irving (Al-Hajj Ta'lim 'Ali) (Brattleboro, VT: Amana, 1985).

42. One of the most famous of these is the Magnificat in Christianity, in which Mary, the mother of Jesus, claims that with the coming of the Messiah, "he has filled the hungry with good things, and the rich he has sent empty away" (Luke 1:53).

43. Even the language we use to talk about these matters betrays a bias. In English, for example, we have a clear word for "violence," but only its negation signifies its opposite. Similarly, in Hindi the opposite of *himsa* is merely *ahimsa*. We have a much better idea of what violence and harm are than nonviolence and nonharmfulness.

44. Gandhi used the *Gita* as a spiritual guide for his daily life and translated it into Gujarati, publishing it on March 2, 1930, the day he marched to Dandi from Sabarmati. While in Yeravda prison, Gandhi received a complaint from a member of his ashram that the Bhagavad-Gita was very difficult to understand. Consequently, the Mahatma (a title popularly bestowed on Gandhi meaning "Great Soul") wrote a series of letters (one for each chapter of the Gita) giving his interpretations (see V. G. Desai's translation into English, Gandhi [1930] 1987).

References

Adriance, Madeleine. 1986. *Opting for the Poor: Brazilian Catholicism in Transition.* Kansas City, MO: Sheed and Ward.

Adriance, Madeleine. 1992. "The Paradox of Institutionalization: The Roman Catholic Church in Chile and Brazil." *Sociological Analysis* 53: S51–S62.

Ammerman, Nancy Tatom. 1987. *Bible Believers: Fundamentalists in the Modern World.* New Brunswick, NJ: Rutgers University Press.

Anthony, Dick. 1990. "Religious Movements and Brainwashing Litigation: Evaluating Key Testimony." in Robbins and Anthony (1990) pp. 295–344.

Assimeng, Max. 1978. "Crisis, Identity, and Integration in African Religion." Pp. 97–118 in Mol (1978).

Babcock, Barbara A., ed. 1978. *The Reversible World: Symbolic Inversion in Art and Society.* Ithaca, NY: Cornell University Press.

Bainbridge, William Sims. 1978. *Satan's Power.* Berkeley: University of California Press.

Bainton, Roland. 1950. *The Reformation of the Sixteenth Century.* Boston: Beacon.

Bainton, Roland. 1960. *Christian Attitudes Toward War and Peace.* Nashville, TN: Abingdon.

Barbour, Ian. 1960. "The Methods of Science and Religion." Pp. 196–215 in *Science Ponders Religion,* ed. H. Shapley. New York: Appleton-Century-Crofts.

Barker, Eileen, ed. 1982. *New Religious Movements: A Perspective for Understanding Society.* New York: Edwin Mellen.

Barker, Eileen. 1988. "Defection from the Unification Church: Some Statistics and Distinctions." Pp. 166–184 in Bromley (1988).

Bayle, Pierre. 1697. *Dictionnaire historique et critique.* Rotterdam: Leers.

Bellah, Robert N. 1964. "Religious Evolution." *American Sociological Review* 29: 358–374.

Bellah, Robert N. 1970. *Beyond Belief: Essays on Religion in a Post-Traditional World.* New York: Harper & Row.

Bellah, Robert N. 1975. *Broken Covenant: American Civil Religion in Time of Trial.* New York: Seabury.

Bellah, Robert N., and Phillip E. Hammond. 1980. *Varieties of Civil Religion.* San Francisco: Harper & Row.

Bendix, Reinhard. 1978. *Kings Or People: Power and the Mandate to Rule.* Berkeley: University of California Press.

Berger, Peter L. 1969. *The Sacred Canopy: Elements of a Sociological Theory of Religion.* New York: Doubleday.

Berger, Peter L., and Thomas Luckmann. 1967. *The Social Construction of Reality.* New York: Doubleday.

Berryman, Philip. 1976. "Latin American Liberation Theology." Pp. 20–83 in *Theology in the Americas,* ed. Sergio Torres and John Eagleston. Maryknoll, NY: Orbis.

Berryman, Phillip. 1984. *The Religious Roots of Rebellion; Christians in Central American Revolutions.* Maryknoll, NY: Orbis.

Bhagavad Gita. 1962. Trans. Juan Mascaró. Harmondsworth, UK: Penguin.

Bhardwaj, S. M. 1973. *Hindu Places of Pilgrimage in India.* Berkeley: University of California Press.

Blanco, José, S. J. "Filipino People Power: An Interpretation in Faith." In Kurtz and Asher (forthcoming).

Boff, Clodovis, and Leonardo Boff. 1986. *Liberation Theology: From Confrontation to Dialogue.* San Francisco: Harper & Row.

Bradley, Ian. 1992. *God Is Green: Ecology for Christians.* New York: Doubleday.

Brecht, Bertolt. 1966. *Leben des Galilei.* English version by Charles Laughton. Ed. Eric Bentley. New York: Grove.

Bromley, David G. 1988a. "Deprogramming as a Mode of Exit from New Religious Movements: The Case of the Unificationist Movement." Pp. 185–204 in Bromley (1988).

Bromley, David G., ed. 1988b. *Falling from the Faith: Causes and Consequences of Religious Apostasy.* Newbury Park, CA: Sage.

Bromley, David G., Anson D. Shupe, and J. C. Ventimiglia. 1979. "Atrocity Tales, the Unification Church, and the Social Construction of Evil." *Journal of Communication* 29: 42–53.

Bromley, David, and Anson Shupe. 1981. *Strange Gods: The Great American Cult Scare.* Boston: Beacon.

Buckley, G. A. 1967. "Sin of Heresy." P. 1069 in *The New Catholic Encyclopedia,* vol. 6. New York: McGraw-Hill.

Buddha, Gautama. 1954. *The Collection of the Middle Length Sayings* [Majjhima-Nikaya], vol. 1. *The First Fifty Discourses* [Mulapannasa]. Trans. I. B. Horner. London: Luzac.

Bush, Richard C. 1988. "Buddhism." Pp. 113–170 in Yates (1988a).

Caplow, Theodore, Howard M. Bahr, and Bruce A. Chadwick. 1983. *All Faithful People: Change and Continuity in Middletown's Religion.* Minneapolis: University of Minnesota Press.

Cardenal, Ernesto. 1976–1982. *The Gospel in Solentiname*. Trans. Donald D. Walsh. 4 vols. Maryknoll, NY: Orbis.

Ch'en, Kenneth K. S. [1964] 1972. *Buddhism in China: A Historical Survey*. Princeton: Princeton University Press.

Chopp, Rebecca. 1986. *The Praxis of Suffering: An Interpretation of Liberation and Political Theologies*. Maryknoll, NY: Orbis.

Christ, Carol P. 1987. *Laughter of Aphrodite: Reflection on a Journey to the Goddess*. Cambridge: Harper & Row.

Christiano, Kevin. 1987. *Religious Diversity and Social Change*. Cambridge: Cambridge University Press.

Christiansen, Drew, S. J. 1992. "Christian Theology and Ecological Responsibility." *America* (May 23): 448–451.

Clark, Elmer T. 1937. *The Small Sects in America*. Nashville, TN: Cokesbury.

Collins, Randall. 1974. "Three Faces of Cruelty: Towards a Comparative Sociology of Violence." *Theory and Society* 1: 425–440.

Comte, Auguste. 1853. *The Positive Philosophy*. Trans. Harriet Martineau. 2 vols. London: John Chapman.

"Constitution of the United States." [1787] 1938. Pp. 180–198 in *American Historical Documents: 1000–1904*, ed. Charles W. Eliot. Harvard Classics. New York: P. F. Collier & Son.

Cousins, L. S. 1984. "Buddhism." Pp. 278–343 in Hinnells (1984).

Cox, Harvey. 1984. *Religion in the Secular City: Toward a Postmodern Theology*. New York: Simon & Schuster.

Cragg, K. 1965. *Counsels in Contemporary Islam*. Edinburgh: Edinburgh University Press.

Crippen, Timothy. 1988. "Old and New Gods in the Modern World: Toward a Theory of Religious Transformation." *Social Forces* 67: 316–336.

Cross, George. 1925. "Heresy (Christian)." Pp. 614–622 in *The Encyclopedia of Religion and Ethics*, ed. James Hastings, vol. 6. New York: Scribner.

Daly, Mary. [1968] 1975. *The Church and the Second Sex*. 2nd ed. New York: Harper & Row.

Dansette, Adrien. 1961. *Religious History of Modern France*. 2 vols. Freiburg: Herder.

Darwin, Charles. [1859] 1952. "The Origin of Species by Means of Natural Selection." Pp. 1–251 in Great Books of the Western World, ed. Robert M. Hutchins, vol. 49. Chicago: Encyclopedia Britannica.

Darwin, Charles. [1871] 1952. "Descent of Man." Pp. 253–600 in *Great Books of the Western World*, ed. Robert M. Hutchins, vol. 49. Chicago: Encyclopedia Britannica.

Deats, Richard. "The Global Development of Movements of Active Nonviolence." In Kurtz and Asher (forthcoming).

Demoulin, Meinrich, and John C. Maraldo, eds. 1976. *Buddhism in the Modern World*. New York: Collier Macmillan.

Diehl, C. G. 1956. *Instrument and Purpose: Studies on Rites and Rituals in South India*. Lund: Gleerup.

Douglas, Mary. 1966. *Purity and Danger: An Analysis of Concepts of Pollution and Taboo*. London: Routledge & Kegan Paul.

Dunne, John S. 1965. *The City of the Gods: A Study in Myth and Mortality*. New York: Macmillan.

Durkheim, Emile. 1961. *Moral Education: A Study in the Theory and Application of the Sociology of Education*, ed. E. K. Wilson. Trans. E. K. Wilson and Herman Schnurer. New York: Free Press.

Durkheim, Emile. [1915] 1965. *The Elementary Forms of the Religious Life*. Trans. J. W. Swain. New York: Free Press.

Durkheim, Emile. [1893] 1933. *The Division of Labor in Society*. Trans. G. Simpson. New York: Free Press.

Ebaugh, Helen Rose. 1991. "The Revitalization Movement in the Catholic Church: The Institutional Dilemma of Power." *Sociological Analysis* 52: 1–12.

Ehrenreich, Barbara. 1981. "U.S. Patriots Without God on Their Side." *Mother Jones* (February/March): 35–40.

Eisler, Riane Tennenhaus. 1988. *The Chalice and the Blade: Our History, Our Future*. San Francisco: Harper & Row.

Eister, Allan, ed. 1974. *Changing Perspectives in the Scientific Study of Religion*. New York: John Wiley.

Eliade, Mircea. 1959. *The Sacred and the Profane: The Nature of Religion*. Trans. Willard R. Trask. New York: Harcourt.

Eliade, Mircea. 1967. *From Primitives to Zen: A Thematic Sourcebook of the History of Religions*. New York: Harper & Row.

Eliade, Mircea. 1987. *The Encyclopedia of Religion*. 15 vols. New York: Macmillan.

Eliade, Mircea. [1958] 1970. *Yoga: Immortality and Freedom*. Trans. W. R. Trask. Princeton: Princeton University Press.

Ellison, Christopher G. 1991. "Religious Involvement and Subjective Well-Being." *Journal of Health and Social Behavior* 32: 80–99.

Ellison, Christopher G. 1993a. "Religious Involvement and Self-Perceptions among Black Americans." *Social Forces* 71: 1027–1055.

Ellison, Christopher, and John Bartkowski. Forthcoming. "Religion and the Legitimation of Violence: The Case of Conservative Protestantism and Corporal Punishment." In Turpin and Kurtz (Forthcoming).

Ellison, Christopher, and Daniel Sherkat. In press. "Semi-Voluntary 'Institutions Revisited: Regional Variations in Church Participation Among Black Americans." *Social Forces*.

Erikson, Kai. 1965. "The Sociology of Deviance." Pp. 457–464 in *Social Problems: Persistent Challenges*, ed. E. C. McDonagh and J. E. Simpson. New York: Holt, Rinehart and Winston.

Erikson, Kai. 1966. *Wayward Puritans: A Study in the Sociology of Deviance.* New York: John Wiley.

"Evangelist Uses Computer Exchange." 1984. *New York Times* (August 24): 15.

Fenn, Richard K. 1972. "Toward a New Sociology of Religion." *Journal for the Scientific Study of Religion* 11: 16–32.

Fenn, Richard K. 1974. "Religion and the Legitimation of Social Systems." Pp. 143–161 in Eister (1974).

Fenn, Richard K. 1976. "Bellah and the New Orthodoxy." *Sociological Analysis* 37: 160–166.

Ferguson, John. 1977. *War and Peace in the World's Religions.* New York: Oxford University Press.

Ferm, Deane William. 1986. *Third World Liberation Theologies: An Introductory Survey.* Maryknoll, NY: Orbis.

Fields, Echo E. 1991. "Understanding Activist Fundamentalism: Capitalist Crisis and the 'Colonization of the Lifeworld.' " *Sociological Analysis* 52: 175–190.

Finke, Roger, and Rodney Stark. 1986. "Turning Pews into People: Estimating 19th-century Church membership." *Journal for the Scientific Study of Religion* 25: 180–92.

Finke, Roger, and Rodney Stark. 1988. "Religious Economies and Sacred Canopies: Religious Mobilization in American Cities, 1906." *American Sociological Review* 53: 41–49.

Finke, Roger, and Rodney Stark. 1992. *The Churching of America, 1776–1990: Winners and Losers in Our Religious Economy.* New Brunswick, NJ: Rutgers University Press.

Frazer, James George. [1922] 1950. *The Golden Bough: A Study in Magic and Religion.* 1 Vol Abridged Ed. New York: Macmillan.

Freud, Sigmund. [1913] 1950. *Totem and Taboo.* Trans. James Strachey. New York: Norton.

Fromm, Erich. 1961. *May Man Prevail? An Inquiry into the Facts and Fictions of Foreign Policy.* Garden City, NY: Doubleday.

Fukuyama, Francis. 1992. *The End of History and the Last Man.* New York: Free Press.

Gandhi, Mohandas K. [1908] 1939. *Hind Swaraj* or *Indian Home Rule.* Revised New Edition. Ahmedabad: Navajivan Publishing House.

Gandhi, Mohandas K. 1962. *The Essential Gandhi,* ed. Louis Fischer. New York: Vintage.

Gandhi, Mohandas K. [1930] 1987. *Discourses on the Gita.* Trans. Valji Govindji Desai. Ahmedabad: Navajivan.

Gard, Richard, ed. 1962. *Buddhism.* New York: George Braziller.

"Gaudium et Spes" [1965] 1976. Pp. 243–335 in *The Gospel of Peace and Justice,* ed. Joseph Gremillion. Pastoral Constitution on the Church in the Modern World (Second Vatican Council, December 7, 1965). Maryknoll, NY: Orbis.

Geertz, Clifford, ed. 1963. *Old Societies and New States*. New York: Free Press.

Geertz, Clifford. 1973. *The Interpretation of Cultures*. New York: Basic.

Gehrig, Gail. 1981. *American Civil Religion: An Assessment*. Society for the Scientific Study of Religion, monograph series no. 3. Storrs: University of Connecticut Press.

Gimbutas, Marija. 1982. *The Goddesses and Gods of Old Europe: 6500–3500 BC Myths and Cult Images*. Rev. ed. Berkeley: University of California Press.

Gimbutas, Marija. 1989. *The Language of the Goddess*. London: Thames and Hudson.

Girard, René. 1977. *Violence and the Sacred*. Baltimore, MD: Johns Hopkins Press.

Glenn, Norval. 1964. "Negro Religion and Negro Status in the United States." Pp. 623–639 in *Religion, Culture, and Society*, ed. Louis Schneider. New York: John Wiley.

Glock, Charles, and Philip E. Hammond. 1973. *Beyond the Classics? Essays in the Scientific Study of Religion*. New York: Harper & Row.

Glock, Charles, and Robert N. Bellah. 1976. *The New Religious Consciousness*. Berkeley: University of California Press.

Glock, Charles, and Rodney Stark. 1965. *Religion and Society in Tension*. Chicago: Rand McNally.

Goffman, Erving. 1959. *The Presentation of Self in Everyday Life*. Garden City, NY: Doubleday.

Goldfarb, Jeffrey. 1982. *On Cultural Freedom*. Chicago: University of Chicago Press.

Goldman, Ari. 1985. "Dream of Being a Rabbi Is in Sight for a Woman." *New York Times* (February 17).

Gopalan, S. 1978. "Identity-Theory Against the Backdrop of the Hindu Concept of Dharma: A Socio-Philosophical Interpretation." Pp. 119–132 in Mol (1978).

Gottwald, Norman K. 1979. *The Tribes of Yahweh: A Sociology of the Religion of Liberated Israel 1250–1050 B.C.E* . Maryknoll, NY: Orbis.

Grant, Robert M. [1963] 1972. *A Historical Introduction to the New Testament*. New York: Simon and Schuster/Touchstone.

Greeley, Andrew M. 1989. *Religious Change in America*. Cambridge, Mass.: Harvard University Press.

Griswold, Wendy. 1987. "A Methodological Framework for the Sociology of Culture." *Sociological Methodology* 17: 1–35.

Griswold, Wendy. 1994. *Cultures and Societies in a Changing World*. Thousand Oaks, CA: Pine Forge Press.

Guth, James L. "The New Christian Right." Pp. 31–45 in Liebman and Wuthnow (1983).

Gutiérrez, Gustavo. 1973. *A Theology of Liberation: History, Politics, and Salvation*. Maryknoll, NY: Orbis.

Gutiérrez, Gustavo. 1977. *Liberation and Change*. Atlanta: John Knox Press.

Gutiérrez, Gustavo. 1983. *The Power of the Poor in History*. Trans. Robert Barr. Mary-knoll, NY: Orbis.

Gyatso, Tenzin, the 14th Dalai Lama. 1990. Personal interview, Dharamsala, India.

Habermas, Jürgen. 1975. *Legitimation Crisis*. Boston: Beacon.

Habermas, Jürgen. 1987. *The Philosophical Discourse of Modernity*. Cambridge, MA: MIT Press.

Habermas, Jürgen. 1994. "'More Humility, Fewer Illusions'"—A Talk Between Adam Michnik and Jürgen Habermas. New York Review of Books (24 March): 24-29.

Haddad, Yvonne. 1988. "Islam and the Transformation of Society." Lecture, University of Texas at Austin, March 2.

Hadden, Jeffrey K. 1969. *The Gathering Storm in the Churches: The Widening Gap Between Clergy and Laymen*. Garden City, NY: Doubleday.

Hadden, Jeffrey K., and Charles E. Swann. 1981. *Prime Time Preachers: The Rising Power of Televangelism*. Reading, MA: Addison-Wesley.

Hammond, Phillip E. 1976. "The Sociology of American Civil Religion: A Bibliographic Essay." *Sociological Analysis* 37: 169–82.

Hammond, Phillip E. 1980. "The Conditions for Civil Religion: A Comparison of the United States and Mexico." Pp. 40–85 in Bellah and Hammond (1980).

Hargrove, Barbara. 1989. *Sociology of Religion: Classical and Contemporary Approaches*. 2nd ed. Arlington Heights, IL: Harlan Davidson.

Harris, Marvin. 1974. *Cows, Pigs, Wars, and Witches*. New York: Random House.

Havel, Vaclav. 1990. "Power of the Powerless." Pp. 43–127 in *Without Force or Lies: Voices from the Revolution of Central Europe in 1989–90*, ed. William Brinton and Alan Rinzler. San Francisco: Mercury House.

Hazarika, Sanjoy. 1984. "An Age-Old Barrier in India Topples: Hindu Women Assume Priestly Role." *New York Times* (July 3): 4.

Herberg, Will. 1960. *Protestant, Catholic, Jew: An Essay in American Religious Sociology*. 2nd ed. Garden City, NY: Anchor.

Hertzberg, Arthur, ed. 1962. *Judaism*. Great Religions of Modern Man Series. New York: George Braziller.

Hesse, Hermann. 1971. *Siddhartha*. Trans. Hilda Rosner. New York: Bantam.

Hinnells, John R., ed. 1984. *A Handbook of Living Religions*. Harmondsworth, UK: Penguin.

Hiro, Dilip. 1989. *Holy Wars: The Rise of Islamic Fundamentalism*. New York: Routledge & Kegan Paul.

Howe, Richard Herbert. 1979. "Max Weber's Elective Affinities: Sociology within the Bounds of Pure Reason." *American Journal of Sociology* 84 (September): 366–385.

Hughes, Philip. 1961. *A Church in Crisis: A History of the General Councils 325–1870*. Garden City, NY: Hanover House.

Hunter, James Davison. 1991. *Culture Wars: The Struggle to Define America*. New York: Basic.

Iannaccone, Laurence R. 1988. "A Formal Model of Church and Sect." *American Journal of Sociology* 94 (Supplement): s241–268.

Iannaccone, Laurence R. 1990. "Religious Practice: A Human Capital Approach." *Journal for the Scientific Study of Religion* 29: 297–314.

Iannaccone, Laurence R. 1991. "The Consequences of Religious Market Structure: Adam Smith and the Economics of Religion." *Rationality and Society* 3: 156–177.

Iannaccone, Laurence R. 1992. "Sacrifice and Stigma: Reducing Freeriding in Cults, Communes, and Other Collectives." *Journal of Political Economy* 100: 271–291.

Iannaccone, Laurence R. 1994. "Why Strict Churches Are Strong." *American Journal of Sociology* 99: 1180–1212.

Ibrahim, Youssef M. 1994. "Fundamentalists Impose Culture on Egypt." *New York Times* (February 3): 1ff.

Jagannathan, Shakunthala. 1984. *Hinduism: An Introduction*. Bombay: Vakils, Feffer and Simons.

Jeyapragasam, S., ed. 1993. *Communalism: The Crisis in India and The Way Out*. Madurai, India.

James, William. [1902] 1960. *The Varieties of Religious Experience*. New York: Random House.

Johnson, Gregory. 1976. "The Hare Krishna in San Francisco." Pp. 31–51 in Glock and Bellah (1976).

Johnson, James Turner. 1981. *Just War Tradition and the Restraint of War*. Princeton: Princeton University Press.

Jones, R. Kenneth. 1978. "Paradigm Shifts and Identity Theory: Alternation as a Form of Identity Management." Pp. 59–82 in Mol (1978).

Jordan, David K. 1985. *Gods, Ghosts, and Ancestors: Folk Religion in a Taiwanese Village*. 2nd ed. Taipei: Cave Books. [First edition, University of California Press, 1972.]

Joseph, Paul. 1993. *Peace Politics: The U.S. Between the Old and New World Orders*. Philadelphia: Temple University Press.

Juergensmeyer, Mark. 1993. *The New Cold War: Religious Nationalism Confronts the State*. Berkeley: University of California Press.

King, Martin Luther, Jr. 1986. *Testament of Hope: The Essential Writings of Martin Luther King, Jr.*, ed. by James Melvin Washington. San Francisco: Harper & Row.

Kitagawa, Joseph M., and Frank Reynolds. 1976. "Theravada Buddhism in the Twentieth Century." Pp. 43–64 in Demoulin and Maraldo (1976).

Klein, Felix. 1951. *Souvenirs*, vol. 4, *Americanism: A Phantom Heresy*. Cranford, NJ: Aquin Book Shop.

Kothari, Rajni. 1970. *Politics in India*. Hyderabad: Orient Longman.

Kurtz, Lester R. 1979. "Freedom and Domination: The Garden of Eden and the Social Order." *Social Forces* 58 (December): 443–464.

Kurtz, Lester R. 1986. *The Politics of Heresy: The Modernist Crisis in Roman Catholicism*. Berkeley: University of California Press.

Kurtz, Lester R. 1988. *The Nuclear Cage: A Sociology of the Arms Race*. Englewood Cliffs, NJ: Prentice-Hall.

Kurtz, Lester R. 1991a. "From Heresies to Holy Wars: Toward a Theory of Religious Conflict." Paper presented at the American Sociological Association, Cincinnati, Ohio, August 1991.

Kurtz, Lester R. 1991b. *Gods and Bombs: An Anthology and Interpretation*. Unpublished manuscript, University of Texas at Austin.

Kurtz, Lester R. 1993. Review of *Culture Wars*, by James Davison Hunter. *Contemporary Sociology* 22 (May): 439–440.

Kurtz, Lester R. 1994. Review of *Culture Wars: The Struggle to Define America*, by James Davison Hunter (New York: Basic Books, 1991). *American Journal of Sociology* 99: 1124–1128.

Kurtz, Lester R., and Sarah Beth Asher, eds. Forthcoming. *The Geography of Nonviolence*.

Kushner, Harold S. 1981. *When Bad Things Happen to Good People*. New York: Schocken.

Lane, Ralph, Jr. 1976. "Catholic Charismatic Renewal." Pp. 162–179 in Glock and Bellah (1976).

Lao tzu. 1972. *Tao te Ching*. Trans. Gia-fu Feng and Jane English. New York: Knopf.

Latin American Bishops. 1979. *The Church in the Present-Day Transformation of Latin America in the Light of the Council: Second General Conference of Latin American Bishops*. 3rd ed. Washington, DC: National Conference of Catholic Bishops.

Latus, Margaret Ann. 1983. "Ideological PACs and Political Action." Pp. 75–99 in Liebman and Wuthnow (1983).

Leach, Maria. 1956. *The Beginning*. New York: Funk & Wagnalls.

Lee, Richard R. 1992. "Religious Practice as Social Exchange: An Explanation of the Empirical Findings." *Sociological Analysis* 53: 1–35.

Lee, Stephen. "The Philippines Revolution." In Zimmerman and Kurtz (forthcoming).

Lenski, Gerhard. 1963. *The Religious Factor.* Garden City, NY: Doubleday.

Leo XIII, Pope. 1899. *"Testem Benevolentiae."* Pp. 5–20 in *Leonis XIII Pontificus Maxima Acta,* vol. 19. Rome: Ex Typographia Vaticana.

Lernoux, Penny. 1982. *Cry of the People.* New York: Penguin.

Lévi-Strauss, Claude. 1969. *The Raw and the Cooked.* Trans. John and Doreen Weightman. New York: Harper & Row.

Liebman, Robert C., and Robert Wuthnow, eds. 1983. *The New Christian Right: Mobilization and Legitimation.* New York: Aldine.

Liebman, Robert C., John R. Sutton, and Robert Wuthnow. 1988. "Exploring the Social Sources of Denominationalism: Schisms in American Protestant Denominations, 1890–1980." *American Sociological Review* 53: 343–352.

Lofland, John. 1977. *Doomsday Cult.* Enlarged ed. New York: Irvington.

Lofland, John, and Rodney Stark. 1965. "Becoming a World-saver: A Theory of Conversion to a Deviant Perspective." *American Sociological Review* 30: 863–875.

Loisy, Alfred. [1903] 1976. *The Gospel and the Church.* Trans. Christopher Home. Philadelphia: Fortress.

Luckmann, Thomas. 1967. *The Invisible Religion: The Problem of Religion in Modern Society.* New York: Macmillan.

Lyng, Stephen G., and Lester R. Kurtz. 1985. "Bureaucratic Insurgency: The Vatican and the Crisis of Modernism." *Social Forces* 63 (June): 901–922.

Macfarlane, Alan. 1979. *The Origins of English Individualism: The Family, Property, and Social Transition.* New York: Cambridge University Press.

Malinowski, Bronislaw. 1954. *Magic, Science and Religion and Other Essays.* Garden City, NY: Doubleday.

Marty, Martin E., and R. Scott Appleby, eds. 1993. *Fundamentalism and Society: Reclaiming the Sciences, the Family, and Education.* Chicago: University of Chicago Press.

Marx, Karl. [1932] 1972. "The German Ideology: Part I." Pp. 146–200 in Marx (1972).

Marx, Karl. 1972. *The Marx Engels Reader,* ed. R. C. Tucker. New York: Norton.

Marx, Karl. [1843] 1972. "Contribution to the Critique of Hegel's Philosophy of Right." Pp. 11–23 in Marx (1972).

Marx, Karl, and Frederick Engels. [1844] 1975. *The Holy Family, or Critique of Critical Criticism.* Moscow: Progress.

Maududi, Sayyid Abdul Ala. 1979. *Purdah and the Status of Women in Islam.* Lahore: Islamic Publications.

McLuhan, Marshall. 1960. *Explorations in Communication,* ed. E. S. Carpenter. Boston: Beacon.

Mead, George Herbert. 1934. *Mind, Self, and Society.* Chicago: University of Chicago Press.

Merleman, Richard. 1984. *Making Something of Ourselves: On Culture and Politics in the United States.* Berkeley: University of California Press.

Messer, Jeanne. 1976. "Guru Mahara Ji and the Divine Light Mission." Pp. 52–72 in Glock and Bellah (1976).

Michnik, Adam. 1992. "The Moral and Spiritual Origins of Solidarity." Pp. 239–250 in *Without Force or Lies,* ed. William Brinton and Alan Rinzler. San Francisco: Mercury House.

Mills, C. Wright. 1959. *The Sociological Imagination.* London: Oxford University Press.

Mol, Hans. 1976. *Identity and the Sacred.* Oxford: Basil Blackwell.

Mol, Hans, ed. 1978. *Identity and Religion: International, Cross-Cultural Approaches.* London: Sage.

Nanji, Azim. 1988. "African Religions." Pp. 32–51 in Yates (1988).

Nash, James. 1992. *Loving Nature: Ecological Integrity and Christian Responsibility.* Nashville, TN: Abingdon.

National Conference of Catholic Bishops. 1983. *The Challenge of Peace: God's Promise and Our Response.* Washington, DC: United States Catholic Conference.

Needleman, Jacob, and George Baker, eds. 1978. *Understanding the New Religions.* New York: Seabury.

Neitz, Mary Jo. 1987. *Charisma and Community: A Study of Religious Commitment within the Charismatic Renewal.* New Brunswick: Transaction.

Neitz, Mary Jo. 1990. "In Goddess We Trust." Pp. 353–372 in Robbins and Anthony (1990).

Nelson, Lars-Erik. 1981. "Goldwater Rips New Right's 'Threat' Tactics." *Austin American Statesman* (Sept. 19): 1.

Novak, Michael. 1986. *Will It Liberate? Questions about Liberation Theology.* New York: Paulist Press.

O'Dea, Thomas F., and Janet O'Dea Aviad. 1983. *The Sociology of Religion.* Englewood Cliffs, NJ: Prentice-Hall.

O'Flaherty, Wendy. 1973. *Asceticism and Eroticism in the Mythology of the Siva.* London: Oxford University Press.

Ogburn, William F. 1922. *Social Change: With Respect to Culture and Original Nature.* New York: Huebsch.

Pargament, Kenneth I., David S. Ensing, Kathryn Falgout, Hannah Olsen, Barbara Reilly, Kimberly Van Haitsma, and Richard Warren. 1990. "God Help Me: (I): Religious Coping Efforts as Predictors of the Outcomes to Significant Negative Life Events." *American Journal of Community Psychology* 18: 793–824.

Paris, Arthur. 1982. *Black Pentecostalism: Southern Religion in an Urban World.* Amherst, MA: University of Massachusetts Press.

Parrinder, Geoffrey. 1980. *Sex in the World's Religions.* New York: Oxford University Press.

Parsons, Talcott. 1960. "Some Comments on the Pattern of Religious Organization in the United States." Pp. 295–321 in *Structure and Process in Modern Societies.* Glencoe, Ill.: Free Press.

Parsons, Talcott. 1967. "Christianity and Modern Industrial Society." Pp. 33–70 in *Sociological Theory, Values, and Sociocultural Change,* ed. Edward A. Tiryakian. New York: Harper Torchbooks.

Parsons, Talcott. 1969. "On the Concept of Value Commitments." Pp. 439–476 in *Politics and Social Structure.* New York: Free Press.

Patrick, Ted, with Tom Dulack. 1976. *Let Our Children Go!* New York: E.P. Dutton.

Pius X, Pope. 1908a. *Lamentabili Sane Exitu.* Pp. 217–230 in Paul Sabatier, ed., *Modernism.* London: Unwin.

Pius X, Pope. 1908b. *"Pascendi domini gregis."* Pp. 71–97 in *The Papal Encyclicals,* ed. Claudia Carlen, vol. 4. Wilmington, NC: McGrath.

Piven, Frances Fox, and Richard A. Cloward. 1971. *Regulating the Poor: The Functions of Public Welfare.* New York: Pantheon.

Plock, Donald. 1987. "Methods for the Time Being." *Sociological Analysis* 47: 43–51.

Poblete, Renato. 1970. "The Church in Latin America: A Historical Survey." Pp. 39–52 in *The Church and Social Change in Latin America,* ed. Henry A. Landsberger. Notre Dame, IN: University of Notre Dame Press.

Pollner, Melvin. 1989. "Divine Relations, Social Relations, and Well-Being." *Journal of Health and Social Behavior* 30: 92–104.

Prabhavananda, Swami. 1963. *The Sermon on the Mount According to Vedanta.* New York: New American Library.

Prebish, Charles. 1978. "Reflections on the Transmission of Buddhism to America." Pp. 153–172 in Needleman and Baker (1978).

Qur'an: The First American Version. 1985. Trans. and Commentary by T. B. Irving (Al-Hajj Ta'Lim 'Ali). Brattleboro, VT: Amana Books.

Ramsey, Paul. 1961. *War and the Christian Conscience.* Durham, NC: Duke University Press.

Ramsey, Paul. 1968. *The Just War: Force and Political Responsibility.* New York: Scribner.

Redfield, Robert. 1957. *The Primitive World and Its Transformations.* Ithaca, NY: Cornell University Press.

"Revive Native Religion." 1947. Editorial in the *Eastern Nigeria Guardian* (May 30). Quoted in Assimeng (1978).

Robbins, Thomas, and Dick Anthony, eds. 1990. *In Gods We Trust: New Patterns of Religious Pluralism in America.* 2nd ed. New Brunswick, NJ: Transaction.

Roberts, Bryan R. 1968. "Protestant Groups and Coping with Urban Life in Guatemala City." *American Journal of Sociology* 73: 753–767.

Robertson, Roland. 1991. *Religion and Global Order.* New York: Paragon House.

Robertson, Roland. 1992a. *Globalization: Social Theory and Global Culture.* Newbury Park, CA: Sage.

Robertson, Roland. 1992b. "The Economization of Religion? Reflections on the Promise and Limitations of the Economic Approach." *Social Compass* 39: 147–157.

Rochford, E. Burke, Jr. 1985. *Hare Krishna in America.* New Brunswick, NJ: Rutgers University Press.

Roof, Wade Clark. 1978. *Community and Commitment: Religious Plausibility in a Liberal Protestant Church.* New York: Elsevier.

Rousseau, Jean Jacques. [1762] 1901. *Social Contract,* ed. C. M. Andrews. New York: William H. Wise.

Ruether, Rosemary Radford, ed. 1974. *Religion and Sexism: Images of Women in the Jewish and Christian Traditions.* New York: Simon & Schuster.

Ruether, Rosemary Radford. 1981. "The Feminist Critique in Religious Studies." *Soundings* 64: 388–402.

Ruether, Rosemary Radford. 1992. *Gaia and God: An Ecofeminist Theology of Earth Healing.* San Francisco: HarperSanFrancisco.

Russell, Bertrand. 1967. *Autobiography,* vol. 1. London: Allen and Unwin.

Ryan, William. 1976. *Blaming the Victim.* Rev. ed. New York: Vintage.

Said, Edward. 1978. *Orientalism.* New York: Pantheon.

Scroggs, Robin. 1972. "Paul: Chauvinist or Liberationist?" *Christian Century* (March 15): 307–309.

Segundo, Juan Luis. 1976. *Liberation of Theology.* Maryknoll, NY: Orbis.

Segundo, Juan Luis. 1985. *Theology and the Church: A Response to Cardinal Ratzinger and a Warning to the Whole Church.* Minneapolis: Winston Press.

Sengren, P. Steven. 1983. "Female Gender in Chinese Religious Symbols: Kuan Yin, Ma Tsu, and the 'Eternal Mother.'" *Signs* 9 (1): 4–25.

Shapiro, Laura, with Daniel Glick. 1993. "Do You Believe in Magick? Witching Hour: 'Fort God' vs. Born-Again Pagans." *Newsweek* (August 23): 32.

Sharot, Stephen. 1991. "Judaism and the Secularization Debate." *Sociological Analysis* 52: 255–75.

Sharp, Gene. 1973–1974. *The Politics of Nonviolent Action.* Vol. 1: *Power and Struggle.* Vol. 2: *Methods of Nonviolent Action.* Vol. 3: *Dynamics of Nonviolent Action.* Boston: Porter Sargent.

Sharp, Gene. 1979. *Gandhi as a Political Strategist: With Essays on Ethics and Politics.* Boston: Porter Sargent.

Sharp, Gene. 1987. "Nonviolence: Moral Principle or Political Technique?" Pp. 29–53 in *Gandhi and Politics in India,* ed. Verinder Grover. New Delhi: Deep and Deep Publications.

Sherkat, Darren E., and John Wilson. Forthcoming. "Preferences, Constraints, and Choice in Religious Markets: An Examination of Religious Switching and Apostasy." Working Paper, Vanderbilt University and Duke University.

Shils, Edward A. 1981. *Tradition.* Chicago: University of Chicago Press.

Simmel, Georg. 1971. *On Individuality and Social Forms,* ed. Donald N. Levine. Chicago: University of Chicago Press.

Simmel, Georg. 1978. *The Philosophy of Money.* Trans. Tom Bottomore and David Frisby. London: Routledge & Kegan Paul.

Sinha, Manju, and Braj Sinha. 1978. "Ways of Yoga and the Mechanisms of Sacralization." Pp. 133–150 in Mol (1978).

Smelser, Neil J. 1963. *Theory of Collective Behavior.* Glencoe, IL: Free Press.

Smith, Huston. 1965. *The Religions of Man.* New York: Harper & Row.

Smith, Morton. 1952. "The Common Theology of the Ancient Near East." *Journal of Biblical Literature* 71: 135–147.

Smith, Morton. 1973. "On the Differences between the Culture of Israel and the Major Cultures of the Ancient Near East." *Journal of Ancient Near Eastern Studies* 5: 389–395.

Snow, David A., Louis A. Zurcher, and Sheldon Ekland-Olson. 1980. "Social Networks and Social Movements: A Microstructural Approach to Recruitment." *American Sociological Review* 45: 787–801.

Spinoza, Baruch. [1670] 1883. *Tractatus Theologico-Politicus.* Hamburg: Kunraht. Trans. R. H. M. Elwes. Vol. 1 in *The Chief Works of Benedict de Spinoza.* London: Bell.

Stark, Rodney, and William Sims Bainbridge. 1980. "Networks of Faith: Interpersonal Bonds and Recruitment to Cults and Sects." *American Journal of Sociology* 85: 1376–1395.

Stark, Rodney, and William Sims Bainbridge. 1985. *The Future of Religion: Secularization, Revival, and Cult Formation.* Berkeley: University of California Press.

Stevenson, M. S. [1920] 1971. *The Rites of the Twice-Born.* New York: International Publications.

Taylor, Robert J., and Linda M. Chatters. 1988. "Church Members as a Source of Informal Social Support." *Review of Religious Research* 30: 114–125.

Thomas, W. I. 1966. *W. I. Thomas on Social Organization and Social Personality.* Chicago: University of Chicago Press.

Tillich, Paul. 1967. *Systematic Theology.* Chicago: University of Chicago Press.

Tocqueville, Alexis de [1862] 1945. *Democracy in America.* Trans. Henry Reeve. New York: Knopf.

Tolstoy, Leo. 1987. *Writings on Civil Disobedience and Nonviolence.* Trans. Aylmer Maud. Philadelphia: New Society Publishers.

Tönnies, Ferdinand. [1887] 1957. *Community and Society.* Trans. by Charles P. Loomis. East Lansing: Michigan State University Press.

Turner, Victor. 1967. *The Forest of Symbols*. Ithaca, NY: Cornell University Press.

Turpin, Jennifer, and Lester R. Kurtz, eds. Forthcoming. *The Web of Violence*. Urbana, IL: University of Illinois Press.

Tylor, Edward B. 1871. *Primitive Culture*. London: Murray.

Vatican Council II. [1965] 1982. "Gaudium et spes, Constitution on the Church in the Modern World." Pp. 17–23 in *Nuclear Disarmament: Key Statements of Popes, Bishops, Councils and Chambers*, ed. Robert Heyer. New York: Paulist Press.

Wach, Joachim. 1944. *The Sociology of Religion*. Chicago: University of Chicago Press.

Wald, Kenneth D., Dennis E. Owen, and Samuel S. Hill. 1989. "Habits of the Mind? The Problem of Authority in the New Christian Right." Pp. 93–108 in *Religion and Political Behavior in the United States*, ed. Ted G. Jelen. New York: Praeger.

Wallace, Anthony F. C. 1966. *Religion: An Anthropological View*. New York: Random House.

Wallerstein, Immanuel. 1984. *The Politics of the World-Economy: The States, the Movements, and the Civilizations*. Cambridge: Cambridge University Press.

Wallis, Roy. 1976. *The Road to Total Freedom*. New York: Columbia University Press.

Warner, Marina. 1976. *Alone of All Her Sex*. New York: Knopf.

Warner, R. Stephen. 1993. "Work in Progress Toward a New Paradigm for the Sociological Study of Religion in the United States." *American Journal of Sociology* 98: 1044–1093.

Weber, Max. [1904] 1958. *The Protestant Ethic and the Spirit of Capitalism*. New York: Scribner.

Weber, Max. 1922–1923. "The Social Psychology of the World Religions." Pp. 266–301 in Weber (1946). Originally published as "Die Wirtschaftsethic der Weltreligionen" [The Economic Ethics of the World Religions]. Pp. 237–226 in Weber (1947).

Weber, Max. 1946. *From Max Weber: Essays in Sociology*. Trans. and ed. H. H. Gerth and C. Wright Mills. New York: Oxford University Press.

Weber, Max. 1947. *Gesammelte Aufsätze zur Religionssoziologie*. Tübingen: Mohr.

Weber, Max. 1968. *Economy and Society*. 3 vols. Berkeley: University of California Press.

Webster's New Collegiate Dictionary. 1974. Springfield, MA: G.&C. Merriam.

Weightman, Simon. 1984. "Hinduism." Pp. 191–236 in Hinnells (1984).

Welch, Holmes. 1972. *Buddhism Under Mao*. Cambridge: Harvard University Press.

White, Andrew Dickson. 1896–97. *History of the Warfare of Science with Theology in Christendom*. 2 vols. New York: Appleton.

Wilkinson, Loren. 1992. "Earth Summit: Searching for a Spiritual Foundation." *Christianity Today* 36 (July 20): 48.

Williams, John Alden, ed. 1962. *Islam.* Great Religions of Modern Man Series. New York: George Braziller.

Williams, Melvin D. 1974. *Community in a Black Pentecostal Church: An Anthropological Study.* Pittsburgh: University of Pittsburgh Press.

Wilson, Bryan. 1959. "An Analysis of Sect Development." *American Sociological Review 24:* 3–15.

Wolf, Margery. 1968. *The House of Lim: A Study of a Chinese Farm Family.* New York: Appleton-Century-Crofts.

Wolf, Margery. 1972. *Women and Family in Rural Taiwan.* Stanford: Stanford University Press.

"Women Studying to Be Conservative Rabbis." 1984 *New York Times* (September 9).

Woodward, Kenneth L., and David Gates. 1982. "Giving the Devil His Due." *Newsweek* (August 30): 72–74.

Wuthnow, Robert. 1976. *The Consciousness Reformation.* Berkeley: University of California Press.

Wuthnow, Robert. 1980. "World Order and Religious Movements." Pp. 57–75 in Studies of the Modern World System, ed. Albert Bergesen. New York: Academic Press.

Wuthnow, Robert. 1987. *Meaning and Moral Order: Explorations in Cultural Analysis.* Berkeley: University of California Press.

Wuthnow, Robert, James Davison Hunter, Albert Bergesen, and Edith Kurzweil, eds. 1984. *Cultural Analysis: The Work of Peter Berger, Mary Douglas, Michel Foucault, and Jürgen Habermas.* London: Routledge and Kegan Paul.

Yates, Kyle M., ed. 1988. *The Religious World: Communities of Faith.* 2nd ed. New York: Macmillan.

Yinger, J. Milton. 1970. *The Scientific Study of Religion.* New York: Macmillan.

Zald, Mayer N. 1982. "Theological Crucibles: Movements in and out of Religion." *Review of Religious Research* 23: 317–336.

Zimmerman, Margaret, and Lester R. Kurtz, eds. Forthcoming. *Experiments in Peace: Student Studies in Nonviolence.* New Delhi: Gandhi-In-Action.

Glossary/Index

in daily life, 76
Hindu yogic, 70
Dharma also Dhamma; Hindu and
Buddhist concept of the law of
the cosmos, the Buddha's teachings, or the duties required by
any given situation, 29, 37, 48, 59,
60, 61, 105–106, 113, 114, 116, 121
Dharshans encounters with God or
others of authority, 86
Dhyani Buddhas, 36
Diaspora the dispersal of Jews from
ancient Israel throughout the
world, 91
Diety. *See* God concept
Dissident movements, religious legitimation of, 14–15
Diversity
in alternative religious movements, 192, 193–203
modernist crisis and increasing cultural, 159, 236
social and institutional, as sociological classification,
25
unity and, in global village,
159, 236–240
Divine Light Mission, 197
Douglas, Mary, 77
sociological approach of, 15
**Dramaturgical approach to sociol-
ogy of religion** a contemporary
approach to religion that stresses
expressive or communicative
properties of culture and its interaction with social structure,
15–16
Duaita Vedanta, 31
Dualistic theodicies explanations of
suffering that posit two opposing
forces in the world such as good
and evil, God and Satan, 58
Durga-Parvati Hindu goddess associated with Shiva embodying his
immanent active energy, 32
Durkheim, Emile, 5, 7, 51, 100–101,
208
definition of religion by, 9
on sacred and profane, 64–65

E

Eastern Orthodox church Christian
churches resulting from the
Great Schism of 1054 C.E. that
produced a separation between
four Eastern churches and the Roman Catholic Church, 89
Eastern religions. *See also* Buddhism;
Hinduism
ahimsa nonviolence principle,
216, 217
ethos of, 104–105
good and evil in, 58
influence of, on new religious
movements in U.S.,
193–197
other-worldly nature of,
48–49
theodicies of, 58–61, 63–64
warfare and violence in,
217–218
Ecclesiastical institutions formal religious organizations organized
into a bureaucracy with a division of labor between clergy and
laity, 83, 84–85
in Christianity, 88–90
in Hinduism and Buddhism,
85–88
in Judaism and Islam, 90–92
Economics
Christian ethics and, 131–132
global, 4–5, 146
Islamic ethics and, 135 136
Jewish ethics and, 129
taboos and, 122–123
Egalitarianism in religion, 118–119
in ancient Judaism, 119
authoritarianism vs., 115
separate but equal policy in
Islam, 119–120
Eightfold Path, Buddhist, 36
Eilberg, Amy, 231
Eisler, Rianne, 231
Elective affinities a metaphor referring to a relationship between
ideas and the interests of a social
group or strata, 13–15
conversion process and, 202
between religious ethics and

ف

dgment is made to the following for permission to reprint:

.from *The Quran: The First American Version*, translated and commentary by T. B. Irving
Hajj TaLimAli), 1985 (Brattleboro, VT: Amana Books); Scripture quotations are from the Re-
vised Standard Version of the Bible, copyright 1946, 1952, 1971 by the Division of Christian Education of the National Council of the Churches of Christ in the USA, used by permission;
Boshongo Cosmogony (page 145-146) from *The Beginning: Creation Myths Around the World* by
Maria Leach and Jane Bell Fairservis, illustrator, copyright © 1956 by Harper & Row, Publishers,
Inc., reprinted by permission of HarperCollins Publishers, Inc.; Ti-ratana in the Pali text (p. 53)
and Edict No. XII from Ashoka (pp. 18-19) from *Buddhism* edited by Richard A. Gard, copyright
© 1962 by George Braziller, Inc., reprinted by permission of George Braziller, Inc.